LIMITS
OF EMPIRE
ROME'S BORDERS

LIMITS
OF EMPIRE
ROME'S BORDERS

SIMON AND JONATHAN FORTY

CASEMATE
publishers

12,631
#2

Acknowledgments

There are a number of go-to websites that proved hugely helpful: for online information on inscriptions, *romaninscriptionsofbritain.org*; Jona Lendering and the excellent *livius.org*, Carole Raddoto's Following Hadrian blog, the UNESCO Frontiers of Empire, intarch. ac.uk, vici.org, and academia.edu were all very helpful We'd like to thank everyone who's helped with the book, in particular Patrick Hook and Sandra for their considerable help with captioning; Mark Franklin for the maps; Eleanor for design and work on cutouts and overlays; Ivana Artuković at the Muzej Brodskog Posavlja; Elena Obuhovich and Olga Novoseltseva at The State Hermitage Museum, St. Petersburg; Mark Cromwell; Pazirik Informatics Ltd for the fabulous reconstructions in Chapter 3 and Balázs Szakonyi for his help; Leo Marriott for the aerial photography. The photos are credited individually on p. 198. Thanks to Mette Bundgaard and Ruth Sheppard at Casemate for their patience and helpful comments.

Published in the United States of America and Great Britain in 2021 by

CASEMATE PUBLISHERS

1950 Lawrence Road, Havertown, PA 19083, USA
and
The Old Music Hall, 106–108 Cowley Road, Oxford OX4 1JE, UK

Copyright 2021 © Simon Forty

Hardcover Edition: ISBN 978-1-63624-076-3
Digital Edition: ISBN 978-1-63624-077-0

A CIP record for this book is available from the British Library

Printed and bound in the Czech Republic by FINIDR s.r.o.

Packaged by Greene Media Ltd
Design: Eleanor Forty

For a complete list of Casemate titles, please contact:

CASEMATE PUBLISHERS (US)
Telephone (610) 853-9131
Fax (610) 853-9146
Email: casemate@casematepublishers.com
www.casematepublishers.com

CASEMATE PUBLISHERS (UK)
Telephone (01865) 241249
Email: casemate-uk@casematepublishers.co.uk
www.casematepublishers.co.uk

DATES
All dates BC are so indicated. Any other date is AD. Where there may be doubt we've inserted AD.

PAGE 1 Arutela was a fort on the *limes Alutanus* in Dacia—today's Calimanesti in Romania. See p. 143.

PAGES 2 and **3** Matilo archaeological park in Leiden-Roomburg, the Netherlands. See p. 92.

BELOW Palmyra in Syria blossomed under Roman rule as an important trading city. See p. 162.

Contents

Introduction

Sycamore Gap and Castle Nick
(milecastle 39) on Hadrian's Wall.

The history of the western Roman Empire, from its first emperor, Caesar Augustus, to its fall in the mid-fifth century, continues to be fascinating because so much of it still exists today, hundreds of years later. While the remains of so many other peoples have disappeared, that isn't the case with the Roman Empire—roads and aqueducts; forts, and fortifications; cities and towns; statuary and art; books, speeches, and letters—the sheer quantity of source material still available is huge. And then there are the stories: the military prowess, the political machinations, the soap operas and personal stories of lives that seem so similar to our own. Their world appears very like our world. And, as in our world today, the borders of their empire were important. Just as we do, the Romans wanted to control the movement of people into and out of their empire. They wanted to collect taxes from them—especially import duties. They wanted to protect the empire from military threats, be that a few raiders or a full-scale onslaught by larger armies. Outside the empire to the north lay Germania or *barbaricum*, and the people who lived there wanted to come in for the same reasons refugees from Africa want to come to Europe, or central Americans into the United States today: protection, wealth, opportunity.

In the time of the Roman Republic, the border between Romans and barbarians was nothing more than a debatable frontier zone with little demarcation. That was sufficient while Rome's armies were conquering huge swathes of territory, and dividing lines were not fixed because they were in flux, but as those frontiers coalesced into borders, so a more systemized approach was needed. Those borders that could be delineated were dictated by the geography and politics of their location. They fluctuated throughout Roman history, but at their height at the beginning of the second century AD, they mainly followed the natural geographical features of the Rhine and Danube to the north, the Atlantic Ocean to the west, the African deserts of Arabia and the Sahara to the south and in the east a mixture of mountains, rivers (chiefly the Euphrates), deserts, and the boundaries of other empires. These features were usually enhanced with a matrix of forts and outposts linked by roads. Continuous linear fortifications were constructed only where necessary, to seal up critical gaps and separate the Roman world from the lands beyond, which were deemed unworthwhile and dangerously hostile. The Roman word *limes* at root means a boundary path or road and its genitive form—*limitis*—is the root of our word limit. Today, the Roman *limes* are preserved through UNESCO's 1987 world heritage grouping of the Frontiers of the Roman Empire. They consist of the various discernible remains of Rome's border systems and constitute the largest body of all existing Roman archaeology visible today. That's what this book is about. It's designed to be an introduction to a subject that is complex, continuously debated, but above all a subject that is visible. The Roman frontiers generate much archaeology but also tourism. There are footpaths and cyclepaths, scenic driving routes, and river cruises. This book will give the reader a guide to what used to be there and a taste of what can be seen today.

We are lucky that the Romans loved building as much as they liked fighting. Building was a statement of possession and intent, a consolidation of conquest that had also a softer, more seductive side for those who were given the franchise—the benefits of Roman civilization. Remarkably, the military also built most of the basic infrastructure of its borders, especially in the uncivilized north. Before they fought, the Roman Army built roads and camps; after the fighting, its camps and fortresses acted as the focus for traders and civilians, often

leading to towns and cities that still exist. The spectacular feats of military engineering also provided a statement of power, presence, and capability that would have had a massive psychological effect—particularly in northwest Europe, although less so in the east.

The army's role in empire building, however, was more than simply its ability to crush resistance and build walls and forts. Military experience was a prerequisite for civic advancement and the army was inextricably connected to the seat of civilian power. The benefits of this were that, particularly after the reforms of Gaius Marius, its soldiers were valued, reflecting the investment in their long-term extensive training, skills, equipment, and experience and they were honored in retirement, some being settled in *colonia* that continued the process of Romanization of new territories.

The army and its veterans played an important role in the Roman economy. The army in the early, expansive days brought in slaves—essential for Rome which was, above all, a slave society—and booty; latterly, once it had moved to the frontiers, it required integrated supply systems and local manufacturing to sustain it. Forts became centers for trade, oversaw markets, and brought with them the crafts to provide the soldiers with things they needed: pottery, tanning, metallurgy. Soon, these skills were in place and locals were learning skills and taking advantage of the markets. Retired veterans provided ready markets for Roman goods. In later years, production of military equipment and weapons was turned over to state *fabricae* located around the empire: this meant they needed raw materials and a road system to get materials to the workplace and goods from it to the customers. Most of the *fabricae* in the west made individual items—shields, bows, arrows, swords etc.

The problems of a powerful politicized army were obvious from early days. The power behind the throne in Rome was often the Praetorian Guard, but in general terms, having a strong standing army whose officers were using their military service as part of their political career was a double-edged sword. Emperors had to keep the army busy and on their side. Those that didn't could find themselves dead or dethroned. The size of the empire didn't help. A schismatic emperor in the extremities could secure his power base and prepare for battle before an emperor hundreds of miles across the Mediterranean was able to react. The crisis of the third century was, in part, caused by a politicized army: between 235 and 285 there were 26 emperors and most of them were elevated by—and as often murdered by—their own men.

The Roman Empire wasn't the only slave society in the ancient world but it was a major player. There was a continuous trade in slaves, and while some of them lived pleasant, even pampered lives, and some could look forward to manumission, many others were worked to death in agriculture, mines or industry, or died in the arena. Many of these slaves resulted from warfare—Flavius Josephus said that the fall of Jerusalem in the first Jewish revolt saw 97,000 become slaves; Dio mentions 50,000 Dacians. However, as the empire's expansion slowed, and there were fewer opportunities to turn the population of conquered countries into a workforce, fewer slaves were freed and more escapees were hunted down. **ABOVE** Chained captives at Mogontiacum.

The seeds of Imperial Rome's destruction were self sown. The fall of the western empire was not purely the result of the failure of the border system and the aggression of "barbarians." Undoubtedly some emperors died at the hands of outside enemies—Decius and Etruscus were killed in battle against the Goths, as was Valens a century later—but most died at the hands of fellow Romans. When you add into the mix a pandemic—the plague of Cyprian (c. 249–270) decimated soldiers and citizens—it's understandable why the third century crisis has been so named. What is even more surprising is that Rome was able to gather itself again and survive for two centuries afterward. Part of that resilience is down to the strength of its frontiers.

The Roman frontiers

Augustus set the tone for the first emperors. He expanded the territorial domination of Rome and his successors continued to do so. When Hadrian succeeded Trajan in 117, the Roman Empire had reached its greatest extent. Today, we know that it covered some 20 million square miles and upward of 50 million people lived within its territories. On his deathbed, Augustus had, however, sounded a note of caution, suggesting (as reported by Tacitus) "*consilium coercendi intra terminos imperii*"—that it would be a good idea to worry about hanging onto what Rome had and sticking to its existing frontiers. Tacitus wondered whether that was due to fear or jealousy—whichever was true, his successors didn't follow the advice. A man, especially an emperor whose hold on power was almost always tenuous, had to be seen to win victories, defeat enemies, and acquire land for Rome—even if, as was the case with Caligula, the victory was against the sea god, Neptune. There may not have been a cult of "Manifest Destiny" but most Romans believed that there were few limits to the empire's power and so no need for hard borders. Where there were problems, money or duress could usually provide a client kingdom or buffer state, and the Roman view was that client states were Roman territory in all but name.

Nevertheless, it became obvious that the edges of Roman control needed oversight—particularly in the north. There were threats that needed to be monitored. For all modern historians' discussions about trading zones and control of markets and entry into the empire, in reality, however, the empire was a tantalizing prize for those outside: the prospects of work, advancement, and citizenship were important, but so was booty. The hard borders that were constructed—Hadrian's Wall, the Germanic–Raetian walls, the Dacian *limes*, the *Fossatum Africae* in Tripolitania—had a plain intent. Watchtowers, forts small and large, legionary fortresses: these all have a military purpose as well as potentially providing a customs barrier. The Romans certainly traded with people outside the empire, either through specially organized *macellae* (markets) or otherwise, but they also recognized the need for a military presence. While, often, that meant an auxiliary *ala* working from a small fortlet and watchtowers, it also included the might of the legions. Rome conquered. Conquered people don't always like the result and revolt. A big part of the Roman Empire's military history was about dealing with these revolts.

To facilitate military control and response to problems, communications had to be good. The Roman road network was already well-established across the Italian peninsula by the end of the third century BC. Augustus developed the network still further, metaling, cobbling, and paving extensively. By improving the quality he was able to establish an efficient commercial postal system with stations spaced a day's journey apart: the *cursus publicus* which became two speed after Diocletian's reforms, the *cursus velox* (fast) and *cursus clabularis* (slow). By land, messages could move at some fifty miles a day; by sea, double that. Having permanent roads also considerably boosted trade and brought in much-needed money to help fund their construction. The Imperial Roman state spent huge amounts on building and upgrading roads right across the empire. By the end of the second century AD more than 56,000 miles had been built, and they formed a vital part of all military planning.

They also helped with logistical support for the army, whether in fixed camp or on campaign. However, while movement of supplies by road was better than without roads, ox carts were slow, whereas movement by river could be a lot faster and a lot easier. The campaign in Britannia was supported from Germania Inferior by ship and much of the provisioning was along the Rhine. The riverine elements of the borders provided a strong element of defense, but the Romans knew only too well that they could be bridged or even walked over when they were iced up—so watchtowers and forts lined the banks of the Rhine and Danube.

In Africa, roads were also built, often to improve existing trade routes, but as well to facilitate military movement. Seapower along the Mediterranean coast was also of prime importance. However, the desert supplied a strong border and, while there were undoubtedly threats from raiders, most of Rome's attention to south and east was directed against threats from the Parthian and, later Sasanian, empires. Until the end of the third century, Rome tended to have the upper hand and again, rivers played their part as the Tigris and Euphrates supplied a natural border. The rise of the Sasanian empire, however, coincided with weakness in Rome and the Sasanians took advantage. The eastern border remained turbulent though into Byzantine days.

What have the Romans ever done for us? Well, their roads were pretty good. This is not to say that there was a complete lack of them before the Roman armies arrived: most of the countries they conquered had large areas of cultivation and many trackways, but they were uncoordinated and had gone up through ancient usage rather than planning. Initially, the roads the Romans built as they advanced had a military purpose. They may, to some extent, have followed existing trackways but they were planned strategically, to take Roman legions where they needed to go, to follow them with their supplies, and to allow them to hurry to places they were needed. This was particularly true in the border areas. The Latin word *limes* means track or pathway as well as boundary, and the military road that went along Hadrian's Wall or the River Rhine or Danube, was probably the most important part of the Roman frontier system because their main frontier defense mechanisms were reactive: they didn't try to defend the border but react to incursions.

ABOVE Moved higher since antiquity because of the Iron Gates hydroelectric system, the *Tabula Traiana* was created to commemorate the military road Trajan had built preparatory to his advance into Dacia. The inscription reads: "Emperor Caesar son of the divine Nerva, Nerva Trajan, the Augustus, Germanicus, Pontifex Maximus, invested for the fourth time as Tribune, Father of the Fatherland, Consul for the third time, excavating mountain rocks and using wood beams has made this road" (translation by Otto Benndorf). Opposite it, on the Romanian side, is a giant modern sculpted head of the Dacian King Decebalus, who opposed Trajan's incursions.

BELOW An example of a high-quality Roman road at at Tel al-Karameh, Syria. This road connected Antioch, the capital of the province of Syria (and, later, Coele Syria) with Chalcis ad Belum and on into Mesopotamia. Partly reconstructed by the French, it was probably built in the second half of the second century during Marcus Aurelius's reign.

The sources

Rome had a long history and a literate society that was only too happy to record it—although not always accurately or truthfully. Roman authors were every bit as prone to propagandize and lack objectivity as modern historians. However, most of what we can read in the form of inscriptions—epigraphy—is a major building block in our knowledge of events and dates, the location of people and military units, and boundaries. Luckily, the Romans spent a great deal of time and effort recording who built what and when, remembering the deeds and lives of the dead, as well as making votive offerings to their gods. The number of inscriptions linked to the army provide a great deal of information.

**Deo
Antenocitico
Et Numinib**(us)
Augustor(um)
Ael(ius) **Vibius**
Leg(ionis) **XX V**(aleriae) **V**(ictricis)
v(otum) **s**(olvit) **l**(ibens) **m**(erito)

To the god
Antenociticus
and to the Divinities
of the Emperors
Aelius Vibius
centurion of *legio XX Valeria Victrix*
willingly and deservedly fulfilled his vow

D(is) **M**(anibus)
**Iulius Valerianus
eques alae I Ulp**(iae) **con
tariorum stip**(endiorum) **XXIII
vixit annis XXXXVI**
Ulp(ius) **Ingenu**(us) **dupl**(icarius)
**alae eiusdem here
s posuit b**(ene) **m**(erenti)

To the Divine Manes
Iulius Valerianus
cavalryman of *ala I Ulpia Contariorum*
served 23 years
He lived 46 years
Ulpius Ingenuus, duplicarius
of the same ala, his heir
had (this stone) erected, as was the dead man's due

LEFT Aelius Vibius's altar Roman soldiers dedicated votive altars to their gods. In this case the god is unusual. Found in a temple at Benwell on Hadrian's Wall, Antenocitico isn't to be found on any other European altar and so is probably a British god. *Legio XX* was one of the four legions that invaded Britain in AD43, helped build the wall and was probably still in Britain when the Romans pulled out in the fifth century.

LEFT Julius Valerianus's tombstone At the other end of the Roman world, *legio II Parthica* had its winter quarters in Apamea, Syria. The cemetery has seven cavalrymen's tombstones, five of them men from *ala I Ulpia Contariorum*. They were brought to the area in the late third century AD because of increased conflict with the Sasanians who were noted horsemen. This *ala* was a Roman heavy cavalry unit of cataphracts. The poor quality of the carving as compared, for example, with that in Britannia (see p. 42) probably means the use of local stonemasons.

1 Brick stamp of *cohors II Flavia Commagenorum* from Micia (Vetel, Romania).
2 Brick stamp of *classis Britannica* from Pevensey.
3 "From cohors V the century of Gellius Philippus (built this)": Hadrian's Wall, Gilsland.
4 From Fort Alauna (Maryport), "Built by a *vexillatio* of legio II Augusta and XX Valeria Vitrix," early third century.
5 Brick stamp of *legio I Italica* in Novae.
6 Brick stamp of *cohors IIII Vindelicorum*, Großkrotzenburg.

1   2   3

4   5   6

In 2004 an inscription was published attesting to the presence of a detachment of *legio II Traiana Fortis* and auxiliary troops at Portus Ferresanus on the Farasan Islands in the Red Sea. Dating to 144, it tells that they built and dedicated a fortified camp—over 2,500 miles from Rome. In 1958, north of Perth in Scotland, a slab from the Shrine of the Standards dated to the Antonine reoccupation of Bertha was found on the bed of the River Almond, over 1,500 miles from Rome. The borders of the empire may have been far-flung, but they were connected by a communality and connectivity that aids study and understanding.

On top of the inscriptions, the Roman military was meticulous in its records and record keeping. Every time veteran *peregrini* (foreign soldiers without Roman citizenship) retired they were given diplomas, military discharge certificates made of bronze that record information that is hugely helpful to historians. The first found is dated AD52 and over a thousand are extant, although fewer after the *Constitutio Antoniniana* of 212 when Caracalla opened citizenship to all in the empire. Made from two bronze rectangular plates around 3.9in. x 4in. and 8in. x 7in. depending on the period, bound together by bronze wire and sealed with witnesses' seals, they identified the date (day and month) of issuing, with the year defined by the names of the two consuls; the unit in which the soldier had last served and its commander; the soldier's rank, name, his father's name, and origin; that of his wife; the names of their children; and confirmation that the official duplicate was stored in Rome. The veteran became a Roman citizen, as did his wife and children, and this document proved it. They were issued in batches so often record a list of units and names. For example, the diploma given to infantryman Vaxadus, son of Vaxadus of Syedra (in Cilicia) after twenty-five years of service in *cohors I Sebastenorum milliaria* based in Syria Palestina, mentions, "citizenship to the cavalrymen and infantrymen who do not already possess it, that served in the three *alae* which are called *Gallorum and Thracum Constantia* and *Antiana Gallorum and Thracum Sagittariora* and *VII Phrygum*, and in the twelve cohorts (infantry) called *V Gemella* and *I Thracum (milliaria)* and *I Sebastenorum (milliaria)* and *I Damascenorum Armeniacum Sagittariorum* and *I Montanorum* and *I Flavia civium Romanorum* and *I* and *II Ulpiae Galatarum* and *III* and *IV Callaecorum Bracaraugustanorum* and *IV* and *VI Ulpiae Petraeorum*"—that's fifteen units. The diplomas give names of governors and commanders, too.

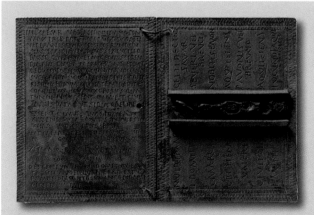

Military diplomas

This is one of the best preserved diplomas found to date. It was discovered during dredging of the River Sava near Slavonski Brod, Croatia in 1997. The recipient was Liccaius, a centurion in the Roman fleet based at Misenum. It is witnessed by seven people, the wax impressions of whose rings are in the covered box at right. The text reads: "Emperor Caesar Vespasian Augustus Pontifex Maximus, with tribunician power for the second time, emperor for the sixth time, the father of the fatherland, and consul for the third time to veterans who fought in the Misena fleet under Sextus Lucilius Bassus, who served twenty-six or more years of military service, who settledin Paestum, and whose names are written below is granted citizenship for themselves, their children and descendants, and the right of legal marriage with the wives they had when citizenship was granted to them, or, if any were unmarried, with those they later marry, but only a single one each. [Dated] February 9, in the consulships of the Emperor Caesar Vespasian Augustus for the third time, and Marcus Cocceius Nerva [AD71]. To centurion Liccaius, son of Birsus, from Marsonia, copied and verified from a copper plate, which was attached in Rome to the Capitol at the foot of the altar of the Julian family."

Of course, the largest collection of written information we have of the Roman world is in their books and letters, whether they are on papyrus (made from the pith of the plant), parchment and vellum (from untanned animal skins), wax-covered wooden tablets, or any available surface: Vindolanda's treasure trove of letters were written on strips of wood; in Graeco-Roman Egypt *ostraca* (shards of broken pots) were recycled and written upon. The British Library's "Writing: Making Your Mark" exhibition mentions an *ostracon* in which two tax collectors give permission to a *hetaira* (a courtesan) to ply her trade on a particular day in 110!

Not all the books of antiquity have survived, unfortunately. There are no surviving Roman histories covering the period before the Punic wars. The work of the first Roman historian we know about, Quintus Fabius Pictor (270–200BC), is almost completely lost as are the *Annales maximi*, the yearly records kept by the chief high priest (*Pontifex maximus*) of the Roman Republic. Some of these "lost" books live on with passages repeated verbatim, in later works; some come to light as palimpsests, cleaned old parchments that reveal their earlier works under ultraviolet light. For the imperial period, however, there is much material—such as the books of Julius Caesar, Publius Cornelius Tacitus, Gaius Suetonius Tranquillus, Dio Cassius, Ammianus Marcellinus, Procopius of Caesare, etc. One book is worth mentioning in more detail: the *Notitia Dignitatum* from end of fourth/early fifth century AD. The *Notitia* lists the offices of the Roman government and army of both Western and Eastern empires, the former from around 420, the latter c. 395. The difference in dates, the time taken in compilation, and gaps mean that it isn't completely accurate, but it's still a fantastic source.

Other than the written word, the most visible source of information on the Roman borders is undoubtedly the archaeological record—what can be seen on the ground: buildings, forts, walls, and ditches. Chapter 4 provides a survey of the structures on the borders, concentrating on those visible today. Dense populations and development of cities have meant that much of the urban remains have been built over. Some of these were recorded before they were obliterated, but unfortunately many were destroyed in the past—and if not destroyed, then certainly robbed for their worked stone. The old joke that most of Hadrian's Wall still survives—but as farm buildings, roads and castles—is a truism that can be extended throughout the Roman world. Their structures were reused for other purposes, sometimes in situ, sometimes many miles away.

While many of their built structures have disappeared, they usually leave a trace and, increasingly, aerial photography has played an important role in unearthing otherwise hidden locations: from an aircraft or a satellite. High-resolution photography—particularly in years of drought—has made outlines of buildings or

The *Tabula Peutingeriana* is a medieval copy of what is said to be a Roman map that shows the roads, cities, and towns of much of the Roman world. Possibly originating from the map produced by Agrippa during the reign of Augustus, it lacks its outside sheet that would have shown Britannia and Hispania.

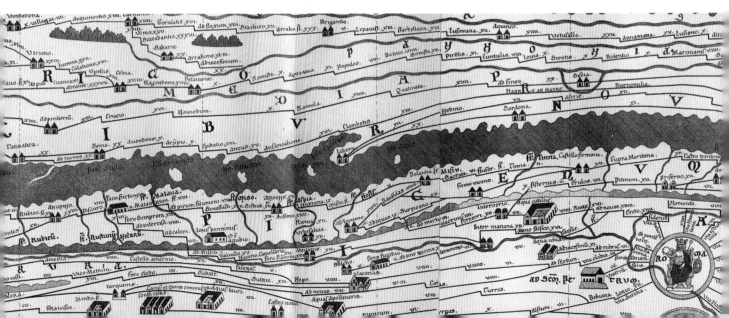

Render unto Caesar ...

The Palmyra Tariff

A document from 137, it specified tariffs to be imposed on imports and exports of certain goods. Palmyra was an important node on trade routes between Mediterranean countries and India, Arabia, and Iran. Many different goods passed through: cloth, spice, jewelry, aromatic oils, olive oil, fat, salted provisions, leather, wine, corn, etc. The tariff on the wall is in Greek and Aramaic and was rediscovered in 1881 by Prince S.S. Abamelek-Lazarev, a Russian amateur archaeologist. Today, it's in The State Hermitage Museum, St. Petersburg. Examples: For each slave exported, 22 denarii.

The customer agent himself shall levy a duty in respect of each camel-load entering Tadmor: 3 denarii.

For each donkey-load imported or exported, he shall collect 1 denarius.

Wool dyed purple. For each fleece imported or exported, 3 denarii.

From those who import male slaves into Tadmor or its territories, the customer agent shall collect 22 denarii per slave.

For each camel-load of aromatic oil imported in alabaster jars, 25 denarii.

Per donkey-load of olive oil , 7 denarii at importation and exportation.

The Ephesus Customs Laws

A inscription from 62 found in Ephesus in 1976, specified the rules about taxation on imports and exports by land or sea from Asia. It identifies that someone has a contract and that on whatever is imported or exported, a portion of one-fortieth shall be given to this tax collector. All importers and exporters should register with a tax collector at specified locations (there were over forty). Tax farmers should raise money from the royal stations the local king kept to collect taxes, and in those areas not subject to the king a 40ft x 40ft building plot should be made available to the tax collector to construct a suitable building so that people can make

declarations or register there. It should be in a public place but not on temple property, a sacred precinct, or on consecrated ground. The tax-farmer gets a tenth of the crops produced by the plough or a fifth of wine or oil, and on minerals, according to the law on mining, four asses per one hundred pounds. Apart from this, they shall not owe any tax. No tax is levied on:

• goods sold within Asia, as long as the transportation is not for the sake of avoiding tax
• boats and their fittings; slaves and anyone they carry; books and tablets that contain writing; all provisions; and animals for the sake of the journey
• imports and exports for private use

forts clear. An important innovator in this field was the French archaeologist Jean Lucien Baradez, who had been an airman in World War I. Attached to the Department of Antiquities of French Colonial Algeria, he was an archaeologist who excavated Tipasa. His aerial surveys showed strong evidence of a frontier made up of ditches, embankments, and watchtowers. His 1949 book *Fossatum Africae; Aerial research on the organization of the Saharan borders in Roman times* was an important step forward in understanding the Roman presence in Africa. While his suggestion that a linear barrier existed for many miles in Africa is largely discounted today, nevertheless his work showed how useful to archaeology aerial surveys could be. Other significant postwar technological developments have also helped: shallow geophysical techniques; ground-penetrating radar; light detection and ranging (LIDAR); drones; and X-ray fluorescence spectroscopy measurers.

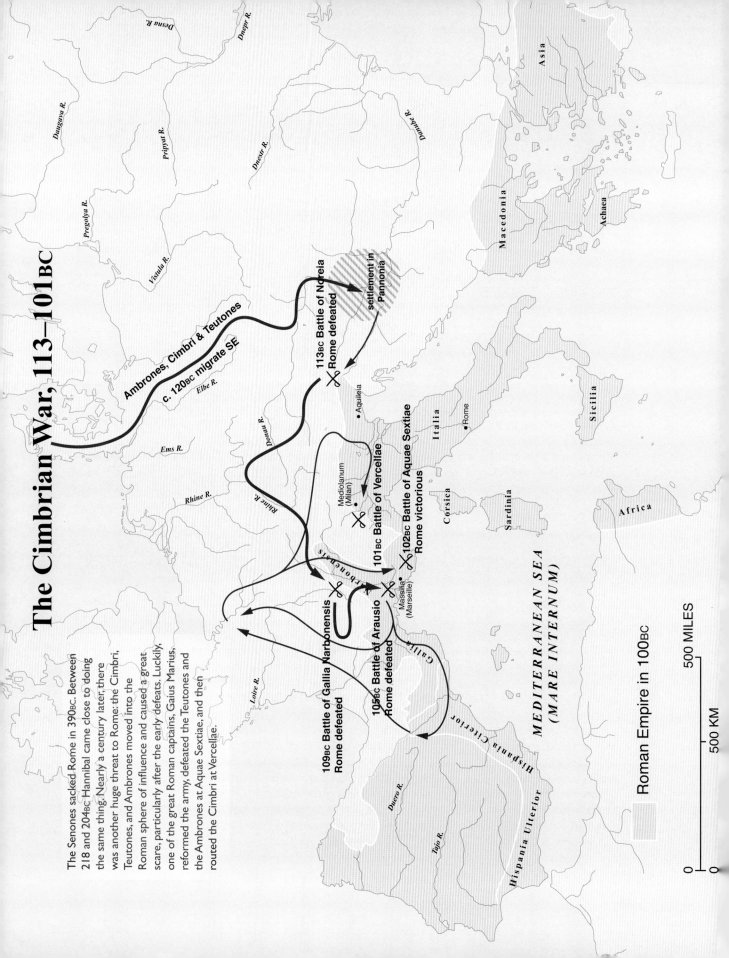

The Cimbrian War, 113–101BC

The Senones sacked Rome in 390BC. Between 218 and 204BC Hannibal came close to doing the same thing. Nearly a century later, there was another huge threat to Rome: the Cimbri, Teutones, and Ambrones moved into the Roman sphere of influence and caused a great scare, particularly after the early defeats. Luckily, one of the great Roman captains, Gaius Marius, reformed the army, defeated the Teutones and the Ambrones at Aquae Sextiae, and then routed the Cimbri at Vercellae.

Ambrones, Cimbri & Teutones

c. 120BC migrate SE

113BC Battle of Noreia Rome defeated

settlement in Pannonia

101BC Battle of Vercellae

102BC Battle of Aquae Sextiae Rome victorious

109BC Battle of Gallia Narbonensis Rome defeated

105BC Battle of Arausio Rome defeated

Mediolanum (Milan)

Aquileia

Massilia (Marseille)

Rome

Narbonensis

Gallia

Italia

Corsica

Sardinia

Sicilia

Hispania Citerior

Hispania Ulterior

Macedonia

Achaea

Asia

Africa

MEDITERRANEAN SEA (MARE INTERNUM)

Duugava R.

Desna R.

Dnepr R.

Pripyat R.

Pregolya R.

Dnestr R.

Visula R.

Elbe R.

Ems R.

Donau R.

Danube R.

Rhine R.

Rhône R.

Loire R.

Duero R.

Tajo R.

Roman Empire in 100BC

0   500 MILES

0   500 KM

1

Border Expansion

Deir el-Munira fort in el-Kharga oasis, Egypt (see pp. 170–71) was built under Diocletian.

The Roman Republic started small around 500BC and had no real concern about frontiers as it fought first for survival and then to control the Italian peninsula. During this struggle it came up against large-scale barbarian attacks—by the Senones in 390BC and the Cimbri in 113–101BC. Its survival gave Romans a sense of destiny that was enhanced when they fought the Mediterranean superpower of the time, Carthage, and won. Victory in the first Punic war gave Rome its first province: Sicily, in 241BC. The second Punic war ended with Rome's strength established having acquired Carthage's possessions and comprehensively defeated its armies.

The second and first centuries BC saw Rome's territories grow even further: Pompey and Caesar ensured that when Octavian Caesar became emperor, his empire stretched from the English Channel to Syria. They had, however, prodded a hornet's nest: the Parthian Empire would be a continuous irritation in the east. The last years of the Republic were riven by internal strife, but a debilitating civil war didn't stop the growth of the empire. By the death of Augustus in AD14, it had expanded far enough that the first serious thought was given to the empire's borders and methods of protecting them.

When Augustus became emperor he had some sixty legions, including those of Mark Anthony, although not all at full strength. He gradually reduced this number to twenty-eight, creating a standing army for the first time consisting of some 150,000 Roman legionaries and about the same number of auxiliaries. The latter were recruited from foreign tribes and those as yet unqualified for citizenship within the empire. He then moved the legions away from the center to the periphery, and tasked them with the continued vigorous expansion and policing of Rome's borders. Augustus was fortunate in having an experienced high-caliber team around him who had fought for his cause in the recent civil wars. This included his close and trusted childhood friend Marcus Agrippa, an outstanding general and administrator who shared Octavian's vision and was responsible for making much of it become reality.

At first, Augustus continued Rome's expansion. Egypt was annexed in AD30 and in the next five years his adopted sons Tiberius and Drusus conquered Noricum and Raetia (now Switzerland, Austria, and Bavaria) while Agrippa completed the conquest of northern Spain. In AD25 Celtic Galatia in what is now central Turkey was annexed, and in AD22 Augustus traveled east to Sicily, Greece, and the new Roman province of Asia (Anatolia) in a huge reorganization of administration and infrastructure. By AD20 he had reached a peace agreement with Parthia which included its acceptance of Armenia as a client kingdom within the Roman sphere of influence. In the north, Balkan and German campaigns aimed to extend Roman control up to a line from the Danube to the Elbe. However, Augustus was running out of family generals. Both Agrippa's sons, adopted by Augustus, had died (in AD2 and 4). Of Augustus's other adopted sons, Drusus died in Germany in AD6, leaving only his brother

The Rise of Rome to Trajan 117AD

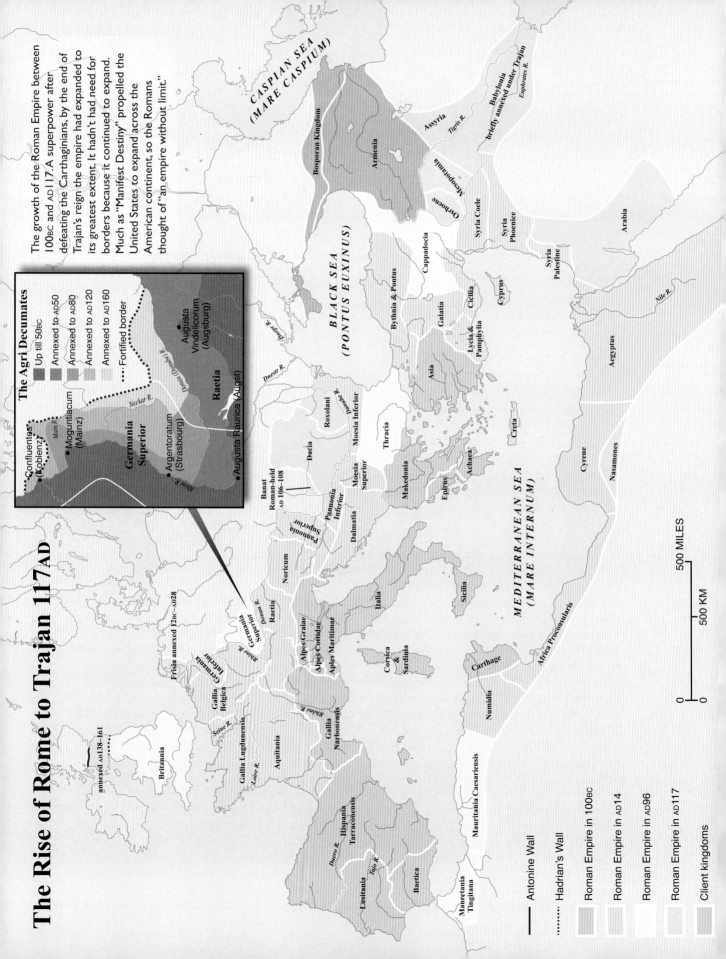

The growth of the Roman Empire between 100BC and AD117. A superpower after defeating the Carthaginians, by the end of Trajan's reign the empire had expanded to its greatest extent. It hadn't had need for borders because it continued to expand. Much as "Manifest Destiny" propelled the United States to expand across the American continent, so the Romans thought of "an empire without limit."

The Agri Decumates

- Up till 50BC
- Annexed to AD50
- Annexed to AD80
- Annexed to AD120
- Annexed to AD160
- ·········· Fortified border

Confluentas (Koblenz)
Main R.
Moguntiacum (Mainz)
Neckar R.
Donau (Danube) R.
Germania Superior
Argentoratum (Strasbourg)
Rhine R.
Augusta Vindelicorum (Augsburg)
Raetia
Augusta Raurica (Augst)

CASPIAN SEA (MARE CASPIUM)

Bosporan Kingdom
Armenia
Assyria
Tigris R.
Babylonia, briefly annexed under Trajan
Euphrates R.
Mesopotamia
Osrhoene
Syria Coele
Syria Phoenice
Syria Palestine
Arabia

BLACK SEA (PONTUS EUXINUS)

Bythnia & Pontus
Cappadocia
Galatia
Asia
Lycia & Pamphylia
Cyprus
Nile R.
Aegyptus

Dnepr R.
Roxolani
Dnestr R.
Danube R.
Dacia
Moesia Inferior
Moesia Superior
Banat Roman-held AD 106–108
Pannonia Inferior
Pannonia Superior
Thracia
Makedonia
Epirus
Achaea
Creta
Cyrene
Nasamones

MEDITERRANEAN SEA (MARE INTERNUM)

Dalmatia
Noricum
Raetia
Italia
Sicilia
Corsica & Sardinia
Africa Proconsularis
Carthage
Numidia
Mauretania Caesariensis

Rhine R.
Germania Superior
Alpes Graiae
Alpes Cottidae
Aples Maritimae
Germania Inferior
Frisia annexed 12bc–AD28
annexed AD138–161
Gallia Belgica
Britannia
Gallia Lugdunensis
Seine R.
Loire R.
Aquitania
Rhône R.
Gallia Narbonensis
Duero R.
Hispania Tarraconensis
Tajo R.
Lusitania
Baetica
Mauretania Tingitana

500 MILES
500 KM

—— Antonine Wall
·········· Hadrian's Wall
Roman Empire in 100BC
Roman Empire in AD14
Roman Empire in AD96
Roman Empire in AD117
Client kingdoms

Tiberius. All of these men had shown great promise as fine generals in their various military exploits, but now they were gone.

On top of the death of his youthful generals, there was a ghastly defeat for Varus's three legions in the Teutoburger Wald in AD9, and then Agrippa died in AD12. Augustus was deeply affected by the former. This was probably the point when consolidation and even caution became the most realistic policy. He withdrew back to the Rhine and began to enhance it with defensive installations. Small forts, watchtowers, and signal stations linked by road were constructed to contain attacks or summon reinforcements, while larger ones covered critical access points. A riverine fleet was formed to patrol and police the river and intercept trouble when it came. As well as a line of defense, these beginnings of a linear barrier enabled the surveillance of tribal movements and also served as a more efficient customs barrier with which to regulate and tax trade.

Augustus continued with his review of his empire's borders, his approach varying from region to region, adjusting for individual circumstances and contingencies. Sometimes a different, more flexible strategy was evolved, seeking to maintain peace through a combination of security, trade, and diplomacy. By allying with friendly local tribes and rewarding their loyalty with cash payments and the promise of mutual protection, he sought to create a buffer zone against those more hostile. He also continued building within the empire, equipping it with a superb network of roads for swift movement and to facilitate trade, and had another fleet formed to fight piracy in the Mediterranean. In his will he advised that the borders of the Roman Empire should be left as they were.

The northern and eastern land borders remained the key problem areas for ingress into the empire, as indeed they would until its demise. The lower reaches of both the Rhine and Danube favored defense and were more stable. It was the watershed mountains, their easily crossed upper reaches, and the gap between the two rivers that were particularly vulnerable. This is where the Roman defenses began to thicken incrementally. It took time for the frontier to stabilize, partly due to further advances. Each successive one left a discernible trace: Domitian furnished his with a clearly demarcated zone of watchtowers, fortlets, and redoubts supported by larger fortresses and linked by road. Further east in the Balkans persistent raiding by the Dacians, Suebi, and Sarmatians was left to Trajan to sort out.

Trajan strengthened the German defenses and in 101 attacked Dacia, determined to solve this decades-long problem once and for all. In fact it took him two attempts, but by 105, he had systematically reduced the Dacian fortresses, destroyed their capital, and brought their king's head back to Rome. The conquest of Dacia produced a salient of territory north of the Danube whose strategic advantage was deemed worthwhile—but this part of the frontier had now become a central axis of the Roman military operations within the empire and sporadic fighting would continue until the territory's defense proved too costly and Aurelian gave it up.

After Dacia, Trajan turned his attention to the east. In 114 he retook Armenia. In 115, he annexed northern Mesopotamia before going on to capture the Parthian capital, Ctesiphon. This was the high watermark of Roman operations in the area as trouble elsewhere in the empire demanded attention and Roman military resources were stretched. Trajan's health was also failing and by 117 he was dead.

Trajan's Column in Rome is a record of the emperor's attacks on Dacia that led to it becoming part of the empire.

Timeline: 753BC–AD117

753BC Foundation of Rome.

509BC Creation of the Roman Republic.

*c.***390BC** A taste of things to come. The Senones (an ancient Gallic tribe) defeated the Romans at the battle of Allia River, and then sacked most of Rome.

340–338BC Latin War: Rome fought the Latin League. Victory saw Rome annex a number of states and expand its territories considerably.

298–290BC Third Samnite War: Rome took control of the bulk of central Italy, in spite of the return of the Senones.

285–282BC Rome advanced into Gallic territory, defeating the Senones at Picenum (283BC), then a combined army of Gauls and Etruscans at Lake Vadimo (283BC), and finally the Etruscans at Populonia (282BC).

264–241BC First Punic War: Rome gained its first overseas possessions—Sicily became a province (in 241BC) and the breadbasket of Rome.

238BC Rome annexed Corsica and Sardinia, which became provinces in 238BC and 237BC respectively.

225BC Another Gallic tribe, the Boii, attacked Rome. They were destroyed first at the battle of Telamon and then at Clastidium in 222BC.

218–201BC Second Punic War: Rome became *the* Mediterranean superpower taking Carthaginian territories in Spain. In 197BC these became the provinces of Hispania Citerior (Nearer Spain) and Ulterior (Further Spain).

156–155BC Dalmatian Wars: after Illyria fell, the northern tribes—who went on to provide many Roman auxiliaries in the future—came into conflict with their southern neighbors. Consul Publius Cornelius Scipio ended the war by sacking the capital, Delminium.

150–148BC Fourth Macedonian War: an uprising was crushed and the province of Macedonia was established in 146BC; shortly after this Achaea was incorporated into the province.

149–146BC Third Punic War: Cato the Censor advocated the city's complete destruction—*Carthago delenda est*. And that's what happened. Punic lands became the Roman province of Africa.

129BC Creation of the province of Asia from the kingdom of Pergamon that had been bequeathed to the Republic by its last king. The Romans had to defeat a pretender first.

120BC Creation of the province of Gallia Narbonensis (hitherto Gallia Transalpina).

113–105BC Cimbrian War: see p. 14.

73–63BC Third Mithridatic War against Mithridates VI of Pontus. Success by Pompey the Great saw Creta et Cyrenaica (69BC) and Pontus et Bithynia (63BC) become provinces. He then moved south to Syria which also became a province. In 63BC, he made Judea a satellite of Syria.

64BC Cicilia became a province. Cyprus was attached 58BC. Caesar reorganized it into Syria about 27BC.

58–51BC Caesar's conquest of Gaul. During this period, Caesar constructed a linear barrier specifically to dissuade the Helvetii moving into or through Roman territory. Eighteen miles long, it comprises a trench and 16ft high wall from Lake Geneva to Mount Jura. Once finished finished, he "distributes garrisons, and closely fortifies redoubts, in order that he may the more easily intercept them, if they should attempt to cross over against his will." It works, to a point. The Helvetii did find another way west, but were defeated by Caesar and then returned to their erstwhile territory as *foederati*. Their oaths were broken when they supported Versingetorix in 52BC.

55BC and **54BC** Caesar leads expeditions to Britain.

46BC Caesar annexed east Numidia to form Africa Nova. In 40BC Octavian annexed west Numidia, and joined the two with Tripolitania to form Africa Proconsularis.

40–33BC Caesar's assassination led to civil war. The Parthian Empire occupied Roman Syria and advanced into Anatolia, where they were defeated. This war with Parthia didn't end formally until 20BC but the two empires continued to lock horns over the next two centuries.

35–33BC Dalmatian Wars: Octavian reconquered the area. The province of Illyricum was formed in 27BC. The Delmatae revolt again in 12BC and again in AD6.

30BC After defeating Anthony and Cleopatra, Octavian became pharaoh of the first Imperial province, Alexandrea et Aegyptus.

29BC Settlements in 27BC and 23BC divided Roman territory into provinces Octavian (as emperor) agreed to oversee (and the legions that were stationed in them) and those overseen by the Senate.

27–19BC Octavian is granted the name Augustus. Cantabrian Wars: the conquest of northwestern Spain led to the complete subjugation of the Iberian peninsula. A hotspot of discontent, it took two permanent legions in the territory for most of the next century to maintain order.

16–15BC Raetia became an Imperial province in 15BC. Noricum was also placed under an Imperial procurator. It became a province in AD43.

14–10BC Pannonian War: rebellions in southern Pannonia and northern Dalmatia.

12BC Germanic Wars: Forces under Drusus crossed the Rhine into Germania, retaliating for persistent raids.

9BC Pannonia annexed and incorporated into Illyricum.

AD5 Tiberius conquered Germania Inferior.

6–9 Batonian War: another rebellion on the Dalmatian coast led to a protracted and bloody war.

9 Judea became a province.

9 Publius Quintilius Varus lost three legions (*XVII*, *XVIII*, and *XIX*) and six cohorts of cavalry, at the battle of the Teutoburg Forest.

The Varusschlacht museum is at Kalkriese, Germany, the likely site of the Teutoburg Forest battle. Its logo is this recreation of a cavalryman's mask. Augustus's reaction is quoted in Suetonius, "*Quintili Vare, legiones redde!*" (Quintilius Varus, give me back my legions!)

Constructed in 81 by Domitian, the Arch of Titus honors his brother Titus's deification, and his and his father Vespasian's victory over the Jewish rebellion of 66–73. This image shows the soldiers taking spoils of war from Jerusalem. Note the menorah candlestick. As with most Roman sculptures, it would have been painted.

14 The death of Augustus led to mutinies on the Rhine and the Danube. Tiberius' adopted and actual son were instrumental in putting the rebellions down, Germanicus in Germania and Drusus in Pannonia respectively.

14–16 Germanicus attacked the tribes over the Rhine and retrieved two of Varus's lost eagles.

42 Aulus Gabinius Secundus regains Varus's final lost eagle from the Chauci.

43 Emperor Claudius invaded Britain with four legions commanded by Aulus Plautius. The same year, Lycia in Turkey was annexed after internal fighting—in 74 Vespasian combined it with Pamphylia.

44 Mauretania, a vassal state, became two provinces—Mauretania Tingitana and Mauretania Caesariensis.

46 Thrace became a province.

58–63 Parthian War: caused by problems in buffer state Armenia, the deciding battle was a Parthian victory in 62 at Rhandeia. The Parthian King Tiridates accept the crown of Armenia from Rome. The loss of Armenia meant that Rome had to rethink its eastern strategy.

66–73 The first of three Jewish rebellions started with the ambush and massacre of the Roman Syrian army and ended with the siege of Masada.

69–70 Batavian rebellion in Germania Inferior, probably encouraged by Vespasian because it tied down troops loyal to Vitellius—*legiones V Alaudae* and *XV Primigenia* were besieged in the fortress at Vetera (Xanten, Germany) and ultimately surrendered and massacred. The revolt was defeated by Quintus Petillius Cerialis, but not before *legiones I Germanica* and *XVI Gallica* had sided with the rebels. After the revolt was squashed, there were repercussions. *Legiones IV Macedonica* and *XVI Gallica* were disbanded (they were reconstituted as *legiones IV Flavia Felix* and *XVI Flavia Firma*). *Legio I Germanica* was disbanded, some of its men joining *legio VII,* which was given the cognomen *Gemina*.

69–70 Julius Sabinus, a Roman officer, set up an independent Gaulish state, but was easily defeated by a local tribe, the Sequani, who remain loyal.

76 Anatolia consolidated into the consular province Cappadocia.

82/33 Domitian campaigned against the Chatti in Germania with new *legio I Minervia*.

c. 100–105 During this period, probably under imperial command, the army in Britannia withdrew to the Stanegate line. The northern Brigantes chased them down.

101–106 Dacian Wars: Trajan conquered Dacia in two wars, after which it becomes a province.

106 Trajan captured the city of Petra and annexes the Nabatean kingdom.

113–117 Trajan started aggressive action in the east against the Parthians, first taking Armenia, killing its Parthian king and creating a province, and then Mesopotamia, before advancing to the Parthian capital, Ctesiphon, creating new provinces of Babylon and Assyria. During his campaign there was a second Jewish revolt that was suppressed by Lusius Quietus.

The Roman Empire had now reached its greatest size, 3.5 million sq miles, with an estimated sixty million inhabitants. In around 350 years—from 264BC, when it gained its first overseas province to the capture of Dacia—the empire had grown exponentially. The next 350 years saw it fighting to maintain sway over its territories, with its main enemies being those thrown up by internal politics.

Three metopes from the Tropaeum Traiani, built to commemmorate Trajan's victory at today's Adamclisi, Romania in 109. (See p. 152.) *Vexillifera* carry their *vexillum* standards; in the middle a *signifer* with his *signum* (**LEFT**); the Emperor Trajan (**CENTER**); Roman killing a Dacian (**RIGHT**), note the latter's long-bladed *falx*.

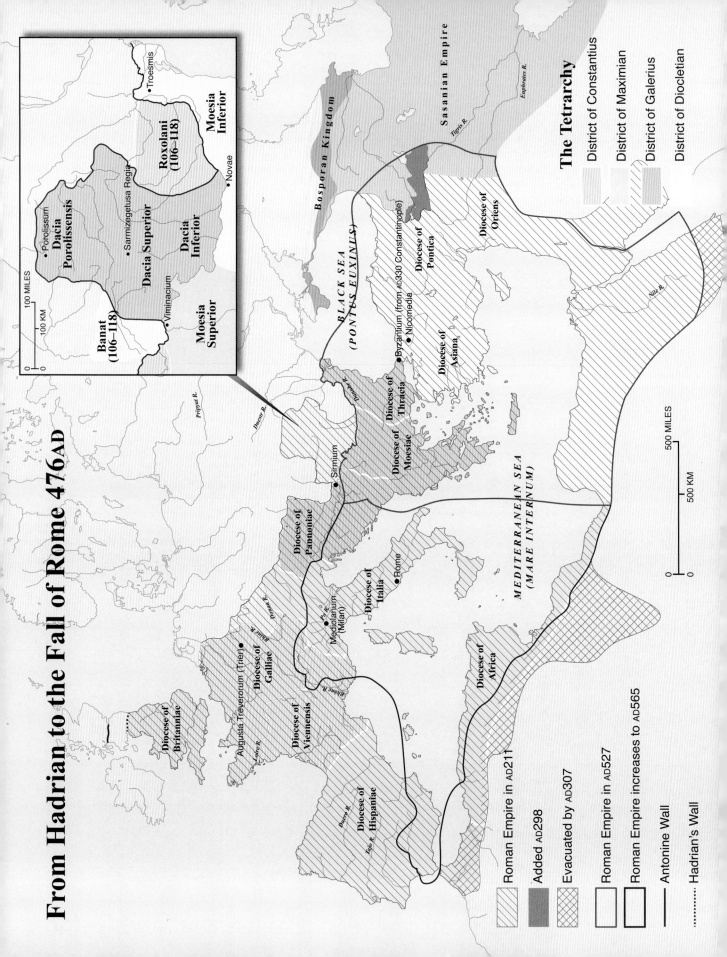

From Hadrian to the Fall of Rome 476 AD

Inset map (Dacia)

Troesmis

Moesia Inferior

Roxolani (106–118)

Novae

Porolissum

Dacia Porolissensis

Sarmizegetusa Regia

Dacia Superior

Dacia Inferior

Banat (106–118)

Viminacium

Moesia Superior

100 MILES
100 KM

Main map

Pripyat R.

Dniestr R.

Dniestr R.

BLACK SEA (PONTUS EUXINUS)

Bosporan Kingdom

Sasanian Empire

Tigris R.

Euphrates R.

Byzantium (from AD330 Constantinople)

Nicomedia

Diocese of Pontica

Diocese of Oriens

Diocese of Asiana

Tigris R.

Nile R.

Diocese of Thracia

Danube R.

Diocese of Moesiae

Sirmium

Diocese of Pannoniae

Drava R.

Danube R.

Po R.

Mediolanum (Milan)

Diocese of Italia

Rome

MEDITERRANEAN SEA (MARE INTERNUM)

Diocese of Africa

Rhine R.

Augusta Treverorum (Trier)

Diocese of Galliae

Diocese of Viennensis

Rhône R.

Loire R.

Garonne R.

Diocese of Britanniae

Diocese of Hispaniae

Duero R.

Tajo R.

500 MILES
500 KM

The Tetrarchy

District of Constantius

District of Maximian

District of Galerius

District of Diocletian

Legend

Roman Empire in AD211

Added AD298

Evacuated by AD307

Roman Empire in AD527

Roman Empire increases to AD565

Antonine Wall

Hadrian's Wall

In AD117 the empire was a colossus. Its lines of control and communication had become too stretched to govern such distances in a world without a more advanced forms of technology. The expense of far-off military operations—particularly in the deserts of Arabia or the forests of northern Europe—was considerable. They also required large armies and local commanders. This often resulted in civil war caused by strong charismatic provincial leaders with the backing of their legions whenever there were problems with the imperial succession. Others on the outside looked in at Rome's tantalizing wealth with envy, as did those to whom the prospects of work, advancement, and citizenship were prized. The empire needed to control access to its markets and improve its finances through regulating as well as defending its borders. All these factors contributed toward a retrenchment and Hadrian started the process.

In 117 Hadrian became the fourteenth Emperor of Rome. An experienced soldier whose senatorial family had Hispano-Roman roots, he had served in various legions all over the empire, including as a tribune of *legio II Adiutrix* in Britain in c. 95. Hadrian was a believer in the Augustan warning to his successors—that they should keep the empire within the natural boundaries of the Rhine, the Danube, and the Euphrates. However this was tempered with a realistic appraisal of the current situation rather than just the implementation of an old ideal. Following many years of almost reckless Roman expansion and military overreach, Hadrian began a stable reign of twenty-one years in which he sought to define and retain what was worthwhile, and give up or contain what was not. In this way—and uniquely for a Roman emperor—he began making lengthy tours of most of the empire, reviewing all infrastructure, especially military, in each province, from a practical, strategic, and geopolitical perspective. He also inspected his armed forces (there's a testament to this in Lambaesis, Algeria; see p. 181). To keep the troops fit, instill discipline, and maintain morale he introduced a system of regular intensive drills and maneuvers. Partly to compensate for the attrition of offensive operations and their drain on Roman manpower, he then instigated a new policy of strengthened defense, with the addition of visible physical fortified barriers to delineate the empire's frontiers wherever necessary. Although unpopular with the militaristic senate, Hadrian's retrenchment of the borders began a period of consolidation, as he sought to end the drive for relentless conquest as a means of advancement in Rome.

In 122 he arrived in Britain, which in the previous two years had seen a major rebellion break out in the north. He reasoned that the number of troops required to hold the glens of Caledonia would not be worth the expense for such meager gains and decided instead that northern Britain should have a unique solid linear barrier which would require fewer troops to garrison. It would be set within a control zone to monitor civilian tribal traffic, intercept problems, and to act as a first line of defense against a determined attack. It was also to be a visual manifestation of the power and capabilities of Rome "*qui barbaros Romanosque divideret*" (to separate the barbarians and the Romans; *Historia Augusta*). It would be built primarily by the three legions based in Britain, with the aid of their attached *auxilia* and men from the Roman British fleet, the *classis Britannica*.

In 123 growing tension with Parthia drew him eastward. Following Augustus, he chose to re-establish the Euphrates as the limit of Roman control and so withdrew from Trajan's recent conquests in Mesopotamia, Assyria, and Armenia. He also personally negotiated a settlement with the Parthian King Osroes I which would last for a considerable time. Hadrian had fought in the Dacian wars himself, but he now considered giving up that province entirely. Unsurprisingly, in the end he decided to keep the part that included the extremely valuable gold mines, content to restore the remainder as a friendly native client kingdom that could once again act as a Roman-influenced buffer zone. On the Rhine–Danube frontier he further expanded Trajan's defenses,

OPPOSITE The Roman Empire was surprisingly resilient in its last 350 years in spite of plague, civil war, and external threats. By the end, however, Rome had lost its position of eminence. In 293 Diocletian attempted to divide the imperial power into four—two senior emperors (Augustus), and two juniors who would be their successors (Caesar). It didn't work. In 324 Constantine I became sole emperor and ruled from Constantinople. This city would take up the mantle of Rome. The Byzantine Empire—mainly in the east, but occasionally extending into the west (as in 565 after Belisarius's victories)—would last for nearly a thousand more years.

adding an extensive 200-mile timber palisade studded with watchtowers and forts, linked with a metaled road and protected by rear defense berms. In the African provinces of Arabia and Tripolitania he added more camps and linear fortifications to augment the natural desert and mountain boundaries. Then, in 132, the province of Judaea erupted in a sustained revolt that took three years to quell and cost Rome another legion's worth of casualties. Hadrian eventually crushed all resistance, destroyed Jerusalem and renamed the province Syria Palaestina.

The growing shortage of manpower within the empire now pressured him to seek soldiers where he could find them, and so to augment the conventional Roman forces of legions and *auxilia* he began to recruit and use less costly *numeri*. *Numeri* were ethnic non-citizen troops under the command of their own leaders and responsible for their own organization and weapons, who could be hired for specific missions or tasks. Such units were drawn largely from the peoples of client states beyond the borders of the empire, but also from some of the more wild tribes within it. As well as saving money and resources, this policy also encouraged more communication and integration between the Roman state, its subject peoples, and its various neighbors, although detractors argued it diluted and degraded the military. Hadrian's provincial roots gave him a different perspective from the conventional Rome-centric stance taken by its aristocracy and usual rulers. He also appreciated and loved Greek art and culture and so sought to develop a more inclusive approach toward other parts of the empire outside Italy. He granted more autonomy, promoted diversity and tolerance, and the empire's provincial urban and tribal centers at this time began to reflect his approach.

Until the beginning of the second century AD, when the borders stabilized, Rome's continuous expansion meant that the legions had moved around continuously, needing permanent camps only for winter quarters. As Hadrian began building more permanent borders, so the legions became more fixed in their locations, with the soldiers allowed to marry and families congregate around the camps in which they were stationed. The highest ranking of these provincial new towns were the official *coloniae*, usually based around land granted to legionaries and auxiliaries on retirement. These veteran soldiers received land and/or a military diploma granting citizenship to them and their dependents, and so there were more Roman citizens in this type of town and they were administered in accordance with Roman customs and practices. Next were the *municipia*, with a more mixed population and more likelihood of local laws, as the local population did not seek to become Roman citizens. Third were the *civitates*, which were usually market towns and capitals of tribal areas. Finally, there were the *vici* and *canabae* that developed around forts and other military sites to provide other unofficial personal services to the troops. In this way the military nature of a border became more established and more firmly anchored within its landscape.

Following Hadrian, a brief highpoint was enjoyed by the empire in the reigns of the last two of the "Five Good Emperors": Antoninus Pius and Marcus Aurelius. But trouble was already coming from both inside and out. The hardened borders had helped to define the empire, but in the succession crises of the late second and third centuries they proved to be insufficient, as a cascade of disasters unfolded. The Marcomannic Wars of 166–180 saw multiple invasions along the length of the Danube that penetrated deep into the empire. Pandemics also raged—the Antonine Plague in 165–180 and later the Cyprian in 249–262—killing millions, brought by soldiers returning from the east and the war with Parthia. The Severan devaluation of the currency to cope with the consequent fall in

The column of Marcus Aurelius in Rome probably depicts the emperor's successful AD176 expedition against the Marcomanni, Quardi, and Sarmatians.

Claustra Alpium Iuliarum (Barrier of the Julian Alps)
The Postojna Gate in today's Slovenia is a mountain pass that allowed access from the east of the empire to Italy and the west. It was a gateway that had been used many times in the past, and after the Great Illyrian Revolt of AD6–9—quelled only by dogged, bloody fighting by Tiberius, Germanicus, and Lepidus—had made use of it, Augustus organized blocking defenses. However, it took the invasion of the Alemanni in 271 to really get things going and it was Diocletian who pushed hard to get a series of *clausurae*—similar to those found in Numidia and Mauretania (see pp. 179–180 and 186–187)—erected. These weren't continuous linear defenses like Hadrian's Wall but shorter elements that blocked access through valleys and passes. They spread from Forum Iulii in Italy to Tarsatica on the Adriatic coast (see map on p. 126), reaching almost to Enoma (today's Ljubljana). The defenses centered on the forts of Ad Pirum (**ABOVE**) and Castra ad Fluvium Frigidum. Ad Pirum had a garrison of 500; Castra had fourteen towers and 11ft-thick walls.

revenues caused a deep and lasting economic depression. The stability and peaceful transfer of power between emperors was lost in savage bouts of self-interest, secession, and civil war. Between 235 and 285, the empire had more than twenty different rulers and split into three parts: Gallic, Roman, and Palmyrene. These visible cracks emphasized the fact that the empire's sheer size made ruling impossible for a single man.

In 284 Diocletian took back control and briefly restored stability, defeating the northern barbarians and Persians, and ending the economic crisis. He also oversaw the end of the Augustus's Principate—where the emperor was first among equals—and the beginning of the more autocratic Dominate period. He created the Tetrarchy by dividing the empire in half and giving each a pair of rulers: a senior *augustus* and junior successor *caesar*. Rome was no longer the capital, but rather Mediolanum (Milan) in the west and Nicomedia in the east. This attempt to forge a new paradigm soon ended in fierce competition after his death and twenty years later Constantine I reunified the whole empire once more. Constantine excelled as a military commander, repeatedly defeating all the tribes along Rome's immense

This well-known porphyry sculpture is in Venice, having been looted from Constantinople during the infamous Fourth Crusade of 1204. It probably depicts the first Tetrarchy made up of the two *augusti*, Diocletian and Maximian, and two *caesars*, Galerius and Constantius I, and is dated to c. 300.

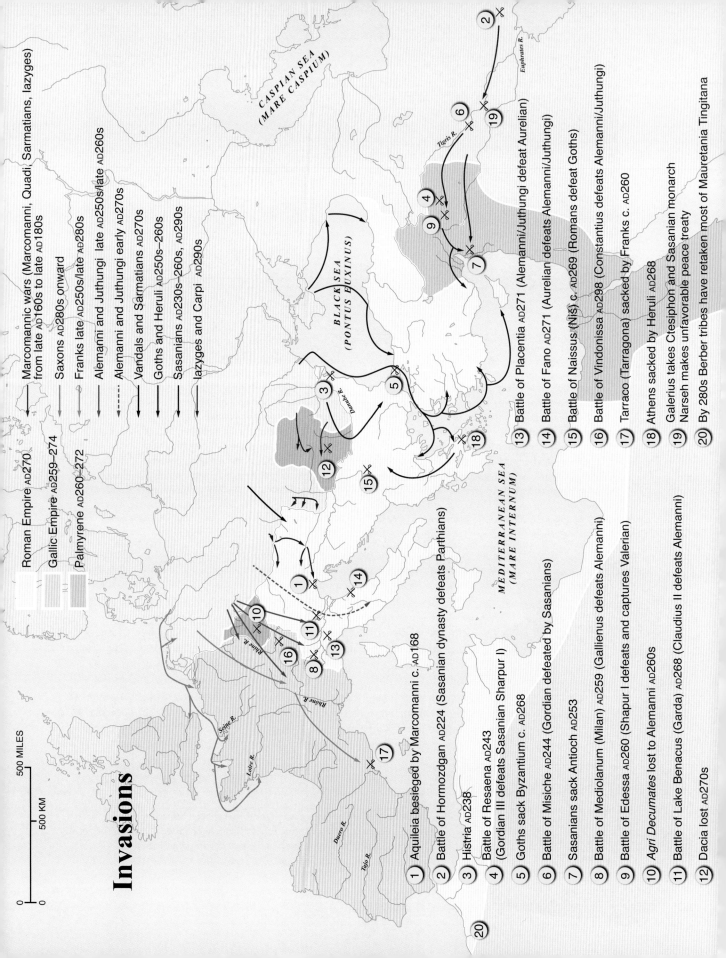

Invasions

0
500 MILES

0
500 KM

CASPIAN SEA
(MARE CASPIUM)

BLACK SEA
(PONTUS EUXINUS)

MEDITERRANEAN SEA
(MARE INTERNUM)

Euphrates R.

Tigris R.

Danube R.

Rhine R.

Rhône R.

Seine R.

Loire R.

Duero R.

Tajo R.

Roman Empire AD270

Gallic Empire AD259–274

Palmyrene AD260–272

Marcomannic wars (Marcomanni, Quadi, Sarmatians, Iazyges)
from late AD160s to late AD180s

Saxons AD280s onward

Franks late AD250s/late AD280s

Alemanni and Juthungi late AD250s/late AD260s

Alemanni and Juthungi early AD270s

Vandals and Sarmatians AD270s

Goths and Heruli AD250s–260s

Sasanians AD230s–260s, AD290s

Iazyges and Carpi AD290s

1. Aquileia besieged by Marcomanni c. AD168
2. Battle of Hormozgan AD224 (Sasanian dynasty defeats Parthians)
3. Histria AD238
4. Battle of Resaena AD243 (Gordian III defeats Sasanian Sharpur I)
5. Goths sack Byzantium c. AD268
6. Battle of Misiche AD244 (Gordian defeated by Sasanians)
7. Sasanians sack Antioch AD253
8. Battle of Mediolanum (Milan) AD259 (Gallienus defeats Alemanni)
9. Battle of Edessa AD260 (Shapur I defeats and captures Valerian)
10. *Agri Decumates* lost to Alemanni AD260s
11. Battle of Lake Benacus (Garda) AD268 (Claudius II defeats Alemanni)
12. Dacia lost AD270s
13. Battle of Placentia AD271 (Alemanni/Juthungi defeat Aurelian)
14. Battle of Fano AD271 (Aurelian defeats Alemanni/Juthungi)
15. Battle of Naissus (Niš) c. AD269 (Romans defeat Goths)
16. Battle of Vindonissa AD298 (Constantius defeats Alemanni/Juthungi)
17. Tarraco (Tarragona) sacked by Franks c. AD260
18. Athens sacked by Heruli AD268
19. Galerius takes Ctesiphon and Sasanian monarch Narseh makes unfavorable peace treaty
20. By 280s Berber tribes have retaken most of Mauretania Tingitana

northern frontier, from the Franks and the Alemanni in 306–308 to the Goths in 323. He then consolidated the Rhine and Danube borders, reasserting Roman control over territory that had been previously abandoned, and pushed the Pannonian *limes* eastward to produce the Sarmatian *limes*, designed to protect his clients the Iazyges. He also enacted the Milan Edict in 313, converted to Christianity, and relocated the capital to Byzantium (which became known as Constantinople after his death), actions that set the scene for the continued survival of the eastern half of the Roman Empire in its future Byzantine form.

At his death his sons divided the empire among themselves before fighting each other for sole supremacy. Constantius II had to concentrate on repeatedly defending the eastern border against Sasanian invasions under the Shapurs and in 363 the last of the dynasty, Julian the Apostate, was killed by the Persians at the battle of Samarra, although he had successfully held the north. Valentinian I had earned his spurs fighting on the northern frontier and continued to have to contend with its problems when in 367 what seemed like (and so was called) a "great conspiracy" of tribes from the far north of Britain to the Rhine surged over the borders or raided by sea. He sent his general, Theodosius, to defeat the Picts and Scots in Britain while he fought against the Saxons and Alemanni to restore order on the continent.

The repeated failures of the frontiers to hold back invaders had made the empire more porous and prompted an evolution in the modes of defense. Established border fortifications in critical areas were still maintained and manned by local garrisoned troops—*limitanei*—but the legions morphed into mobile field armies (*comitatenses*), with a high proportion of heavy cavalry in their ranks. Kept close by emperors for their own personal reassurance, they were also capable of responding as a rapid reaction force against any internal or external threats. Disgruntled provincial cities, the targets of marauding raiders, began to resent paying tax and hardened their own individual defenses, building walls, towers, and citadels to protect themselves. Thus the reality of defense in depth evolved in having to cope with deeper barbarian penetrations, as well as the instability engendered by the high turnover of emperors.

In the end nothing could stop the exodus from the far north, as another climate-driven mass movement of peoples began around 376. It was to have devastating consequences for the western empire. Pushed inexorably southward, Huns, Goths, Vandals, and Germanic tribes gradually overwhelmed the cities and provinces that were left to fend for themselves. The Roman way of interfacing with tribes and peoples they had encountered was usually to beat them in battle then seduce them with trade, technology, and civilization, to synthesize a Roman-flavored composite. They were not averse to adopting new weapons and industrial processes, finding compatible gods or even adopting new ones wholesale, nor in making use of the skills of others when superior to their own.

ABOVE Constantius I's son, Constantine, was proclaimed emperor in York, north England, in 306 when his father died. Eighteen years later, after beating off his rivals, he was the only one left standing. He espoused Christianity and moved his capital to Byzantium, which was renamed after him: Constantinople.

OPPOSITE The crisis of the third century was caused by internal issues—specifically, the inability of the imperial establishment to maintain continuity of succession. Without secure succession, it seemed as if any leader with military backing could throw his hat into the ring and take his chance at glory. Ever since the days of Gaius Marius, Pompey, and Julius Caesar, leaders who looked after their legions had built-in backing. The trouble was that in the third century, few of them stayed in power long enough to ensure continuity. Unsurprisingly, this in-fighting meant that the external threats were not dealt with prophylactically and the empire had to deal with direct attacks by Alemanni, Sasanians, Marcomanni, Vandals, Goths, and others.

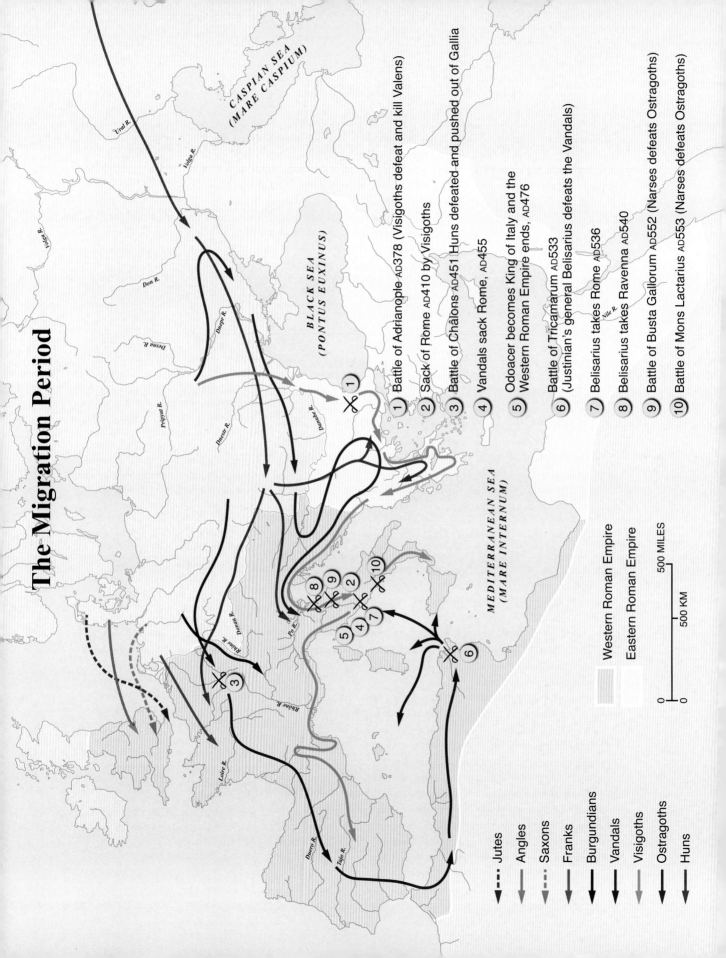

The Migration Period

CASPIAN SEA
(MARE CASPIUM)

BLACK SEA
(PONTUS EUXINUS)

MEDITERRANEAN SEA
(MARE INTERNUM)

Ural R.
Volga R.
Don R.
Dnepr R.
Desna R.
Pripyat R.
Dnestr R.
Danube R.
Drava R.
Rhine R.
Po R.
Rhône R.
Loire R.
Duero R.
Tajo R.
Nile R.

1. Battle of Adrianople AD378 (Visigoths defeat and kill Valens)
2. Sack of Rome AD410 by Visigoths
3. Battle of Châlons AD451 Huns defeated and pushed out of Gallia
4. Vandals sack Rome, AD455
5. Odoacer becomes King of Italy and the Western Roman Empire ends, AD476
6. Battle of Tricamarum AD533 (Justinian's general Belisarius defeats the Vandals)
7. Belisarius takes Rome AD536
8. Belisarius takes Ravenna AD540
9. Battle of Busta Gallorum AD552 (Narses defeats Ostragoths)
10. Battle of Mons Lactarius AD553 (Narses defeats Ostragoths)

Western Roman Empire
Eastern Roman Empire

500 MILES
500 KM

Jutes
Angles
Saxons
Franks
Burgundians
Vandals
Visigoths
Ostragoths
Huns

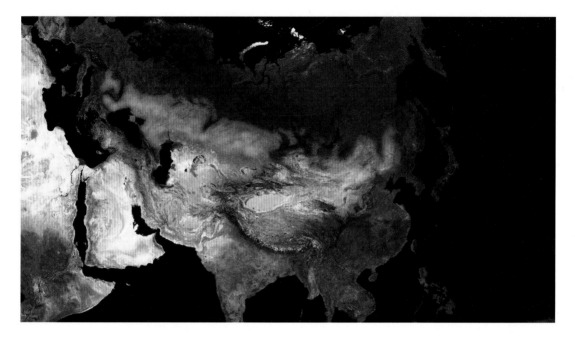

OPPOSITE From the fourth to the sixth century large bands of Germanic and Asian tribes moved west and south. The Germans call it the "*Völkerwanderung*." Many of them saw service with the legions, and some were allowed to settle within the empire, usually as *foederati*, those who had agreed a treaty with Rome. Their reliability was uncertain.

ABOVE This cleverly colored image shows the Eurasian steppe belt running from Manchuria to Hungary. This was the route that so many steppe nomads used to reach Europe, perhaps the best known being Genghis Khan's Mongol hordes. For the Romans, it meant the Scythians, Sarmatians, Iazyges, Goths, Vandals, Visigoths, Franks, Ostragoths, and Huns.

This had begun with Julius Caesar's Gallic cavalry, was formalized with the creation of the *auxilia* and continued, spurred on by a growing shortage of manpower, with the *foederati* (tribes who had agreed by treaty to fight for Rome—an old idea repurposed). However, in the face of such large and continuous migration this system was overwhelmed and began to collapse. Emperors came to rely increasingly on the *foederati*. Eventually whole tribes were granted permission to settle or increasingly, like the Goths, invaded and stayed, making no effort to integrate. Many of them (especially their leaders) had served in the Roman military and assimilated their training and tactics, which made their combat more purposeful, and as they began to organize in ever larger confederations they became dangerously capable and volatile. In 378 Emperor Valens was killed in battle at Adrianople by an army of rebel Goth and Alan *foederati*. Theodesius (379–395) briefly retained control by allowing yet more large numbers of barbarians to settle within the empire in exchange for *foederati* status and military service. Just as Constantine I can be considered one of the critical progenitors of the Byzantine Empire, so too was Theodesius, who made Christianity the official state religion and fortified Constantinople with such massive walls that it remained unconquered until the fifteenth century. On his death the empire was officially divided in half for the last time, between his sons Arcadius and Honorius. It would never be one again.

The eastern half, assigned to Arcadius, was destined through luck and geography to continue in Byzantine form for another thousand years, while the west went through its final death throes. Ravenna became the capital in 402 and Stilicho, regent for the underage emperor Honorius, defeated or dealt with various invasive tribes and won back lost ground until his execution in 408. With his death, a final collapse began. Britain was abandoned,

Gaul conquered by Visigoths and Franks, Hispania taken the Suebi, and North Africa fell to the Vandals. In 410 a Visigoth invasion led to the sack of Rome for the first time in 800 years: a momentous symbolic event despite the fact that it hadn't been the capital for some time. Another general, Constantius, helped Honorius fight off various usurpers and regain some control of Hispania and Gaul by 420 and was rewarded by being made co-emperor.

It was a brief respite. Carthage fell to the Vandals in 439, and in 444 the Hun tribes, united under their famous ruler Attila, intensified their raiding on the provinces of the northeastern frontier in the Balkans, then switched to cross over the Rhine and into Gaul. In 451 a Roman coalition with federated elements of Germanic tribes (Burgundians and Visigoths) managed to defeat Attila in Gaul, but he regrouped and invaded Italy the following year. He was persuaded not to storm Rome through a mixture of negotiation, plague among his troops, and an invasion of the Hun home territory by the Eastern Roman Emperor Marcian. The chaos continued. Another general, Orestes, deposed Julius Nepos in 474 and made his own teenage son, the ironically named Romulus Augustulus, emperor—of nothing much, just most of Italy and a very small part of Gaul. Finally, in 476 another rebel Germanic *foederati* officer, Odacer, stormed the capital Ravenna, deposed Romulus Augustulus, and had himself crowned King of Italy. The western empire had come to its end.

The historical surge of the northern tribes changed the nature of Europe, but Roman culture was not destroyed in the process. Much had been absorbed by the tribes through many centuries of contact. Many of them had served in the Roman military, used Roman weaponry and were Christian in some form or another. The Germanic kingdoms that replaced Rome were, therefore, not a clean sweep of all that had gone before, but rather a rewilding or rebalancing of the elements that make up the European dynamic.

The pharos at Dover, on the south coast of England, is dwarfed by Henry II's rebuild of the original eleventh-century Norman castle. It sits alongside the church of St Mary in Castro. The pharos (**A**) acted as the medieval church's belltower. The octagonal pharos was built at the same time the Romans built a fort for the *classis Britannica*. (The first three levels are Roman; the final is medieval.) There was another on the western shore and they served as navigation beacons for the fleet. The fort was rebuilt in 270.

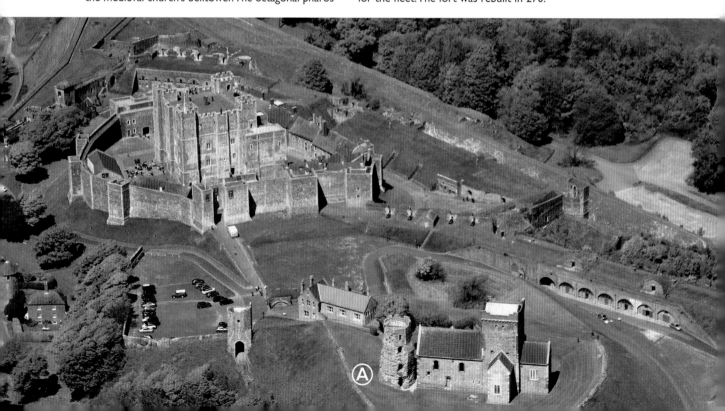

Timeline: AD117–527

118 New emperor Hadrian was forced to fight in Dacia where the Roxolani and Iazyges rebelled after Trajan stopped paying them subsidies. Hadrian beat them, but restarted the payments and returned to the Roxolani the part of Dacia that had been given to Moesia Inferior. Dacia was reorganized and in 120 split into Superior and Inferior. By 123 Dacia Porolissensis was established from NW Dacia Superior.

c. 119–122 Fighting in Britain. The *Expeditio Britannica* was sent from the continent with 3,000 legionaries. At some time in this period *legio IX Hispana* left Britain and *legio VI Victrix* arrived.

121–126 On Hadrian's first voyage, he visited Britain. His eponymous wall was probably planned and started during this visit. Most of the wall was constructed by 126. The vallum was added after the forts were built, running from around Milecastle 5 to Bowness, with a short disruption in the marshy area from Milecastle 73 to 76.

140–144 The Romans moved north to the Forth–Clyde line and built the turf and timber Antonine Wall. Around this time, the defenses of Hadrian's Wall were decommissioned.

148 An attack on the Antonine Wall. This would be a continuing story.

154 Revolt of the Brigantes.

161–166 Parthian War: in 162, the Parthians invaded Armenia; successful Roman defense ended with the counter-invasion of Parthia 165–166.

162–165 The Chatti and Chauci invaded Raetia and Germania Superior but were repulsed.

165–180 The Antonine Plague—perhaps a smallpox or measles pandemic—decimated Rome and the Roman Army, reducing capabilities on the Rhine. Probably introduced by soldiers returning from Parthia, the death toll was as many as ten million—up to a third of the Roman population.

166 Rome threatened by the Marcomannic wars: an invasion of Raetia, Germania Superior, and Dacia.

177 Second Marcomannic War started with a rebellion by the Quadi, followed by the Marcomanni.

182 Third Marcomannic War: further Roman victories don't hide the fact that the Germanic frontier required a permanent military presence—up to as many as sixteen legions would be garrisoned there.

184–185 Northern tribes—the Caledonii—took advantage of the death of Marcus Aurelius and crossed the wall.

192–195 Civil war followed the murder of Commodus at the end of 192 (a plot that may well have involved Lucius Septimius Severus, governor of Upper Pannonia). Among the many claimants, Severus (with sixteen legions along the Rhine and Danube) was the closest to Italy and defeated the opposition.

RIGHT Tombstone of Vonatorix, a cavalryman, found in Bonn in 1891. Dating to the start of the second century AD it shows key military features: the four-horned saddle; lack of stirrups (they wouldn't arrive in Europe until the seventh century AD); a long spear raised for thrusting; sword and hexagonal shield. The inscription reads: *Vonatorix Du/conis f(ilius) eques ala/ Longiniana an/norum XLV stipen/ diorum XVII h(ic) s(itus) e(st).* This translates as: "Vonatorix, son of Duco, trooper of the cavalry regiment Longiniana, lived forty-five years, served seventeen years. He lies here."

195–196 Parthian War: Severus attacked the Parthians and annexed the kingdom of Osrhoene, but had to move west to deal with Albinus, who invaded Gaul.

196–197 Civil war: battle of Lugdunum (Lyon) in February 197, leaves Severus as undisputed emperor. In Britain, the Maeatae, Brigantes, and Caledonii cross Hadrian's Wall to cause major problems. They are too strong for the weakened Romans and the new governor, Virius Lupus, has to buy peace.

197–198 Raising three new legions (*legiones I*, *II*, and *III* all with the cognomen *Parthica*), Severus invaded Parthia with *I* and *III*, leaving *legio II* near Rome—partly as a strategic reserve and partly to secure his rear.

197 Severus captured Ctesiphon, and rebuilt the province of Mesopotamia (leaving new legions as a garrison).

202–203 Severus returned to Africa, advancing the frontier south into the Sahara.

c. 211 Britain divided into two provinces: Britannia Inferior, run from Eboracum by a praetorian governor, and Britannia Superior, commanded by a consular governor in London. The victories of Severus kept the north fairly quiet for some years.

211 Death of Severus at Eboracum. He was succeeded by his sons, Caracalla and Geta. Hadrian's Wall became the boundary of empire once again. Caracalla went on to kill Geta.

212 Caracalla granted Roman citizenship to most freeborn inhabitants of the empire—a significant change for the Roman Army; until then, there had been a citizenship distinction between legions and *auxilia*.

214 Caracalla changed the provincial boundary of Pannonnia Inferior to take in Brigetio (and, therefore, *legio I Adiutrix*). Each of the Pannonian provinces now had two legions.

218 The so-called "crisis of the third century" had its roots in the early years of the century after Caracalla and then Macrinus were assassinated.

Hadrian's Wall runs on top of the Whin Sill making the best of the geography. Septimius Severus came to Britain in 208 to extend Roman control over Scotland. He campaigned for three years before dying in York. During this period, he retook the Southern Lowlands and rebuilt Roman forts and military establishments in the north of England, probably resuscitating the Antonine Wall, but after his death his successors (his sons Caracalla and Geta) made peace and his gains did not survive for long, the border returning to Hadrian's Wall.

Ignominy. This relief at Naqsh-e Rostam near Persepolis in Iran shows the result of what was possibly the greatest military disaster to befall a Roman emperor. Shapur I, the Sasanian king of kings, triumphs over the Emperor Valerian at Edessa in 260. The result was havoc in the empire as a number of new emperors were declared. Poor old Valerian lived out his life in captivity, the sources divided as to the conditions.

220 The first Saxon raids started on southeast Britain.

224 A new, more vibrant enemy arrived in the east after the battle of Hormozdgan saw Ardashir the Unifier of the Sasanian Empire defeat the Parthians, whose empire fell. A few years later, in c. 230 the Sasanians launched a war to reconquer lost lands in the Roman east.

234 Germanic and Sarmatian tribes invaded over the Rhine and Danube. Alexander Severus took an army north.

235 Severus was killed by his troops near Mogontiacum (Mainz). Maximinus Thrax, commander of *legio IV Italica*, became emperor and continued the campaign against the Alemanni successfully, before moving to Pannonia where he campaigned against the Dacians and Sarmatians.

237 Persians invaded the province of Mesopotamia.

239 Gothic invasion of Lower Moesia repelled.

244 Philip the Arab negotiated peace with Persia and paid a large indemnity. He had to do this in order to get back to Rome to secure his position and then to deal with the troubles on the Rhine/Danube border. Significantly, he was forced to cut payments to client states north of the Rhine/Danube border.

245 Philip campaigned against the Carpi, who had crossed into Moesia.

248 A real *annus horribilis* for Rome. Rebellions by the army in Pannonia and Moesia. Many tribes invaded the northern provinces.

249–253 Goth invasion: King Kniva crossed the Rhine into Roman territory; defeated by Aemilianus in Moesia.

249–262 Plague of Cyprian—possibly smallpox, influenza, or even ebola—badly affected the army.

252 King Shapur I of Persia attacked again, invading Armenia. He defeated a Roman army at the battle of Barbalissos and invaded the province of Syria.

254–260 In the east, Valerian regained Antioch and Syria, but plague at Edessa cut down his men and he was defeated there in 260 and captured by Shapur I (**ABOVE**).

256–260 The Franks, a Germanic tribe made up of the Cherusci and Chatti, invaded Gaul and Spain. The Alemanni invaded Italy but were defeated outside Rome by the Praetorian Guard, and then at Mediolanum (Milan) by Gallienus. Scared by this encroachment into Italy, Gallienus introduced a mobile cavalry army to stay at Mediolanum to protect Italy. Unfortunately, the commander of the cavalry, Aureolus, eventually claimed the throne himself. Gallienus was assassinated in 268 while besieging Aureolus.

259–275 Britain and Gaul revolted. Marcus Cassianus Latinius Postumus, declared himself emperor (259) of the Gallic provinces.

260 In the east, Odaenathus of Palmyra pushed the Sasanians back, retook all Roman land lost since 252, and ruled the east only nominally under the aegis of the emperor. In the west, *Limesfall*: the Romans abandoned the *limes* in the *Agri Decumates;* the new border was the Rhine–Iller–Danube (see pp. 112–117). There may have been a reassertion of Roman dominance over the area 270–282 under Aurelian and Probus.

267–269 Ship-borne invasions by Goths attacked the Black Sea coast, Byzantium, etc. Defeated by the navy, they attacked southern Greece where Gallienus (or Claudius II with future emperor Aurelian commanding his cavalry: there's debate) defeated them at Naissus River in 268 or 269. The Alemanni, who invaded Raetia and north Italy, were defeated at Lake Benacus (268 or 269) and then headed for the Balkans where a second wave of Goths was invading.

270 The army of Queen Zenobia of Palmyra invaded Egypt and entered the city of Alexandria. Zenobia declared herself empress. She cut off Rome's grain—always something that forced an emperor into action.

270 Aurelian inherited an empire split in three (Rome, Gallic, and Palmyrene empires) with external threats along the Rhine and Danube. His first action was to expel the Vandals, Juthungi, and the Sarmatians from Italy.

271 Battle of Placentia: an invasion of the Alemanni, Marcomanni, and Juthungi ambush Aurelian's army. He defeated them at Fano, again at Pavia, and chased the remnants down and destroyed them in Raetia. He started building the defensive walls around Rome—the Aurelian walls. He then defeated the Goths beyond the Danube but abandoned the province of Dacia and created a new province, Dacia Aureliana in Moesia. It was later split into two: Dacia Ripensis and Mediterranea.

272 Aurelian moved east and defeated Zenobia at the battle of Immae, outside Antioch, then at Emesa before taking Palmyra. Aurelian's general Marcus Aurelius Probus retook the other African provinces.

273 Palmyra revolted. The city was destroyed by Aurelian.

274 Aurelian returned to Europe and defeated the army of the Gallic Empire at Châlons, reannexing it after thirteen years of schism. Aurelian was honored with the title *Restitutor Orbis* (Restorer of the World).

277 Probus and his generals defeated the Burgundians, Longiones, Alemanni, and Franks, cleared the Goths and Germanic tribes from Gaul, and followed them across the Rhine to ensure they stayed put. He exacted tribute from them in the form of manpower, which he settled in border areas to help provide auxiliaries. He rebuilt Hadrian's frontier between Rhine and Danube.

278–280 Probus campaigned against Germanic tribes in Raetia and Vandals in Illyricum.

282 Carus defeated the Quadi and Sarmatians on the Danube. He then thrust deep into Persia. The Sasanian Empire was going through a moment of internal weakness so the attack was well timed.

286 Diocletian's co-emperor, Maximian, gave Carausius—based with the fleet at Gesoriacum Bononia (Boulogne)—the job of dealing with Frank and Saxon pirates in the Channel and North Sea. Carausius later rebelled and took over Britain and northern Gaul as Emperor in the North. He beat Maximian in battle in 288/289, but was assassinated by Allectus who became Emperor of Britannia.

296 Constantius Chlorus was finally strong enough to recover Britain from Allectus.

296 After Constantius takes Britain he instituted a regime of repair and renovation along the wall.

296 Pannonia was divided into four by Diocletian—Prima and Savia in the west; Secunda and Valeria in the east. Other changes saw Noricum split into Ripense and Mediterraneum; Moesia, too, was divided into four: Prima and Dardania out of Superior; Inferior becomes Secunda and Scythia Minor.

306 Constantius died at Eboracum and Constantine was proclaimed emperor. It took till 324 for him to beat his rivals and become sole emperor. He ruled until 337, the last seven years from Byzantium.

312 Constantine defeated Maxentius at the battle of Milvian Bridge. The Praetorian Guard and *equites singulares* (Imperial bodyguard) both of which had fought for Maxentius were disbanded.

324 Constantine pushed the Pannonian *limes* east and created the "Devil's Dykes"—earthworks along the new border. This enraged the Quadi and led to a major incursion into Pannonia in 374.

367 The "great barbarian conspiracy" saw the biggest rebellion against Roman rule in Britain since the Iceni. Valentinian's general, Theodosius, cleared Britain of the invaders and restored the wall.

368 Valentinian I initiated a major overhaul of the *limes* defenses, building many small forts (*burgi*) and watchtowers.

375 Valentinian I retook Pannonia from the Quadi and reestablished Constantine's *limes*. However, he died of a stroke at Brigetio (famously, while berating Quadi envoys) and soon the area was retaken by the barbarians.

376 Pushed south by the Huns, the Visigoths became *foederati* and were allowed to settle south of the Danube.

378 The Visigoths rebelled and Valentinian's brother and co-emperor, Valens, was killed as the Eastern Empire's forces lost the battle of Adrianople to the Goths.

379 Theodosius's son became emperor. On his death in 395, the empire was split into east and west and was never reunited. The *Notitia Dignitatum* was compiled.

402 Alaric I and the Visigoths invaded Italy. they were checked by Stilicho and defeated at Pollentia. Ravenna became imperial headquarters.

406/7 Invasion of Gaul by the Sueves, Alans, and Vandals over the frozen Rhine. Gaul is ravaged. They were defeated by the Visigoths. The Vandals crossed over to Africa in 428/9.

410 Visigoths sacked Rome but their king, Alaric, died soon after.

429 The Vandals migrated under Geiseric from Spain to Africa.

441 Attila crossed Danube and invaded Thrace; invaded again 447.

451 Attila invaded Gaul but was heavily defeated by Roman general Aetius and Visigoth King Theodoric I at Châlons.

452 Attila invaded Italy but spared Rome and retired.

475 Romulus "Augustulus" became the last western emperor but was deposed in 476 by Odoacer, who then ruled nominally as the viceroy of the Eastern Emperor.

527 Justinian the Great (**RIGHT**) became Byzantine emperor. His generals, Belisarius and Liberius, reconquered Italy, bits of North Africa and Spain.

"*La carmagnola*," a porphyry head said to be of Justinian I, probably looted from Byzantium during the infamous Fourth Crusade, today in St. Mark's Square, Venice.

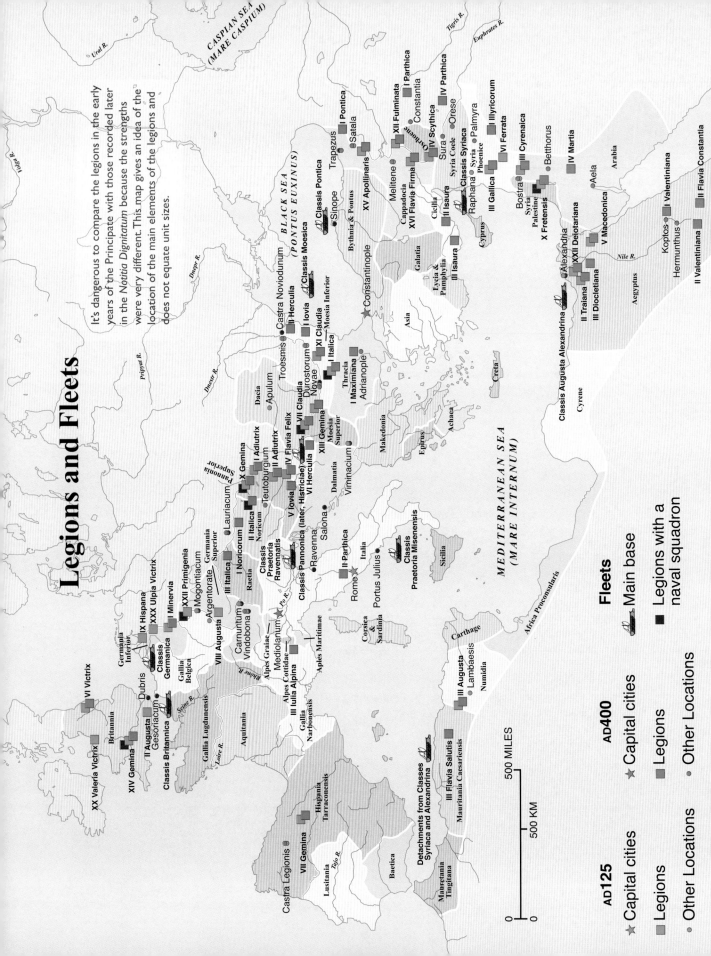

Legions and Fleets

It's dangerous to compare the legions in the early years of the Principate with those recorded later in the *Notitia Dignitatum* because the strengths were very different. This map gives an idea of the location of the main elements of the legions and does not equate unit sizes.

Fleets

AD400
⭐ Capital cities

AD125
⭐ Capital cities
🟦 Legions
• Other Locations

Fleets
⛵ Main base
🟦 Legions with a naval squadron
🟦 Legions
• Other Locations

Ural R.

Volga R.

CASPIAN SEA
(MARE CASPIUM)

Tigris R.

Euphrates R.

Dnepr R.

Dnestr R.

Pripyat R.

BLACK SEA
(PONTUS EUXINUS)

I Pontica
Satala
Trapezus
Classis Pontica
Sinope
Bythinia & Pontus
XV Apollinaris
Melitene
Cappadocia
XVI Flavia Firma
Galatia
Lycia & Pamphylia
III Isaura
II Isaura
Cicilia
Cyprus

I Parthica
Constantia
IV Parthica
Orese
IV Scythica
Sura
Osrhoene
XII Fulminata
Palmyra
Syria Coele
Raphana
Syria Phoenice
Classis Syriaca
III Gallica
VI Ferrata
III Illyricorum
III Cyrenaica
Bostra
Syria Palestine
X Fretensis
Betthorus
IV Martia
Aela
Arabia

II Traiana
III Diocletiana
V Macedonica
XXII Deiotariana
Alexandria
Classis Augusta Alexandrina
Aegyptus
Koptos
I Valentiniana
Hermunthis
II Valentiniana
II Flavia Constantia
Nile R.
Cyrene

Constantinople ⭐

Castra Noviodunum
Troesmis
II Herculia
I Iovia
Classis Herculia
Classis Moesica
XI Claudia
Durostorum
Moesia Inferior
Novae
I Italica
Dacia
Apulum
VII Flavia Felix
XIII Gemina
Moesia Superior
Viminacium
I Maximiana
Thracia
Adrianople

Asia
Makedonia
Achaea
Epirus
Creta

MEDITERRANEAN SEA
(MARE INTERNUM)

I Adiutrix
X Gemina
Teutoburgium
IV Adiutrix
Pannonia Superior
Lauriacum
VI Herculia
V Iovia (later; Histriciae)
III Italica
Noricum
Raetia
Carnuntum
Vindobona
Classis Pannonica
Dalmatia
Salona

IX Hispana
XXX Ulpia Victrix
Minervia
XXII Primigenia
Mogontiacum
Germania Superior
Argentorate
Germania Inferior
VIII Augusta
Classis Germanica
Gallia Belgica
Dubris
Classis Britannica

VI Victrix
XX Valeria Victrix
Britannia
II Augusta
Gesoriacum
XIV Gemina

Alpes Graiae
III Iulia Alpina
Alpes Cottidae
Mediolanum ⭐
Classis Praetoria Ravennatis
Ravenna
Italia
Po R.
Rome ⭐
Portus Julius
Classis Praetoria Misenensis
II Parthica

Apes Maritimae
Gallia Lugdunensis
Gallia Narbonensis
Aquitania
Loire R.
Seine R.
Rhone R.

Corsica & Sardinia
Sicilia

Castra Legionis
VII Gemina
Hispania Tarraconensis
Lusitania
Baetica
Tagio R.

Detachments from Classes Syriaca and Alexandrina

III Flavia Salutis
Mauritania Caesariensis
Mauretania Tingitana
III Augusta
Lambaesis
Numidia
Carthage
Africa Proconsularis

500 MILES

500 KM

2

Border Troops

Replica of a *navis lusoria* (see p. 50) which was used to ferry troops along the Rhine.

Rome's heavy infantry legions reflect their origins in the armored hoplite phalanx of the Greeks, the Etruscans, and the Macedonians. Such an organized formation was almost invariably successful against a disorganized barbarian horde, in spite of the latter's greater numbers. Each Roman legion was a discrete stand-alone unit, based in a fortress within its own specific province—a complete self-contained army in miniature, with all its weapons, artillery, support staff, transport, stores, and ancillary equipment. It was subdivided into sections called cohorts that could operate as one or independently. It was also a Roman society in microcosm, consisting of rank and file legionaries who were all Roman citizens, staffed by centurions—the most experienced soldiers who had risen through the ranks—and officered by men of the senatorial and equestrian classes. It was the forerunner of all modern armies in many ways, being endlessly active and constantly practicing: a professional standing army, undoubtedly the most evolved in the world in its day in the arts of siege warfare and military engineering.

However, more than any modern army, as well as fighting, the legions also built. Using wood, turf, and stone they built roads, bridges, forts, towers, walls, amphitheaters, temples, baths, water and sewage systems, granaries, cemeteries, and monuments—all of which created a radical new infrastructure that increased the spread of Roman civilization. To be capable of doing this a legion contained soldiers who were also craftsmen, including stonemasons, carpenters, plasterers, lead workers, tool-makers, potters, and tilers. Such skilled specialists were termed *immunes* and although they still had to fight when the legion was on active service, they were spared the everyday jobs of guarding, patrolling, firewood collection, and latrine cleaning that were the lot of less qualified men, recruits, or those on punishment details. Because of all these combined capabilities an entire legion was seldom present in one place, except, perhaps, when parading for an emperor or a change of commander, or when involved in a major martial task or relocation. Otherwise, individuals and units were seconded where and when required. Like a modern-day formation it had its central headquarters, but cohorts and specialist subunits would be considerably spread out across its sphere of operations, as could individuals—the *beneficiarii*, for example (see p. 109). However, while a legion's presence would always be obvious within its area noticeable through flags, shields, symbols, and inscriptions, for the most part it was the *auxilia*—the non-citizen soldiers recruited usually from within the empire—that permanently or continuously manned the majority of positions and defenses once they had been built (see p. 40). The legions were kept further back from the front line for their wider strategic capability.

After the Marian reforms of 101BC the legions were standardized and put on a full-time professional footing, with wages paid thrice yearly, a twenty-five year service contract (twenty years plus five years as a reservist for soldiers; twenty-six years for naval troops) and on retirement the choice of a land grant or a sum of money. By recruiting from the poorer classes and unemployed, and later granting all Italian legions Roman citizenship, the army was both considerably democratized and increased in size, thus enabling Rome to field larger forces, maintain its security, and continue its successful expansion. While on active service soldiers were not supposed to get married, but many did unofficially with the obvious tacit compliance of their superiors, for their families often lived just outside their forts in the local civilian settlements known as *vici*. Just as today, if they did not return to their homeland, soldiers tended to retire in the area they had been stationed, where perhaps their wife was from and their children grew up.

Surprisingly perhaps, it is not known precisely how many men were in a legion. Just as with an equivalent modern formation there would be a difference between its strength on paper and in reality, with a steady attrition of manpower through war, accident, illness, retirement or postings to other units, and the officers and commander—tribunes and legates—regularly moving off on their own career trajectories. What can be said is that a legion consisted of approximately 5,500 men, primarily heavy armored infantry, organized into ten cohorts (*cohors*; pl *cohortes*) each of 480 soldiers, but with the first cohort being double the size of the other nine and containing the best and most experienced fighting men.

This mosaic from Mogontiacum (Mainz, Germany) shows the Capricorn symbol of *legio XXII Primigenia*. The legion, which numbered the emperors Hadrian, Didius Julianus, and Laelianus among its alumni, spent most of its existence in Mainz although *vexillationes* are known to have been as far north as the Antonine Wall (an inscription at Blatobulgium) and as far east as Parthia.

The cohort was the basic tactical unit of the legions. A cohort itself was made up of six *centuriae* (centuries) of eighty men, each commanded by a senior centurion with an *optio* serving as his second-in-command. A *centuria* (century) was divided into ten *contubernia* (tent/mess unit) and was commanded by a junior centurion. A *contubernium*, the smallest sub-unit of a legion, was made up of eight men, lead by a *decanus* (not to be confused with the cavalry *decurio*). These eight men shared a leather tent when on campaign or a pair of rooms when in barracks —one for accommodation and the other for equipment.. The other two (to make up the ten) would have been slaves or support troops. Additionally each legion had a 120-man cavalry unit (an *ala*—wing; pl *alae*), called the *eques legionis* who were used as scouts for reconnaissance and as messengers for fast communication. It also had some non-combatants. Being sticklers for record keeping, there was an administrative staff of clerks, along with orderlies for the doctor and the quartermaster, and carters to transport equipment and supplies.

By the third century BC the Roman military assemblage of the late Republic and early Principate period had become the classic legionary equipment most associated with the Roman Empire. It consisted of hooped armor called *lorica segmentata*, although scale armor (*lorica squamata*) and chain mail (*lorica hamata*) were also increasingly used. The helmets worn were full Imperial Gallic, edged in brass, dropping down at the back to a wide, ridged neck protector and with large hinged cheek guards. The primary weapon was the *gladius*, a double-edged and pointed short sword perfect for close-quarter infantry work and used in conjunction with the long semi-cylindrical shield (*scutum*) for slashing and chopping as well as thrusting with its tapered point. Personal equipment was completed with the *pilum*, a type of javelin. It was designed with a hard iron point and a softer, thin shank which bent on contact and rendered the weapon useless until beaten out straight once again, so it could not be reused by the enemy.

Manpower

Recruiting for the Roman Army was always a difficult proposition once Roman wars spread far from home: long years of service, poor pay, death—it's not surprising that the wealthy citizens became more and more reluctant to be called to arms. Substitutes—*vicarii*—were used, and accepted so long as they met the recruitment requirements (height, physical condition, etc). Conscription—*dilectus*—was the standard method of recruitment in the early Republic and continued on into the Principate in provinces as it was needed. It would become a requirement again during the Dominate.

In the early Republic, enfranchisement of the Latins helped, as did the loosening of the property rules—to fight for Rome originally you had to own property. Gaius Marius accepted men below the wealth line—as had happened in extremis in 212bc in the fight against Hannibal. Slowly, the firm link between Italians and service in the legions was broken. Indeed, the salaries of the respective arms of service saw the Italians plump as often as not for the *auxilia*. The process had started during the Republic—Caesar needed troops to fight against the Helvetii he recruited from outside Italy. Commodus, when he made a treaty ending Marcus Aurelius's wars with the Marcomanni and Quadi, demanded recruits as part of the settlement. In the Julio–Claudian period the *auxilia* was almost completely made up of *peregrini*; between 117 and 170, they were overtaken by the numbers of Roman citizens.

Septimius Severus, who died in 211, had instituted reforms. He had increased soldiers' pay (to cover inflation); set up a tax levied in foodstuffs (*annona militaris*) collected by the military (hitherto the cost of their food had to be paid by the soldiers themselves); allowed soldiers to be married—or live with women—while in service (although there is debate about this); improved promotion opportunities; and created a new Praetorian Guard from the provincial legions. He told his sons to look after their troops and by the 212 *Constitutio Antoniniana*, Caracalla did his bit by extending citizenship to all free men within the empire. This immediately meant more taxation—particularly useful being the *decima hereditatum* that paid into Augustus's *aerarium militare* (the military treasury that provided the army pension fund).

The Plague of Cyprian struck in 249 and for twenty years till 270, it killed thousands in both the army and Rome. Increasingly, the Romans needed to fill gaps in the ranks. They did so with *foederati*. Also, as units became more fixed on specific locations in stone fortesses, so recruitment for those units was primarily from their regions—latterly including the children of the soldiers, something Diocletian made mandatory.

The ultimate centurion reenacted by the Ermine Street Guard. Note the *vitis* stick that served as a badge of rank and a purveyance of punishment, transverse crest on his helmet, greaves, and sword on the left (legionaries carried theirs on their right). He's also wearing his decorations: the disk-like *phalerae*, torcs, and *armillae* (bracelets).

Picking off individual targets or hurled en masse in a barrage, a well-thrown pilum could pierce armor or else stick in an enemy's shield and drag it down, exposing him to the oncoming crunch of the Roman front rank.

Artillery

Torsion artillery learnt from the Greeks was further refined by Roman metallurgical skill, giving it greater strength, range, and accuracy. A legion came equipped with some powerful missile weapon systems. Vegetius details fifty-five *carroballista*, with their own specialist crews who operated and maintained them. The heaviest were the onagers (*onagri*) large one-armed catapults firing the biggest of mainly stone ammunition and named after the wild ass because of their huge recoil. Requiring a specially built firing base and a crew of eight to operate, Vegetius writes that ten such weapons were assigned to each legion, one for each cohort. Next came the smaller two-armed catapults. Crossbow-like in appearance and design, they were operated by winding back a windlass held by a rack and pin or cog. The bigger ones were known as *ballistae* and the smaller as *scorpiones*, but there is some confusion between the two in the primary Roman sources. The *ballistae* had a crew of two or more while the *scorpiones* were one-man operated. They all fired iron-headed bolts of different sizes and were sometimes mounted upon carts for mobility and they had a considerable reputation for accuracy.

Vexillatio *(pl* vexillationes*)*

When trouble or distance made it necessary, a *vexillatio* could be detached from a legion to be sent on a particular mission. Usually consisting of a number of cohorts, a *vexillatio* was a task force assembled and sent off separately or combined with elements from other legions into a temporary ad hoc battlegroup. (The name comes from the *vexillum*, a square flag born by such a unit which would feature its parent formation.) In the case of *legio III Augusta* in northern Africa, for example, vexillation went from the legionary fortress at Lambaesis to fight the Parthians in Syria in 115, the Jewish revolt in 132–136, Parthia again in 162–166 and 215–216. By the second century the separation of some detachments from their parent units had become permanent. As time went on all Roman formations became generally smaller as resources dwindled.

The *auxilia*

The Roman legions themselves fought above all as infantrymen, and the pre-Marian Roman army had relied on aristocratic knights, the *equites*, for its horsemen. However the Marian's reforms discouraged this custom and instead the Romans began to develop auxiliaries (*auxilia*), initially from those Italians who did not have citizenship, then from foreign tribes of recently conquered territory, and eventually even from outside the empire. At first these were mainly "horse people," skilled in the art of mounted warfare, who filled a gap in the Roman military and who became steadily more important as the empire grew. As with the legions, recruitment was voluntary and the reward for twenty-five years' service was citizenship for the soldier and his family. Julius Caesar put the process on a proper footing with his recruitment of Gallic horsemen, transforming them and the *auxilia* cavalry with a standardized structure similar to that of the legions. Later, after the Augustan reforms, the *auxilia* was developed to become an integral part of the Roman Army, including light and heavy cavalry, light infantry, and specialized units such as archers or slingers specifically to support and supplement Rome's armored punch of heavy infantry.

Following various revolts carried out by enlisted *auxilia* in their province of origin, such as the Batavian revolt of 69–70, the Roman rule became that of relocation for all *auxilia* units, away from their homelands, with the option to return individually on retirement. The *auxilia* recruited in the western provinces took their unit names from their original tribes or regions. Based on a foreign frontier such a unit maintained its identity with recruitment from the homeland when it could, but as time and the empire went on and units became settled they began to lose their unique identity to their locality, through intermarriage and retirement as well as local replacement. They kept their unit name although most of the personnel were no longer from that location.

It was the *auxilia* that manned many of the defenses on the empire's frontier, *cohortes* and *alae* levied in the countries that Rome had conquered; others, less well defined, are the *numeri*. The *Notitia* records a *numerus barcariorum Tigrisiensium*—bargemen from the Tigris— at Arbeia, the logistical center for Hadrian's Wall. As an example of the widespread nature of the *auxilia*, take the units that we know—through attestation— that were in Moesia during the Flavian period (information from Matei-Popescu, 2012). There were ten *cohortes*—all *quingenaria equitata* (mixed cavalry and infantry with around 480 infantry and 120 cavalry) unless noted:

- *I Antiochensium* (from Antioch in Roman Syria; later given the indication *sagittaria*—archers)
- *I Flavia Bessorum* (from the Besser tribe from Thrace)
- *I Cilicum* (infantry from Cilicia)
- *I Cisipadensium* (from today's Libyan coast)
- *I Cretum* (a Cretan *peditata sagittaria*—foot archers)
- *I Lusitanorum* (from the province of Lusitania— western Spain and Portugal)
- *I Thracum Syriaca* (from Thrace and Syria).
- *II Flavia Commagenorum* (*equitata sagittaria* horse archers from Syria)

- *V Gallorum* (Gauls who would later serve on Hadrian's Wall at Vindolanda)
- *V Hispanorum* (from the province of Hispania—Spain)
- *ala Claudia nova* (a cavalry unit)

ABOVE LEFT Reproduction of the tombstone of the auxiliary standard bearer Tiberius Iulius Pancuius of *cohors Lusitanorum* from Neuss-Grimlinghausen, Germany.

ABOVE CENTER Reproduction of the tombstone of *auxilia* cavalry signifer Oclatius of the *ala Afrorum* (a unit of some 500 cavalrymen from Africa Proconsularis), found at Neuss-Grimlinghausen.

ABOVE RIGHT Statue of an auxiliary at the location of the *porta principalis sinistra* of the cohort fort Niedernberg, Bavaria, Germany, that housed *cohors I Ligurum et Hispanorum civium Romanorum*—soldiers originally raised from the Alpes Maritimes (the Ligures tribe) and from Hispania who had been grouped together. The honorific "*civium Romanorum*" indicated that at some stage the unit had been granted Roman citizenship, a great achievement, but this didn't carry over to later recruits.

Almost all the permanent garrisons on the borders were *auxilia*. By the second century AD, large numbers of such troops had been recruited in Spain, Gaul, Thrace, Anatolia, and Syria and the *auxilia* reached parity in numbers with the legions in infantry and provided all the Roman Army's cavalry and archer support. Citizens often joined the auxilia rather than the legions because the cavalry pay was better. In 212 Emperor Caracalla granted Roman citizenship to all free inhabitants of the empire and the manpower distinction between legions and *auxilia* blurred.

The *auxilia* wasn't formed into legions but rather into six basic types of *alae* (wings) and *cohortes*. The cavalry were organized into *alae* composed of *turmae*—a *turma* had 32 men. An *ala quingenaria* had 16 *turmae* (nominally 512 men). An *ala milliaria* had 24 *turmae* (768 men). The infantry *cohortes* were organized in much the same way as their legionary counterparts: a *cohors quingenaria peditata* had six centuries (480 men), while the *cohors milliaria peditata* consisted of ten centuries (800 men). Finally, there were also units of mixed infantry and cavalry: the *cohors equitata quingenaria* was made up of six centuries and four *turmae*—608 men; the largest formation of all was the *cohors equitata milliaria*, which had ten *centuriae* and eight *turmae* (1,056 men). There was generally only one *ala milliaria* in any province and there were only seven in total. There were also specialist units of archers and slingers, light and, later, heavy cavalry and also barge and boatmen. Living quarters were arranged by *contubernia* on the legionary model: ten for infantry cohorts and eight for cavalry units, with one barrack block for each centuria while two turmae occupied one barrack and one stable block.

The highest-ranking officer in the *auxilia* was a senatorially appointed tribune who commanded an *ala milliaria*. An *ala* was commanded by a prefect who was an equestrian officer or else a native noble with Roman citizenship. A *turma* was commanded by a *decurio* with two *principales* as subalterns, and a *signifer* (standard bearer) making up the command group. Infantry were commanded by prefects and their centuries were commanded by centurions.

The equipment and attire of the *auxilia* infantry was similar to that of the legions, receiving almost identical weaponry, armor, and training. However, the cavalry arm of the *auxilia* was different with its equipment considerably lighter and with quite a few specialist variations reflecting their particular country of origin in dress and weapons. The legionary *scutum* was obviously impractical on horseback, as was the *lorica segmentata* so the *auxilia* tended to favor round or oval shields. They wore a simpler helmet and chain or scale mail. They also used

BELOW A range of late-empire cavalry at Augusta Raurica, Switzerland, with. Note the Draconarius with his oval shield and dragon banner (**A**) that was adopted first into the Roman cavalry during the second century AD, the different helmets including ceremonial helmet with visor (**B**), and hexagonal shields.

BELOW RIGHT Flavinus, a *signifer* of *Candidus turma, ala Petriana*, found at Hexham Abbey, England. Dating to the first century AD, wearing parade uniform with a plumed helmet, his horse is posed over a cowering enemy.

longer spears, sometimes had a quiver of light javelins or darts attached to the saddle, and had a longer sword—a *spatha*—adopted from the Celtic cavalry auxiliaries.

At this point in time, stirrups had not been invented and although special saddles prevented a man from being unhorsed, it still required much skill to fight on horseback but certain tribes were renowned for their horsemanship and eagerly recruited—many came from the *numeri*, tribes outside the empire.

Late-empire military organization

In the tumultuous third century, the Roman Army evolved in the face of mounting internal and external pressures. Politically, the century ended with the reforms of Diocletian and advent of the Tetrarchy. There had also been a break between the senate and the military. Hitherto, the *cursus honorum* had been predicated on a career path for the senatorial class that took them from military tribune to consul in a mixture of military and civil positions. Latterly, the miltary positions taken by senators were given to the equestrian class: the commander of a legion changed from being senatorial *legatus* to an equestrian *prefectus*. This certainly ensured a more professional army, but it also meant a lot of ambitious people in charge of legions and it's probably no coincidence that the century saw many "barracks emperors," of which Diocletian would have to be included.

The make-up of the army changed significantly. The forerunners of the new systems were Septimus Severus, who had ensured a sympathetic legion, *legio II Parthica*, was stationed near Rome both to protect the city and also discourage would-be usurpers, and Gallienus, who had concentrated a field army, with a large cavalry contingent, near his capital of Mediolanum (Milan). Whereas in the first two centuries AD the army—based on the legion as the building block—was concentrated on the borders of empire, key points in a defensive system that spread legionary *vexilliationes* and the *auxilia* along fixed forward lines, the new system saw the division of the army into field armies manned by *comitatenses*, and a fixed border force. These were the *limitanei* who guarded the *limes* under the command of regional *duces*. The legions had multiplied, although they had been reduced in size. New ones were created by a number of emperors. Diocletian, for example, created *legio I Noricorum* in Noricum, *V Iovia* and *VI Herculia* in Pannonia Secunda, *I Iovia* and *II Herculia* in Scythia.

The *Notitia* identifies twelve field armies: five in the east under two Master of the Soldiers in the Imperial Presence (*Magister Militum Praesentalis* I and II), and Masters of the Soldiers (*Magistri Militum*) of the *Orientem* (east), *Thracum* (Thrace), and eastern *Illyricum* (in the Balkans). There were seven in the west: the Army in Italy under the Master of Infantry (*Magister Peditum*) and in Gaul under the Master of Cavalry (*Magister Equitum*) along with the armies of the counts of western *Illyricum*, *Africae*, *Tingitaniae* (Mauretania), *Britanniae*, and *Hispenias* (Spain). These armies were made up of imperial guard cavalry (*scholae*), *catafractarii* and *clibanarii* (heavy cavalry), *palatini* (elite units), *comitatenses*, and *pseudocomitatenses* (troops seconded from the *limitanei*). The *limitanei* for its part had smaller forts but with stronger, better defenses

LEFT Reenactor wearing typical equipment of a late third-century foot soldier. The helmet is a Niederbieber type, with cross-pattern reinforcing ridges on the top of the bowl, and cheek-guards which can be fastened together. The sword is a *spatha* (c. 36in. long), hitherto in the first and second centuries used exclusively by the cavalry. This soldier carries a *spiculum*, a heavy *pilum*-type javelin. Note the chain mail (*lorica hamata*) shirt and oval shield. He wears a long-sleeved tunic, trousers, and boots. A fourth-century infantryman would look very similar to this, save that the *spiculum* was usually replaced by a thrusting-spear (*hasta*) and the helmet would be of the Intercisa type.

(stone walls with more towers). Many cities were also erecting walls—Aurelian started the walls around Rome but died shortly before completion.

Despite the upgrading of many border forts and the increasing use of *foederati* in the third and fourth centuries, in the end weakened by years of civil war and following economic collapse and plague, the army could no longer be provided with regular supplies by the state. Instead, it slowly devolved into armies manned by hereditary soldiers paid in kind from local sources. It remained a formidable fighting force until the political disintegration and barbarian invasions of the west in the mid-fifth century finally brought about it and Rome's demise.

The foederati *and* laeti

The Romans used many different names and labels for the peoples from outside the empire who fought for them—such as *socii* or *symmachiarii* (allies). Some of these peoples came to live within the empire; some were part in *barbaricum* but part of the border buffer zone. Back in the days of the Republic, the *foederati* were tribes—allies—that were bound by treaty to Rome to supply troops when they were needed. Fast forward to the third and fourth centuries AD and the Romans made similar arrangements with the barbarian tribes prowling their borders. In return for—initially—money or food, the *foederati* were supposed to be bound to mutual assistance.

ABOVE The back row shows late-empire soldiers, probably *foederati*, on a bas-relief on the base of Theodosius I's obelisk in Constantinople (c. 390). A regiment of *palatini* detailed to guard the emperor (at left), more than a third of the *palatini* were barbarian-born by this time. Note the necklaces with regimental pendants and long hair, in contrast to the short hair that was the norm in the Principate.

Later, *foederati* or *laeti* were allowed to settle on Roman territory, with mixed results. Marcus Aurelius allowed capitulating Naristi to settle in the empire and an inscription shows they went on to fight for Rome. (A key word is capitulating: *deditio*, the act of surrendering, had great significance.) Probus (emperor 275–282) settled tribesmen in Thrace and along the Danube but they seized ships and ransacked Greece, Sicily, and Africa before returning to their original home on the Rhine. The Salian Franks were allowed to settle in Gaul by Emperor Julian in 358. They held the borders until 406/7 when the Vandals and Alans crossed the frozen Rhine. Even then, groups of Franks continued to hold their areas into the mid-fifth century. On the other hand, the Goths were allowed to settle in the empire in 374. It didn't go well. Badly treated by Roman provincial commanders, they rebelled and destroyed Emperor Valens's army at Adrianople in 378. Theodosius I subsequently made peace with the Goths and once again allied with them.

The *numeri* were also associated with the Roman Army from the final years of the Republic, although it's likely that use of the term to mean units of tribesmen (such as the *numeri Palmyrenorum Porolissensium et Tibiscensium*, archers who fought in Trajan's Dacian wars) came in later. In the *Notitia*, "*numerus*" was used simply to mean unit (and of the seventeen described, sixteen were in Britannia).

Naval organization

The Roman navy had played an important role when it was needed—such as against the Carthaginian fleet—but had little to do after the Mediterranean had become "Mare nostrum." Its importance on the *limes* was to exploit the rivers of Europe for the movement of supplies to aid logistics. Later, in the third and fourth centuries, the navy had

ABOVE AND BELOW RIGHT The Museum of Ancient Seafaring in Mainz, Germany, opened in 1994. Its primary exhibits are the wooden remains of Roman military ships from the fourth century AD found in Mainz during the winter of 1981/82 as the Hilton Hotel II was built in Löhrstraße. Parts of ten were found—the five principal vessels were four troop transports (Type Mainz A) and a patrol craft (Type Mainz B). The museum has reconstructed them (see pp. 46 and 50–51) and other vessels and has a gallery dedicated to the history of shipbuilding and construction techniques. This photo (**ABOVE**) shows a 1:10 model of the ships depicted on Trajan's column (**BELOW**).

BELOW LEFT Cargo ships came in many forms, this is a third-century Gallo-Roman ship at a jetty.

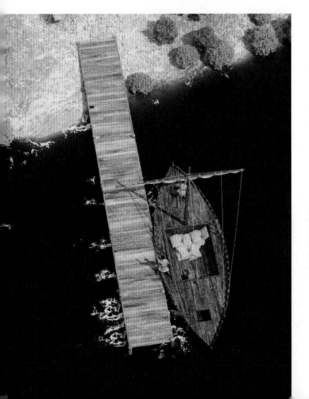

LEFT This *navis actuaria* Type Mainz B reconstruction represents a patrol vessel used for border control on the Rhine. It shows Ship three of the five found in the winter of 1981/82. Dating to the end of the third/early fourth century, it's 45ft long and c. 11ft wide, with a mast and sail. Conservators made a number of discoveries that allowed them to extrapolate the existence of the deck and the use of an outrigger for the fourteen oarsmen.

BELOW Type Mainz A *navis lusoria*, demonstrated by the thirty-two-oar reconstruction in Mainz's *Museum für Antike Schifffahrt*. The main characteristics of this type are that it's slim with a flat-bottomed hull. Crewed by three men (helmsman and two to handle the sail), they could sail or be rowed at a decent speed. Ammianus Marcellinus in *The Roman History* mentions that Julian (351–363) had 40 of these based at Mainz—which was sacked in 407. It was around the start of the fifth century that the docks in Mainz fell into disuse and the Mainz ships were sunk. The version in the Mainz museum has places for 30 oarsmen. Other replicas, such as *Lusoria Rhenana*, a 59ft-long replica with twelve rowers each side, have shown that they are maneuverable craft.

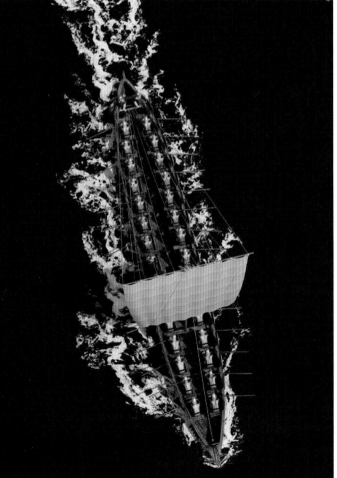

LEFT Computer recreation of a *navis lusoria* troopship moving at speed—between 6 and 10 knots.

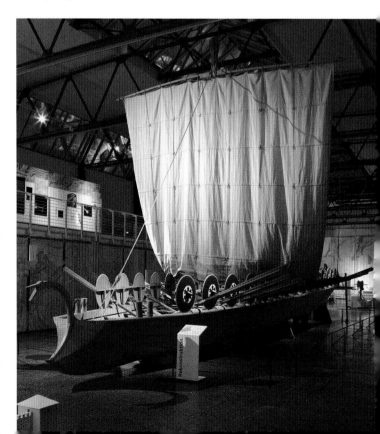

to protect the Saxon Shore from raiders. It was ill-equipped to face the Goths and Vandals, particularly after the latter had taken control of the fleet and shipyards when it took Carthage. This enabled the Vandals to invade Sicily, Corsica, Sardinia, the Balearic Islands—and ultimately Rome itself.

After the end of the civil wars Augustus had downsized his navy as there were no threats to the empire which required one of such a size. The largest ship kept in service was a flagship hexareme, but mainly lighter three-tiered triremes and bireme *liburnae* were used. The latter originated in coastal Liburnia (Croatia) and soon formed the mainstay of the Roman fleets, particularly in the provinces. At just over a 100ft long and powered by a double row of oars, they were small, fast and maneuverable. The Romans added rams and screens for missile protection. From Augustus's reign the imperial navy consisted primarily of two main fleets stationed in Italy acting as a central naval reserve, tasked with policing the Mediterranean, suppressing piracy, and escorting important food imports such as the vital grain shipments to Rome. The *classis Misenensis* was based at Portus Julius with detachments at Ostia, Puteoli, Centumcellae, and other harbors, while the *classis Ravennas* was based at Ravenna.

The waterways and rivers of the empire were patrolled by specific smaller provincial fleets. One of the first (30BC) was the *classis Alexandrine*, based in Alexandria, to control the eastern Mediterranean, escort grain shipments to Rome and police the Nile river. 46 saw the creation of the *classis Perinthia* operating in the Propontis (Sea of Marmara) following the annexation of Thrace and in 64 the *classis Pontica* controlled the eastern end of the Black Sea, based in Trapezus and Byzantium. Fleets based in Libya, Mauretania, and Syria were established some time after 180 to control the African coast and the western Mediterranean.

The Rhine and the Danube

With these rivers playing such an important role in defining borders, the Romans ensured that there were naval units available to patrol, monitor, and intercept as well as transport troops. There were three main provincial fleets, the *classis Germanica* (diplomas attest this was under the army of Germania Inferior; established by Drusus in 12BC to control the Rhine it also ventured out into the North Sea), the *classis Pannonica* under the army of Pannonia Inferior, and the *classis Moesica* under the army of Moesia Inferior. A number of legions had naval squadrons. In Moesia, it looks likely that the *classis Moesica* patrolled the Black Sea and Danube delta, while *legio I Italica*, based at Novae, had a squadron of smaller ships to patrol the river. Elsewhere, similarly, certain legions had squadrons of what eventually became universally known as *liburnae*, to perform riverine operations. In Noricum, the Danube was controlled by ships of the *legio II Italica*, based in Lauriacum from 172/173, joined from the end of the third century from *legio I Noricorum* in Favianis. Pannonia Superior was covered by *legio X Gemina* in Vindobona and *legio XIV Gemina Martia Victrix* in Carnuntum. An interesting addition to this is that the Danube was still patrolled in Moesia (by *legio VII Claudia* based in Viminacium) while the province of Dacia was in existence. The same was true on the Rhine and the Neckar, in the *Agri Decumates*, where *legio XVI Gallica* (in the Claudian period) and *legio XXII Primigenia* at Mogontiacum (Mainz) did the job. It was here that the ships illustrated (left and on p. 50) were discovered in the 1980s. The final stretch of riverine border, in Raetia, was patrolled by boats under an *auxilia* unit (two craft, similar to those discovered in Mainz were excavated at Oberstimm).

Classis Britannica

Formed in the early AD40s at Gesoriacum for the Claudian invasion of Britain and following its success was then based at Rutupiae (Richborough) until c. 85 when it relocated to Dubris (Dover). It remained in the Channel area until the Flavian expansion (69–96), when it was used by Agricola to aid and supply his progress northward, during which it attacked the eastern coast of Caledonia, and reached as far as the Orkney Islands (c. 84)—as attested in Tacitus's biography of Agricola. It then continued to supply Roman forces in the north of Britain, with an important base at the mouth of the Tyne supporting Hadrian's Wall during the second and third centuries. In the late third century Carausius was appointed its commander, with the added task of suppressing piracy in the Channel area. When he was accused of treachery c. 287 he seceded from Rome and declared himself emperor of Britannica and northern Gaul, but by 300 the fleet was back on side. Its final role before the Roman withdrawal from Britain was in the defense of the eastern and southern coasts against increasing Saxon incursions.

Roman army logistical support was often based on rivers. The world of antiquity may have had problems with pirates and shipwrecks but it was still easier to move men and materiel on water than overland. (Although it must be noted that Germanicus's use of ships to transport troops by sea AD 15 and 16 ended in disaster with the ships inundated by heavy seas.) On rivers, flat-bottomed boats with ramp-like sloping ends were perfect and many are recorded north of the Alps, some measuring up to 40m long. This one (**OPPOSITE**) is shown during excavation at Zwammerdam in the Netherlands on November 28, 1972. Three barges and three canoes were found there and six other Roman ships were found in Woerden 1978–2004, including one almost identical to this Zwammerdam barge.

ABOVE There are few working reconstructions of the Zwammerdam barges. This one is from De Meern, another location where a Roman vessel has been found.

BELOW Trajan's column shows stores for the Dacian campaign being unloaded from barges. The forts on the Rhine and Danube were important to retain control of the logistical highway, and it's worth remembering that the supplies for the invasion of Britannia, as well as subsequent trade to and from the province, would have been routed along the Rhine.

The Roman legions grew accustomed to building in stone as all over the empire the original turf and wooden structures were improved and rebuilt. Many of the key locations had multiple levels—Vindolanda has twelve—as they were rebuilt to house different units. The quality of stonework across the empire varies. Analysis of the work on the wall shows that little is of top quality, but that it was completed quickly and would certainly have impressed the locals—something it still continues to do today.

3

The Roman bridge at Trier is the oldest in Germany, dating back to the second century AD.

Border Engineering

The Roman army built in wood, stone, and turf according to availability and time. Turf and timber constructions needed less time and presented fewer logistical problems, so were used for temporary camps on campaign or when enemy proximity necessitated speed; more permanent stone replacements came along later, with timber being used in both. Turf was a tried and tested technology for the Roman military, and was considerably stronger than one might think. Revetted with timber and huge back-berm earthen banks—enabling swift mass-access to the top rampart—and filled with cores of rubble, a turf wall was just as effective as a stone one but required rather more maintenance. Regardless of the difference in size, whether a marching camp, auxiliary fort, or legionary fortress, all Roman military installations were called *castrum* (plural *castra*). The very smallest fortlets were known as *castellum* (plural *castella*). Army regulations required any major unit on campaign to retire to a properly constructed camp each night—as a precautionary defensive measure. No Roman *castra* were made to fight from. The Roman Army fought as heavy infantry in the open, where its superior organization would have the most impact and an outcome could be swiftly reached. Thus the primary purpose of a *castrum* was not to withstand attack but to provide a safe staging area for troops to organize and assemble before deployment.

Forts

All Roman camps or forts essentially followed the same basic idealized template, with variations only when demanded by the constraints of time, terrain, and materials available—and, of course, by the size of the unit and its constituent elements of infantry and cavalry. Such a protocol maintained organization and discipline, for every soldier knew where everything was and where he was supposed to be whether in a legionary fortress or an overnight marching camp. Marching or night camps on campaign were inevitably slighter and more swiftly erected than their more permanent counterparts. Both were chosen with an eye for a good defensive position either on high ground or in the open and sited near water. They were marked out in flags and rope lines by a specialist advance squad that was sent on ahead so that they could be laid out quickly and clearly. When the main body of troops arrived, the visible plan of the camp could then be swiftly realized. The shape and ground plan of these night camps rarely strayed from a round-cornered rectangular playing-card shape, consisting of a wooden palisade (*vallum*) atop an earthen rampart (*agger*) built up from the earth excavated from the ditch (*fossa*) or ditches in front, with a gate on each side leading to the camp's principal roads. Just behind the *vallum* a road or track ran right around the camp and was known as the *intervallum*, enabling swift movement to any part of the defenses as well as acting as a safety margin against incoming missiles. Inside, the camp was then divided into four quarters by the two roads that bisected each other: the *via principalis* and the *via praetoria*, with the command and supply sections always in the center. (Sometimes the *via praetoria* did not pierce its walls dead center, creating three thirds rather than four quarters but with the middle third still the command

1930s' tourism: these photographs are from the Matson (G. Eric and Edith) Photograph Collection at the Library of Congress and were taken on "A Motorboat trip around the Dead Sea." They show Camp F (built by *legio X Fretensis*), one of the camps below Masada (**ABOVE**), and the ramp the Romans built to storm the fortress in AD73 (**BELOW**). The Romans were seldom daunted by obstacles, even if that meant moving a big bit of mountain. The 375ft high ramp was made from earth and stone with timber bracings. Before it was constructed, the Romans built a wall around the mountain to ensure no defenders could get away.

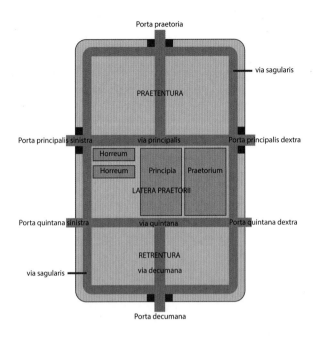

Porta praetoria

via sagularis

PRAETENTURA

Porta principalis sinistra · via principalis · Porta principalis dextra

Horreum

Horreum · Principia · Praetorium

LATERA PRAETORII

Porta quintana sinistra · via quintana · Porta quintana dextra

RETRENTURA

via sagularis · via decumana

Porta decumana

ABOVE The main elements of a Roman fort. Note: *sinistra* = left; *dextra* = right; *praetentura* = the front tent area; *retentura* = back tent area; *latera praetorii* = on either side of the commander's tent or the HQ building. The construction of the fort was under the control of the *praefectus castrorum*.

and control section.) On Hadrian's Wall, the positioning of the gateways on the early forts put the two side entrances ahead of the wall. This meant that the unit could exit the forest and counter any attack more quickly. This would often lead to another set of gates on a second cross street, the *via quintana*.

In the middle of the camp were the important people and buildings: the *praetorium*, the command center where under the Republic, the *praetor* (first officer), the unit's standards, pay chest, and command staff were housed. The use of *praetorium* continued in use under the Principate and came to mean the commander's tent or, in a fixed fort, house. The rank and power of the commander depended on the size of the unit and the commander's political role. In fixed camps the *principia* was the headquarters and housed the standards and safe for pay and the *praetorium* sat alongside.

In front of the *praetorium*, the *praetentura* (the front tented area) the legate's tent with those of the tribunes ranged in front. In the Republic, the term *legatus* indicated a power, usually conferred on a consul or proconsul. By the time of the Principate, the *legatus legionis* commanded a legion. There were six tribunes in a legion, one of whom— the *tribunus laticlavius*—was second in command. The other tribunes were staff officers or officer candidates.

At the center, the *via principalis* was used as an assembly area and parade ground. On one side of the *praetorium* there might be a hospital (*valetudinarium*) and on the other was the *quaestorium* (*quaestor*, the officer responsible for pay and provisioning) where the unit's stores and supplies were kept. The cohort's tents occupied either side of the command section and sometimes part of this space was also left open in which to muster, hold prisoners and booty or horses and supplies. If especially anxious and expecting imminent attack, more ditches could be dug and the gateways further protected with frontal hemispherical berms. When time was available these ditches could be made more elaborate and deadly, with their backs cut vertically making a counterscarp to prevent escape, an ankle breaker bottom slot, and the addition of various sharpened wooden stakes—some huge and obvious while others were more trap-like, being hidden in pits covered in brushwood. Wide, deep ditches created a killing zone for the soldiers on the ramparts, armed with javelins and supported by artillery.

In the more permanent barracks or forts virtually the same plan was followed using stone, often almost exactly over the top of the wooden original, which was usually ceremonially burnt. (The Romans regularly burnt and broke up their own forts—when they were timeworn to start afresh with a rebuild, to make a larger version as required, or else to deny an enemy any possibility of using their own defenses against themselves.) The *praetorium* was built in stone and resembled a Mediterranean Roman villa. The *quaestorium* was also constructed in stone and featured the heavy-set *horreum* (plural *horrea*—granaries or storehouses) with its double-skinned walls and a raised floor to aid airflow and prevent the vital grain supplies from rotting.

Gates in the camp walls were no longer flush with the wall but protruding, often doubled to make a dual entrance and built of stone, with towers on either side as well as at each corner of the camp, while other

These images show Pazirik Informatics Ltd's reconstruction of elements of two Roman forts in Hungary: Arrabona (today's Győr) and Lussonium (see p. 136). Of course, while there are great similarities between all Roman forts, there are significant differences in size between a fortress large enough to house one or two legions (50–60 acres), and one that would house a *vexillatio* (25–35 acres), *numerus*, or *ala*.

Roman forts went through a number of building stages on the *limes*, as time went on and in the face of new threats. Initially, they started as locations which the troops would leave to fight. Many of the forts on the *limes* were started in Augustus's reign or during those of the Flavian dynasty. The early forts had turf walls with wooden palisades, later faced in stone; were playing-card shaped and surrounded by ditches. Sometimes (as with Rough Castle) they had—also surrounded by ditches—annexes which could contain workshops, amphitheaters, or baths. The ditches were carefully constructed with ankle-breaker slots at the bottom and carefully landscaped with the addition of obstacles, *lilia* pits, caltrops, etc.

Later, many of the forts were rebuilt completely in stone with towers inside the walls and stone double gateways, as at Arrobona (**1**). As time went on, they ended up more like medieval castles, with towers projecting outside the walls, platforms for projectile weapons—catapults and javelin throwers—and powerful gatehouses such as in **5** below.

Later still, as personnel numbers were reduced, the large forts were abandoned, sometimes to civilians, and smaller forts were built in one corner.

Arrabona's first garrison around 25/30–69 may have been *ala Pannoniorum* followed in the Flavian period by mounted archers (*ala I Augusta Ituraeorum sagittaria*)—there's a tombstone to Acrabanis Ababunis from that unit. In the early second century, the fort was demolished by *ala I contarorium milliaria* and rebuilt in stone. In the late third century the camp was scaled down, but more heavily fortified. The garrison left Arrabona in the late fourth century.

1 Arrabona after rebuilding in stone.
2–4 Barrack blocks—a cavalry *ala* would have housed the horses and riders together.
5 Lussonium's stone gatehouse and wall walkway.
6–7 Granary (*horreum*).
8 Entry to the *saecellum* and the standards.
9 Lussonium's latrines.

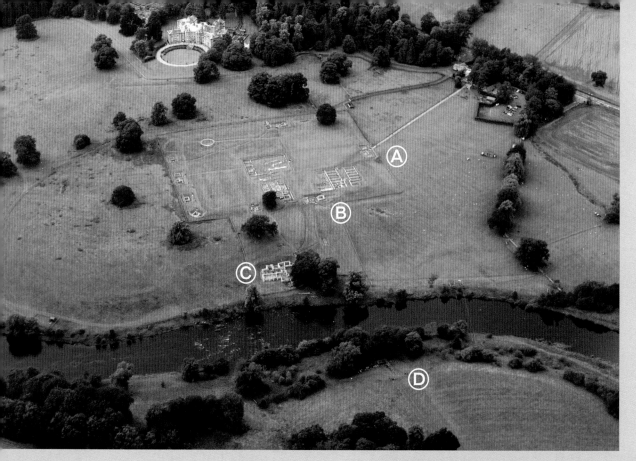

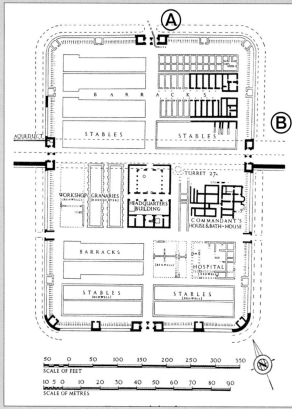

ABOVE AND LEFT This is Cilurnum—Chesters in north England—built in 124, and Eric Birley's beautifully drawn ground plan of it, with the bits that can't be seen on the ground filled in using evidence from other locations. Compare the locations of **A** (*porta praetoria*) and **B** (*porta principalis*) for orientation. **C** is the bathhouse and **D** the abutments for the bridge over the River Tyne—part of the reason for the fort's construction. In fact, we know today that this isn't quite right: there's a granary in the *retentura* and the barrack blocks were divided into rooms in which three cavalrymen and their horses lived, rather than there being separate stables. Note that Hadrian's Wall extends below the west and east gates on the *via principalis*. Originally, the forts were to lie back from the wall but that was changed after construction began. In the case of Cilurnum, an existing stretch of wall and a watchtower had to be demolished. Texts in the RIB that help identify units involved with Cilurnum, include a tombstone mentioning *cohors I Vangionum* (Germans), building inscriptions from *ala Augusta ob virtutem appellata*, *legio VI Victrix*, and the Spanish *ala II Asturum*. The latter was probably the garrison from the later second century while *ala I Asturum* was at Condercum in the third century.

watchtowers also studded the walls. Baths were usually built outside the camp because of the ever-present danger of fire breaking out, unless the fort was large enough to accommodate them—such as a massive legionary fortress, which could encompass 50 or 60 acres. The vital bread ovens would also be built into the back of the rampart minimizing the risk of fire. Temples were often built close by rather than inside the forts. Deeply superstitious, Iron Age people spent much time and energy trying to placate or beg help from different gods as well as honor their dead. The Romans were not exempt from these preoccupations and with their knack of taking what was useful from other cultures their acceptance of other gods is quite apparent. They were always perfectly comfortable finding a Roman equivalent to combine with a local deity or even to adopt an attractive exotic import like Mithraism wholesale. The latter seemed to have had a particular appeal to soldiers as did Jupiter Dolichenus. Other changes or evolutions occurred in camp and fort construction over the course of time and reflected the change of military emphasis away from infantry to different kinds of auxiliary troops—often cavalry or mixed units. Later forts tended to be square rather than rectangular.

The day-to-day running of forts required sophisticated control mechanisms to operate successfully. Aside from the military duties—patrolling, guarding the camp itself, and training—there was fuel to be gathered, food supplies to be arranged and prepared; animals needed to be watered and exercised. The supply administration of a permanent camp was run as a business with money as the exchange medium. Native tribes that supplied the army's needs for food, animals, fodder, and construction materials accrued considerable wealth in the process. Extra workshops producing building supplies such as tiles, pipes, and lime mortar could also be sited outside the defenses—some *vici* or *canabae* (outside legionary fortresses) grew to be substantial—see Chapter 5.

The Roman Empire lasted for hundreds of years and during this period strategies and threats, building techniques and styles changed. Portchester Castle (see also aerial view on p. 86) was built in the late third century AD and then modified—there's a Norman castle in one corner. It's probably the Portus Adurni mentioned in the *Notitia* as one of the forts under the *comes litoris Saxonici*. It's square, with serious bastions that were designed to allow defenders to enfilade attackers—very different to the playing-card-shaped earlier Roman forts.

Fortlets and watchtowers

A vital component of the *limes*, small forts (*castella*) can be found all over the empire. They came in a variety of forms and their garrisons also had a variety of duties. The most plentiful in Britannia and Europe were similar to that at Pohl (**OPPOSITE, ABOVE**) or Würzberg. Their purpose was to supply the troops for local watchtowers (sometimes termed *specula* or *vigilaria*)—a number of which would have been in line of sight from the fortlet—and act as the first line of defense against raiding parties. If something happened that they couldn't deal with, the local cohort fort would be the next step up the chain of command. On Hadrian's Wall, the equivalent is the milecastle (see p. 78). These were part of the wall and protected a gateway. The garrison's duties would have been to monitor the entry into and egress out of the empire and to ensure that duties were paid on requisite items. Other small forts guarded road junctions and in the east, where water is so important, water sources. The final form of the fortlet is best seen in the *burgi* that were initiated during Valentinian I's reign. While similar structures to the *burgi* can be seen from earlier periods, it was in the late fourth century during his seven-year residence in Trier that Valentinian I's major building program saw an overhaul of the *limes* as attested in Symmachus's second oration. Some of the *burgi* were in *barbaricum* and included landing stages to control river passage. They were square towers on mounds and surrounded by ditches as **OPPOSITE, BELOW**.

BELOW LEFT The *numerus* fort at Würzberg, Germany on the Odenwald *limes* would have been manned by 160 troops of the *auxilia*, some of whom would have been rotated as watchtower units. It was built in a number of stages: first, a Trajannic earth and wood structure; then, during Hadrian's reign, double dry stone walls filled with rubble; finally, c. 140–150, a mortared stone wall was built. After all that effort, the site was abandoned c. 159 as the *limes* moved eastward. Würzberg also boasts a well-preserved bathhouse. These weren't a luxury for the legionaries; they were a necessity. Most forts—large or small—had theirs, as is well exemplified by this superb example.

OPPOSITE, ABOVE A reconstructed fortlet and watchtower on the *limes* at Pohl in Germany shows a number of important features: the turf walls of the fort with its wooden barracks; the whitewashed walls with fake stone courses delineated in red; the watchtower, wooden on a stone base surrounded by a ditch and palisade. The small forts—and a number of local watchtowers—were probably manned by the same unit and rotated. Set back from the line of the frontier, these small forts were linked to cohort forts and, further back still, the legionary fortresses.

OPPOSITE, BELOW LEFT AND RIGHT The later *burgi*—this fine computer reconstruction is of the *burgus* at Visegrád-Kőbánya on the Danube in Hungary—would have had garrisons of around fifty men. Nearly 30ft square with a ditch 15ft wide and 6ft deep, this *burgus* was built around 370. There's an inscription panel for *legio I Martia*.

1) Road with clearway through forest

2) Wooden watchtowers are added, forest clearance is extended

3) Improved watchtowers with stone base and a wooden palisade added in front

4) Stone watchtowers replace wood

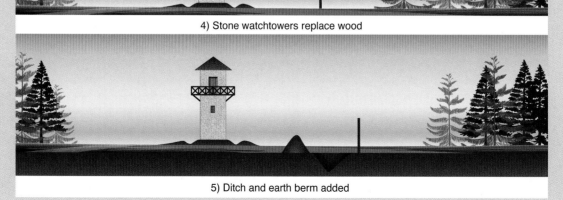

5) Ditch and earth berm added

OPPOSITE The development of the *limes*, starting with the road, which gains towers, a palisade, ditch, and earth berm. In some areas the palisade is replaced by a stone wall. The forests are cut back to improve sightlines.

RIGHT Experimental archaeology at Vindolanda—turf and stone walls with stone and wood towers. The turf wall has been found to have sunk over the years, although this one had to face an enemy the Romans probably introduced: rabbits. The Romans were used to building in turf: their marching camps were turf and much of the German *limes* were of turf with a palisade.

BELOW LEFT AND RIGHT Watchtowers, like forts, went through various stages of construction: first wood, then wood on a stone base, and then stone. Initially they would have had their own ditch and palisade, and slate roofs. When the stone tower replaced the wooden version, it was on different foundations behind the palisade and any ditch(es) that had been added. Access is on the first floor, the ground floor being a storeroom and the top floor the viewing platform.

Pfähle am Mönchsroth-
Wege. Westliche Hälfte.

The palisade

LEFT Proof, if it were needed, that the palisade existed. An original *Limeskomission* photo taken at Mönchsroth, Germany, in 1894.

BELOW LEFT Trajan's column shows a watch-tower with palisade next to a beacon. The integrated defense system would respond to a incursion by notifying the forts and larger response forces.

OPPOSITE Two different palisade reconstructions in Germany at Zugmantel (**ABOVE**) and Mainhardt (**BELOW**). The latter used 20in. oaks split in half lengthways and strengthened with crossbeams; the ditch is 26ft wide and the berm 8ft high. In some areas a 10–15ft high wall was also included. A typical *limes* border setup (**INSET**) shows the development from the original watchtower with its own ditch and palisade (**1**) abandoned for a new stone version (**2**). The road to/from barbaricum would be monitored—some would have had a stone gateway.

The *vallum*

The Romans knew all about turf, using turf walls on their marching camps and the longer linear barriers. On Hadrian's Wall just outside Birdoswald (**ABOVE**) there's a section of the original turf wall. Much of the way along its length, the *vallum* is visible. Nobody's quite sure what it was for. It was about 115ft wide, made up of two earth banks separated by berms and a ditch. Here it is (**RIGHT**) just east of Onnum (Halton Chesters) and, delineated by frost, near Housesteads (**BELOW**). It certainly produced an obvious wall zone that could be easily policed as there were few crossing places (see opposite).

As with any border, crossing the *limes* ditch and wall or Hadrian Wall's *vallum* was carefully controlled. This artist's impression (**ABOVE**) gives an idea of a rural border post. This wouldn't have provided a strong defensive location, but would have allowed the equivalent of passport control, inspection of the people and goods entering the Roman world, and the levying of border dues and taxes.

This is the *vallum* crossing at Condercum (Benwell) at the Newcastle end of Hadrian's Wall. The causeway is about 160ft from the fort's southern gate and shows evidence of a large stone archway that would have been an impressive structure. Note it was south of the wall, and so would have been inspecting and charging people moving from south to north. Material finds north of Hadrian's Wall and the European *limes* show that trade was definitely a two-way process.

Bridges

Bridges were as important to the Roman Army as they were to Wellington and Napoleon, Lee or Grant. Cassius Dio observed, "The Romans bridge streams and rivers with the greatest ease, because the soldiers are always practicing it like any other military exercise on the Ister, Rhine or Euphrates. This is how they do it. They use flat-bottomed boats, anchored upstream a little above the place where the bridge is to be constructed. When the signal is given, they first let one ship drift downstream close to the bank they hold. When it's in the spot to be bridged, they anchor it with a basket filled with stones on the end of a cord. Once it's made fast the ship is joined to the bank by planks and bridgework, and a floor is laid to the farther edge. Then they release another ship at a little distance from the first and another after that until the bridge reaches the opposite bank. The boat nearest the hostile bank carries towers and a gate with a crew of archers and catapults." That technique is well shown on the columns of Trajan and Marcus Aurelius (**ABOVE**). Otherwise, more permanent bridges were significant on the *limes* because of the sheer number of small watercourses to be crossed—examples here are the abutments for the crossing at Cilurnum (Chesters). This would have carried the military way across the Tyne (**BELOW LEFT**). Matilo archaeological park has this reconstruction of a Roman bridge (**BELOW RIGHT**).

Possibly the most remarkable structure of the ancient world—certainly one of them—was the bridge built over the Danube by Apollodorus of Damascus, a Nabatean who also designed Trajan's Column (he and his bridge are seen behind the emperor in this frame on the column—**RIGHT**). Little of the 1,240yd structure remains other than a couple of the pilings on the bank in Serbia (**ABOVE**). There's a reconstruction on the Romanian side (**BELOW**).

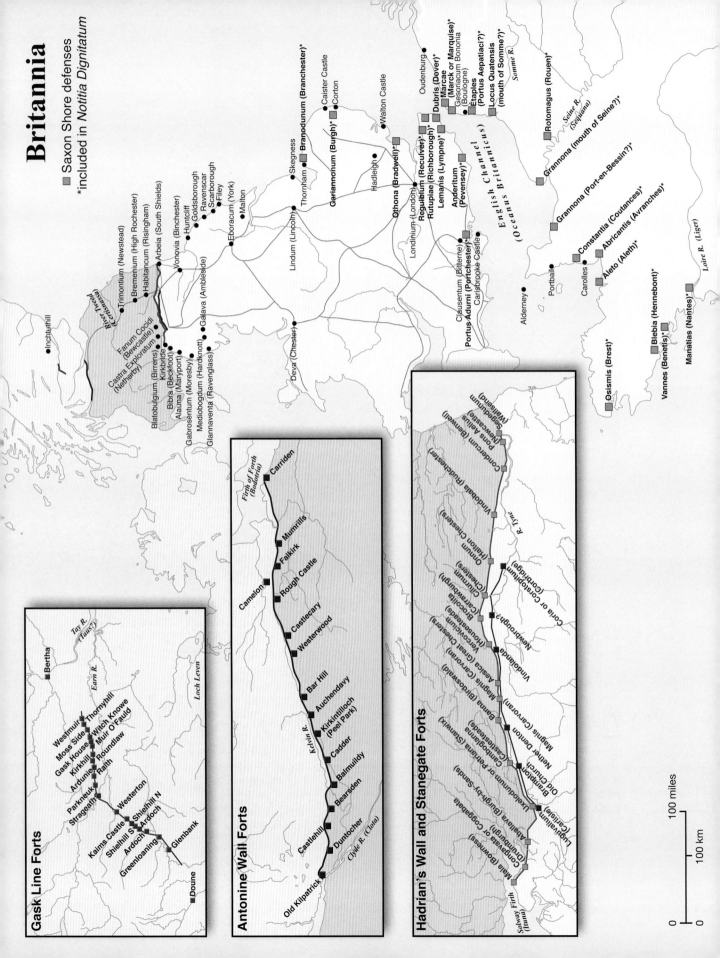

4

The Borders

ABOVE Saalburg cohort fort north of Frankfurt, Germany, was reconstructed at the start of the twentieth century.

OPPOSITE Britannia's northern and later Saxon Shore defenses.

The construction of the hard borders fell into three fairly distinct periods: first, the erection of wood and earth defenses. These started under Augustus and continued on into the second century AD. Next, some time later, the wooden forts became stone-built and *vici* built up around them. The border evolved into a network of forts and forward operating bases linked by roads and supplied by depot towns that were themselves originally forts. Some of these became much more civilian in nature over time, set further back in safer home territory. In particular areas of the empire where tension and hostilities prevailed, defenses thickened into more continuous barriers to seal up vulnerable gaps. Finally, in the last years of the western empire, there were new fortresses, looking more like medieval castles than the playing-card derivatives of earlier years, these had thicker walls and bastion towers. There were also the *burgi* forts, started in Valentinian's reign, designed to let the mobile force inland know of an enemy incursion so that they could deal with it (see p. 59).

Hadrian was probably the most influential early emperor when it comes to fixed borders. The architecture of his frontiers led to practical and functional defensive and administrative structures, set within wider defense zones, but they were also highly symbolic statements of power and possession. The first of his frontiers started in Germania, where the thick forests provided an ample supply of timber for palisades and watchtowers along the Rhine, but the most famous and substantial was built in the north of Britannia, where a lack of trees would necessitate stone as the primary building material.

Britannia

Some provinces more than others suffered from unruly inhabitants and hostile neighbors. There's no doubt that Britannia would classify as one of these. The hostile neighbors at one stage were just the tribes in the north, but as peoples shifted living areas on the continent of Europe, so the southern coast of the island required its own defenses. However, it is with Hadrian's iconic and eponymous wall that we start our tour of the Roman *limes*.

Hadrian's Wall

First, came the Stanegate, a military road that stretched from Luguvallum on the Eden to Corstopitum on the Tyne, and probably further. Along the road was a line of forts, two of which are among the most important archaeological sites in Britain: Vindolanda and Corstopitum. This certainly wasn't a linear barrier, although watch and signal towers make it obvious that it was supposed to provide a defense against incursions. However, with its main forts a day's march away from each other, it was certainly a porous barrier.

In around 122 Hadrian came to Britannia and the legions started to construct his famous wall. It's worth looking at it in some detail because its development provided a template for others that followed. Hadrian's decision to build a solid barrier was ultimately based on hard facts. The Romans had briefly conquered the whole island and built a legionary base at Inchtutil, as well as a series of glen-blocking forts (the Gask Ridge) in the Highlands. The potential rewards just did not match the manpower required to maintain stability in the region. There was a danger, too, in the number of legions a governor of Britannia would require to have under his sole control. A compromise choke point was therefore chosen. The original intent was to build a continuous stone wall just north of the pre-existing Stanegate defenses, that would run for 80 miles across the neck of northern Britain from Newcastle to Bowness, incorporating the natural barriers of rivers and the high central dolerite escarpment of the Whin Sill. It was to be 10ft wide and 15ft high, and at every mile along the wall was placed a gate, protected by a small fortlet termed a milecastle—a two-floored building equipped with a signalling capability for a *contubernium* of eight men. Between each pair of milecastles two small stone observation/signaling turrets were evenly spaced, with room for two–three men. Building began from east to west with these features, the actual wall being filled in between them afterward.

Almost straight away changes were made. The overall width of the wall was reduced from the original broad ten-feet wide to sometimes as little as six feet, and the western part from the river Irthing to Bowness was originally constructed from turf and only later replaced with stone. It was also soon apparent that the forts along the Stanegate would be too far behind the new wall to be able to respond quickly enough to any incursions from the north, so it was decided to build seventeen forts at regular intervals on the wall itself—some of them over existing milecastles and watchtowers. The forts were of two main designs: an infantry version that was completely within the wall and formed part of it, and a cavalry fort that straddled the wall, jutting out, with its northern, western, and eastern gates outside to serve as sally ports.

Within a short time of the wall being built, a military exclusion zone called the vallum was created behind it. This comprised a linear earthwork of a wide median ditch flanked on both sides by higher earth berms, which ran the length of the wall from west to east until it reached Newcastle. Along the west coast the installations extended southwestward in the form of ditch and timber palisades (the Western Sea Defenses), linking a number of forts, fortlets, and watchtowers. It took units from all three of Britain's legions six years to construct most of the wall: *legio II Augusta*, based in Caerleon in South Wales; *legio VI Victrix* from York, and *legio XX Valeria Victrix* from Chester, aided by units from the *auxilia* and the *classis Britannica*, using primarily roughly dressed local limestone and turf. There was a clear decline in standards of craftsmanship with the later structures much more shoddily finished off than earlier ones and it is difficult to know when it was finally completed. An inscription suggests that one fort was not finished until after 128.

To confound the undoubted and inescapable military aspects of Hadrian's Wall and its structures, there are various contradictions that imply a much more nuanced motivation for their creation, as well as their continued evolution. From its inception there were multiple openings that pierced the curtain wall throughout its entire length and the water to some of the forts was supplied by aqueducts from the north, indicating that it was never intended to be solely an impenetrable defensive structure. Except at its main forts, the ramparts could not have been wide enough to move men along easily or to defend. This lack of necessary weapons and space to defend the wall appropriately indicate a more complicated purpose. The number of troops stationed along the wall was not sufficient to fight along its entire length, but rather they were assembled in mobile strike groups (many of the units were cavalry) at critical points covering their own sections.

The vallum is also enigmatic. It varies its course. Most of the time it is close to the wall but sometimes nearly a mile away. While its primary function seems to have been to act as a barrier to restrict access from the south, it was not made to fight from. It was also the only link between the forts along the wall until much later. Twenty years after Hadrian's armies built his wall, under Antoninus Pius the border was pushed forward into Scotland. This advance did not last and under Marcus Aurelius the Romans withdrew back to the Hadrian's Wall. At this stage the western length that had been built from turf was rebuilt in stone, and a metaled road was constructed, running from fort to fort.

Planetrees, England
Here the broad footings changed to a narrower profile (as shown at **A**).

Ⓐ

Vindolanda (Chesterholm, England)
The jewel in the crown—thanks to three generations of the Birley family—the life of soldiers on Rome's northern border has been brought back graphically. The discovery of over 7,000 shoes and 500 letters—most written using ink made from gum arabic, carbon, and water on strips of birch, alder, and oak—and many other finds have made Vindolanda a treasure trove of information about its ten periods of occupation from about AD80 to the middle of the sixth century. This aerial view shows clearly the playing-card outline of the third-century fort (left)—and to its right the *vicus*. Note the third-century bathhouse complex at **A**. The complicated history of the fort and its many iterations make fascinating reading and an even better place to visit. Note **B** *praetorium* (CO's house with its own bath; **C** *principia* (HQ building); **D** *horrea* (granaries).

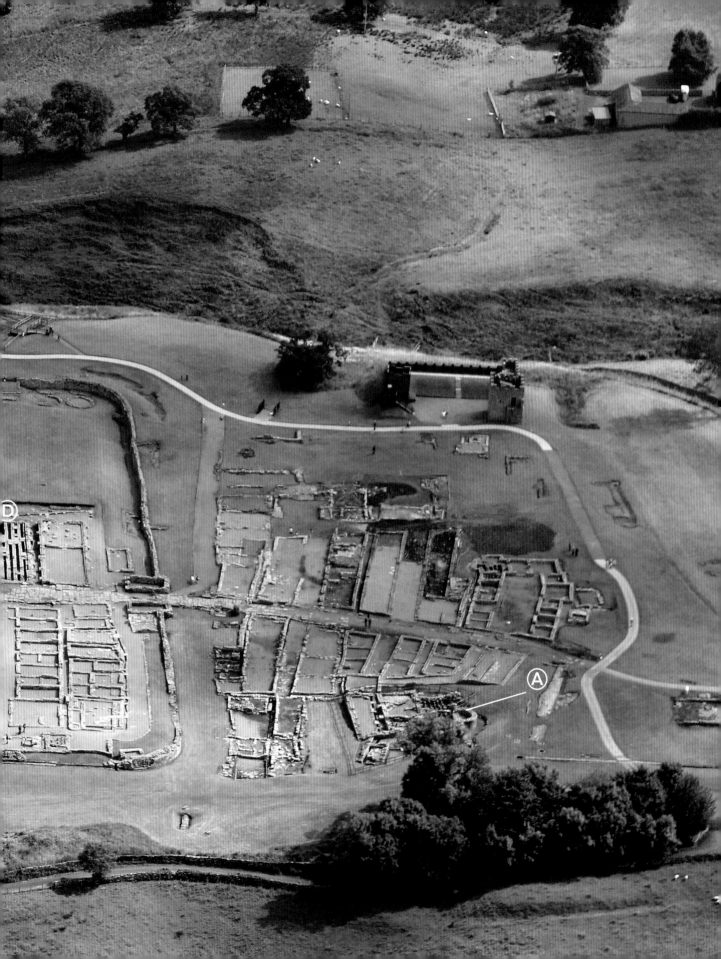

As a critical part of a defense zone, the vallum's crossing points and gates (see p. 65) could stream and monitor traffic, control and tax trade, and intercept trouble by preventing the import of weapons and filtering the travelers for undesirables. By funneling people through such a concentrated area while lightly policing other parts of the line, the number of troops required to police the frontier was decreased. This was surely another important reason driving Hadrian's border policy, as shortages in manpower became an ever-increasing problem for Rome.

A similar approach and design is reflected in other Hadrianic fortifications around the peripheries of the empire, most of them considerably longer and fronted by rivers or deserts, and so not requiring a stone curtain wall as in Britannia. The benefits of these barriers was to enhance the ability of the Romans to oversee and control the areas surrounding the walls, for they were usually sited farther back than the actual extent of Roman control.

Mediobogdum
(Hardknott Fort, England)
It was crucial that the rear areas behind the borders were defended in depth and their supply routes were secured. Mountain passes were particularly important. The Hardknott Pass on the way to Glannaventa (Ravenglass) and the English northwest coast is a case in point. Built during Hadrian's reign it was manned by *cohors IV Delmatarum*, abandoned during the period that the Antonine Wall was active, and reoccupied afterward. Note the bathhouse at **A**.

Corstopitum (Corbridge, England)

A key crossroads on the Stanegate, the Roman fort of Corstopitum—and the town that developed around it—was where the road north, Dere Street, crossed the Stanegate and, nearby, the River Tyne. The bridge was substantial and although stones have been removed over the centuries (some as right, removed for their own protection), the six piers are visible. A 1995 evaluation of the effects of river erosion on the site revealed the remains of the ramp carrying Dere Street onto the bridge which was "a massive and elaborately decorated bridge and has close similarities with the second century bridge at Chesters."

ABOVE Arbeia (South Shields, England)
Built in c. 129 by *legio VI Victrix*, Arbeia protects the mouth of the Tyne. Originally garrisoned by auxiliary cavalry, it became a supply base for the Severan advances north. It retained this role when Scotland was abandoned and rebuilding led to a configuration of granaries, later repurposed again in 300. Attested units include *ala I Pannoniorum Sabiniana* (cavalry from Pannonia), *cohors V Gallorum* when infantry took over, and finally, *numerus Barcariorum Tigrisiensium*—bargemen from the Middle East. This is the reconstructed gatehouse.

BELOW Segedunum (Wallsend, England)
The easternmost fort connected to the wall, Segedunum was built on an extension designed to cover the low tide area on the Tyne east of Pons Aelius (Newcastle). The wooden elements of the original fort (mainly the barracks) were replaced with stone c. 160 when a hospital (*valetudinarium*) was added (**A**). Note the reconstructed bathhouse at **B**. Attested units include *cohors II Nerviorum civium Romanorum* (from Belgium) in the second century, who were replaced by fellow-countrymen *cohors IV Lingonum equitata*.

ABOVE Brocolita (Carrawburgh, England)
There's not much to see of the fort which has lost its top
end to the road. Excavations found a bathhouse outside
the west gate and a small *vicus*. There are three shrines
close by: a water-based shrine to the local spirits (*genius
loci*), to the Romano-British water goddess Coventina,
and a *Mithraeum* (at **A**) in which three altars were
dedicated by a third-century *cohors I Batavorum*
commander. Units attested to Brocolita include *cohortes I
Tungrorum, I Aquitanorum, I Cugernorum, I Frisiavonum,
II Nerviorum civium Romanorum*, and *cohors V Raetorum*.

BELOW Vercovicium (Housesteads, England)
Built around 122, Vercovicium was occupied by
infantry—*cohors I Tungrorum*—from Belgium from the
second to fourth centuries, although many other units
are attested. It had an extensive *vicus*, which was
abandoned by the end of the third century, no doubt
for the security of the walled camp, whose west (**A**)
and north (**B**) gates were blocked; **C** *horrea* (granaries);
D *principia* (HQ); **E** *praetorium* (CO's house);
F *valetudinarium* (hospital); **G** barracks; **H** latrines;
I *vicus*; **J** Hadrian's Wall.

ABOVE Milecastle 37 (west of Housesteads, England)
Hadrian's Wall was built by men from all three legions in Britain at the time, *II Augusta* from Isca (Caerleon), *VI Victrix* from Eboracum (York), and *XX Valeria Victrix* from Deva (Chester). This milecastle was probably built by *legio II Augusta*. There are remains of barrack blocks that would have housed up to thirty legionaries who would have policed the comings and goings through the gateway. Excavations showed that latterly the gate was blocked and then demolished.

BELOW Banna (Birdoswald, England)
Hadrian's Wall was originally a turf wall in the west and when it was rebuilt in stone, Banna's configuration was altered. The yellow line shows the original military road; the white line the original turf wall and later line of the military road. Attested units are *cohortes I Thracum civium Romanorum* at the start of the third century and *I Aelia Dacorum* (Dacians), which left Britain around 410. There was a substantial *vicus* which extended along the military way. Note (at **A**) the *horreum* (granary).

ABOVE Walltown Crags, England

As with so much of the *limes*, Hadrian's Wall has
suffered over the years from robbers who took stone
for building or use as hardcore for roads. Quarries also
took their fair share at Greenhead and here, Walltown
Quarry, which gobbled up the section of wall before
Magna (Carvoran) fort. All of the stone buildings in the
fort have also disappeared.

BELOW Concavata (Drumburgh, England)

The central section of the wall benefits from the
escarpment of the Whin Sill, but the western end is
flat and coastal. Here the yellow lines show the path
of the wall; the white the *vallum*. Nearby Aballava (Burgh
on Sands) is commemorated for having the first recorded African community in Britain: from 253 onward,
numerus Maurorum Aurelianorum: Numidian cavalry.

The Antonine Wall (Vallum Antonini)

The final hard fortification that was built from scratch in the north of Britannia was the Antonine Wall. Begun in 142, just twenty years after the construction of Hadrian's intricate border system, it ran for approximately thirty-eight miles across the critical gap between the Firth of Forth and the Firth of Clyde. This is Scotland's largest and most important river valley system, today containing its two major cities: Edinburgh and Glasgow. Using the high ground along the southern edge of this central isthmus and similar in height and width to Hadrian's stone wall, it was built from wood and turf on stone foundations, though a 6-mile section in the east was built of clay, or earth revetted with clay blocks. Stone was used for some of the forts, or parts of them and their principal buildings. A deep forward ditch exaggerated the height of the wall, which was completed with *lilia* anti-personnel stake pits and anklebreaker slots. Six large forts spaced about 8 miles apart were planned, with fortlets every mile between them— but again there were changes made during construction. So far, some sixteen forts of various sizes have been found, all but two built into the back of the rampart, spaced about 2 miles apart. Most have bathhouses and other unusual features have been noted: the addition of extra facilities

Rough Castle, Scotland

Of the forts along the wall, Rough Castle, although one of the smaller, is probably the best preserved. The defenses along the outside of the wall included *lilia*: pits filled with sharpened stakes. In the aerial view, the yellow line shows the path of the wall. The fort is behind and the *lilia* are opposite the front gate (**A**). Trees would not have been allowed and there would have been good sightlines from the fort. The main fort (**B**) contains the headquarters building, a granary and another stone building, possibly the officers' quarters; the annex (**C**) has a bathhouse. Note the triple ditches (**D**) on the annex side. An inscribed tablet and an altar to the goddess Victory named *cohors VI Nerviorum* as the builders.

Bar Hill, Scotland
Built c. 142, excavations found the remains of a stone *principia*, a *horreum*, and a narrow stone bathhouse and possible latrines. Postholes point to four probable barracks. Unusually, the fort didn't connect to the wall but was set back with the military road between the two. Building inscriptions identify *legiones II Augusta* and *XX Valeria Victrix*, and *cohors I Baetasiorum*. The garrison was probably *cohors I Hamiorum Sagittaria,* auxiliary archers from Syria.
An altar to Silvanus dedicated by Caristianius Iustianus, a prefect of the cohort, and the similarity between Bar Hill and Carvoran where the Syrians were also garrisoned, suggest this.

added to some forts so that transiting troops or work parties could be kept safe and supplied during construction, and some mysterious large platformed areas whose use has not been positively identified. All the forts, fortlets, and watchtowers between them were linked by a road, about 18ft wide, that ran behind the length of the wall enabling swift movement along its course. The remarkable survival of various distance slabs, denoting the legionary builders of sections, have provided much information about its construction.

From a purely military perspective the new wall seems to make sense, for it was a proper Roman military engineering structure, with (one must presume) a palisaded rampart furnished with fighting platforms. It is also the shortest gap between the two coastlines, with the best sea and river access. But on closer examination, like Hadrian's Wall, the Antonine Wall is also not what it seems. First, although it was undoubtedly a functioning border, various shortcuts were taken in its construction that fail to use high ground or leave areas of dead ground not visible from the wall, which would imply a decision of speed or convenience over military considerations. Second, the extra troops required to police this area beyond Hadrian's Wall would not have been justified by the gains, for the land conquered could not support them. Economic rewards and resources were important drivers of Roman military policy. Finally, a fourth legion permanently in Britain was not feasible or advisable.

It seems more likely that the wall was built as part of a imperial media campaign to present the new emperor with the right military credentials. Antoninus Pius was, by all accounts, a supremely unmilitary man with no interest in warfare, but nevertheless came from a conservative senatorial

family. His reign is unique in being the most peaceful of the Principate, for he never left Italy, nor did he launch any campaigns—other than this one into Caledonia. Having assumed the mantle of emperor, he had to be typecast in a more predictably Roman fashion and get at least one campaign under his belt. Unlike Hadrian, Antoninus never came to Britain and never saw his wall, but a triumph was still celebrated in Rome, coins struck, and statues raised. On his death twenty years later, the Romans almost immediately burned the timber forts, took down the wall and withdrew back to the more established Hadrianic defense system.

Later, in 208–210, Septimius Severus decided to focus on northern Britain and arrived with his two sons Caracalla and Geta and a substantial army. No doubt the Caledonii had become more organized in their raiding after the usurper Clodius Albinus had earlier taken the British legions across to Gaul. Severus briefly reused the Antonine Wall along with some of Agricola's Gask Ridge forts in his punitive actions against the Caledonii and especially the Maeatae. Evidence of extensive Severan-era fortifications in the Scottish central lowlands indicate an army of about 40–50,000 and serious intent. Cassius Dio alludes to a projected policy of extermination of the natives.

It was not to be, for having made good progress and with the defeated Caledoni suing for peace, Severus fell ill and died in Eboracum (York) in 211. With his death the campaign came to an end, the Romans returned to the Hadrianic frontier fortifications, and his sons returned to Rome to conclude their personal internecine battle.

Replica of the Bridgeness Slab in Bo'Ness, Scotland. Created around 142, it was discovered in 1868. The original is in the National Museum of Scotland. The inscription reads "*Imp(eratori) Caes(ari) Tito Aelio Hadri(ano) Antonino/ Aug(usto) Pio p(atri) p(atriae) leg(io) II Aug(usta) per m(ilia) p(assuum) IIII(milia)DCLII fec(it).*" This translates as, "For the Emperor Caesar Titus Aelius Hadrianus Antoninus Augustus Pius, Father of his Country, the Second Augustan Legion completed [the Wall] over a distance of 4,652 paces." The images show a Roman cavalryman and four defeated Britons (left) and a *suovetaurilia* ceremony (right) which saw the sacrifice of a sheep, pig, and bull in a purification ritual. There's one on Trajan's column, as the emperor purifies and blesses the army.

The Saxon Shore forts

The island province of Britannia was connected to the continent by the *classis Britannica*, which operated from a number of ports in Britain, the largest being Portus Dubris (Dover). In Gaul, the main port used was Gesoriacum Bononia (Boulogne), the largest and most important on the Gallic coast. It provided a safe and short route to Britain, taking between six and eight hours. Lighthouses were built on both shores to aid navigation. Other ports were also used on each coast, as listed in the *Notitia Dignitatum*. The bad weather often encountered in the Channel was dealt with by using ships with high bows and sterns, capable of handling the heavy storms and swells, with flat bottoms to enter shallow water and cope with ebb tides.

The original purpose of the ports and the fleet was to keep the troops stationed in Britannia supplied and to deter piracy, but this came under increasing pressure in the third century, from secessionists within and raiders without. The Germanic and Sarmatian invasions of 234 that surged over the Rhine and Danube caused ripples across the western empire and Emperor Severus Alexander, last of the Severan dynasty, moved units from Britannia's northern frontier to strengthen the east coast of the province. New forts were added and the existing ones upgraded. This process continued throughout the 270–280s and so, too, on the Gallic coast.

Severus Alexander, however, made a mistake that would cost him his life. In trying to appease the German tribes he triggered the legions to mutiny and he was assassinated on March 19, 235. This marked the beginning of a period of provincial secession and internal civil war that lasted for the next half century and seriously degraded the western empire. In 260 Marcus

OPPOSITE Anderitum (Pevensey Castle, England) The Saxon Shore fort was built in the 290s and housed a *limitanei* garrison and fleet. When the Romans left it became an Anglo-Saxon oppidum. William the Conqueror's invaders sheltered here on their first night in England. The *Notitia Dignitatum* identifies the garrison as being the *numerus Abulci*—an infantry unit.

ABOVE Burgh Castle, England (possibly Gariannonum) This fort and neighboring Caister-on-Sea (the other possible Gariannonum) defended the Norfolk coast. Burgh's garrison was a rapid reaction force of 300 cavalry men from the *equites Stablesiani*.

RIGHT AND BELOW Portchester Castle, England (probably Portus Adurni)
The best preserved of the Saxon Shore forts. dated to the late 260s by coin finds, it was possibly built by Carausius before he declared himself emperor of *Imperium Britanniarum* (Britain and Gaul). The strength of the castle and its strategic location meant it retained its importance into the seventeenth century. The size of its walls and towers show off later Roman building prowess.

OPPOSITE, ABOVE AND BELOW Rutupiae (Richborough Castle, England)
Though now inland, in Roman times it was on the coast and could have been the site of the first Roman landing in AD43. Around 85–90 a triumphal arch was built to remember the conquest (note the cross-shaped footings at **A**). The town was flattened c. 250 so the monument could be used as a signal station (note the V-shaped ditches and single entrance **B**). Twenty years later, all had gone: town, monument, signal station. Rutupiae became part of the Saxon Shore defenses with later Roman walls and towers. The garrison was the *legio II Augusta*. This was the last significant Roman presence in England.

Postumus, a general of Batavian origin commanding the Rhine frontier, was declared emperor by his troops (again concerning the acquisition and distribution of booty). Postumus was recognized by most western and northwestern provinces—Hispania, Gallia, Britannia, Germania, and Raetia—and he lasted for almost a decade, content to hold Gaul, his powerbase province, establishing an alternative administration and defense structure from the rest of the empire. He also continued to defeat and check the encroaching Germanic tribes.

Postumus was, in turn, assassinated by his troops when he tried to prevent them from looting Mogontiacum (Mainz), as were several more Gallic emperors. In 274 Aurelian defeated Tetricus and reunited the empire. Barely a decade had passed before it all happed again. This time Carausius, commander of the *classis Britannica*, was accused of corruption and sentenced to death, so he promptly declared himself emperor of Britain and Gaul, seceding those provinces for almost another decade. Carausius must have been capitalizing on the growing disatisfaction with Rome increasingly felt by the provinces. Nevertheless, the crisis of the third century was ameliorated by the steadying hand of Diocletian. Once again the center slowly resumed control over its peripheries.

Constantius Chlorus reincorporated the Britannic Empire back into the Roman, but the northern barbarians continued to grow in menace, regularly breaking through the frontiers and moving deeper into the empire. Saxon and Frankish pirate raids would soon inevitably overwhelm the Saxon Shore system. The *Notitia Dignitatum* lists the forts on the southeast coast of Britannia and the northwest coast of Gaul (see map p. 67). They were substantial cohort forts, with ramparts, bastions, artillery platforms, and ditches. They were usually located at natural harbors or at the mouths of estuaries to control access to the interior. On the British side they were under the command of the Duke of the Saxon Shore. The northern coast of Gaul was divided into two commands, one covering the estuaries of the Somme and the Scheldt, and the other the coasts of Normandy and Britanny. Because of their strategic locations, most of the forts continued to be occupied by successive waves of defenders and invaders, through the feudal, medieval, and Napoleonic periods.

Germania

The Roman border fortifications in Germania were started by Augustus, who having tried to realize a Roman Germania Magna encompassing all land between the Rhine, the Danube, and the Elbe, eventually decided on a frontier that followed a line linking the Rhine and Danube rivers. Just like the rivers, the border was rarely straight, but followed the vagaries of geography and politics. Once built it was maintained in some form until the fifth century. The two provinces of Germania, Superior and Inferior, were created c. 16–13BC as military zones out of the northern parts of Gallia Belgica.

In the northwest, the depth and size of the lower Rhine provided a perfect defensive setting that endured (with the occasional devastation) until the empire fell. As the forward area of Roman incursions, it was also the original springboard and supply route for the Augustan attempt to occupy Germania Magna, since its secure setting enabled the construction of the earliest major bases in the region at present-day Neuss (Novaesium), Xanten (Vetera), Köln/Cologne (Colonia—the short form of Colonia Claudia Ara Agrippinensium, or CCAA), and Bonn (Bonna). The width of the downstream channels made crossing precarious and precluded the necessity of a continuous defensive palisade, requiring only a series of watchtowers linked by road with small forts set further back, but access points and ports assumed a vital importance as the river was the major mode of transport and trade in the region. Colonia (Köln/Cologne) was the largest, the capital of Germania Inferior and military headquarters with a legionary fortress at Divitia, as well as being the home of the *classis Germanica*, the largest and most important of Rome's provincial fleets. Following the destruction of most Roman facilities during the province-wide Batavian Revolt in AD69–70, new stone forts were added to the rebuilt infrastructure and the Batavian capital at Nijmegen was taken over as a legionary base, becoming Noviomagus.

Further to the south, defenses were much more problematic for Rome, especially the critical 300-mile land corridor between the pronounced bend of the westward Rhine at Mogontiacum (Mainz) and the main flow of the eastward Danube at Castra Regina (Regensburg). The Romans called this watershed region, which roughly separated the Gallic and Germanic tribes, the *Agri Decumates*. Always a troublesome area, over time this part of the frontier steadily accrued more infrastructure according to the threat level and it was here that the main defenses of the German *limes* were concentrated.

Mogontiacum itself had a massive fortress capable of housing two entire legions. Connected to the Rhine by its navigable river (the Main), its centralized position covered the whole southern sector in conjunction with the legionary fortress at Castra Regina, it was the critical lynchpin of this part of the frontier defense system and became the capital of Germania Superior.

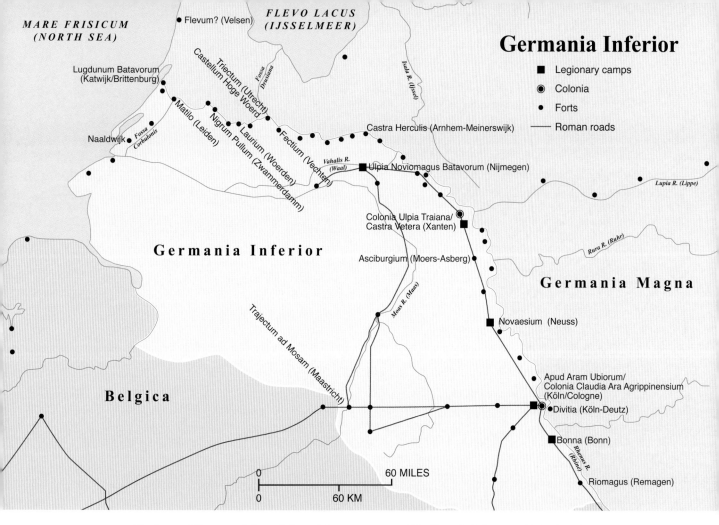

Germania Inferior

- ■ Legionary camps
- ◉ Colonia
- • Forts
- — Roman roads

MARE FRISICUM (NORTH SEA)

FLEVO LACUS (IJSSELMEER)

Flevum? (Velsen)

Lugdunum Batavorum (Katwijk/Brittenburg)

Fossa Drusiana

Isala R. (IJssel)

Triectum (Utrecht)
Castellum Hoge Woerd

Matilo (Leiden)

Nigrum Pullum (Zwammerdamm)

Laurium (Woerden)

Fectium (Vechter)

Castra Herculis (Arnhem-Meinerswijk)

Naaldwijk

Fossa Corbulonis

Vahalis R. (Waal)

Ulpia Noviomagus Batavorum (Nijmegen)

Lupia R. (Lippe)

Germania Inferior

Colonia Ulpia Traiana/
Castra Vetera (Xanten)

Asciburgium (Moers-Asberg)

Rura R. (Ruhr)

Germania Magna

Moas R. (Maas)

Novaesium (Neuss)

Trajectum ad Mosam (Maastricht)

Apud Aram Ubiorum/
Colonia Claudia Ara Agrippinensium (Köln/Cologne)

Belgica

Divitia (Köln-Deutz)

Bonna (Bonn)

Rhenus R. (Rhine)

Riomagus (Remagen)

0		60 MILES
0		60 KM

ABOVE The *limes* of Germania Inferior followed the path of the Rhine to its North Sea mouth. The path fluctuated over the years, as did the coastline, so much so that Lugdunum Batavorum has been completely eroded away. Because of the river border, the Roman presence was confined to forts and watchtowers—not walls and palisades—linked by the frontier road.

BELOW The *Fossa Corbulonis* canal linked the Rhine with the Meuse, meaning ships for Britannia could load and sail from a more peaceful stretch of water. It was probably built in AD50 under the direction of Gnaeus Domitius Corbulo and improved during Hadrian's reign. This trench was part of a 2017 dig and shows the clay that would have been brought in (the local area is peat).

Manufacturing weapons

For most of the early years of Rome's history, the army's weapons were made privately, probably against government contract. Bishop (2006) mentions Calpurnia Piso's *officina armorum* (arms factory) in Macedonia from where Piso's father had supplied weapons during the Social War (91–87BC). In the east, there were a number of cities that had weapons workshops. Tacitus tells (*Historiae* II: 82) that "strong towns were selected to manufacture arms" by Vespasian who "visited each place in person, encouraged the workmen." As well as these private sources, the legions may well have had some weapon-making capacity—although there is some dispute as to the type of weapons and quantities they could produce: Vegetius (*Epitome* II: 11) suggests that the legion's *praefectus fabrorum* oversaw workshops where arms of every type were made. However, archaeology has found little more than recycling or reuse of scrap, so this may not mean large-scale workshops—although a Vindolanda tablet talks about 343 men working in the fort's workshops. The spread of the legions to the frontiers and the distance from Rome, meant that other solutions had to be found, and the *Notitia* identifies state-owned *fabricae*—probably set up by Diocletian: fifteen in the east and twenty in the west, most on the borders, in Italy, or in Gaul.

Initially just a patrol road cleared through forest linking watchtowers, under Hadrian the *limes* defenses became more substantial with the addition of a ditch whose earth was used to build a berm; a thick palisade was added. Behind this almost 1,000 watchtowers with at least sixty supporting forts and fortlets were set a little farther back. Despite this density the defenses that ran through the Black Forest were relatively light, with sections often raided, overwhelmed, and burnt by the tribes, but they served their purpose in acting as a warning system for the legions to launch punitive action or to prevent the easy escape of any heavily laden raiding party, making such attempts less profitable and more hazardous. With peace many forts grew *vici* around them and by 150, the towers and forts had been rebuilt in stone.

In the turbulent third century the pressures both within and without the *limes* forced various ruptures. Dangerous confederations of warlike and migrating tribes or internal civil war ensured regular mayhem. In 256–258 both were combined when the Franks infiltrated Germania Inferior and marched into Gaul. The Roman general guarding the Rhine, Postumus, ended up being declared Emperor of the West, seceding Gaul and Britain from the empire for some fourteen years. Postumus changed the organization of the military at the frontier, positioning more cavalry units along the fort line behind watchtower screens for quick response and layering defenses to create a deeper defense zone through which hostiles had to advance.

In 277–280 Marcus Aurelius Probus expelled more Alemannic and Frankish invaders, restored the Rhine frontier and defeated the Burgundians and Vandals in Raetia. In 293 Constantius defeated another Frankish invasion and rebuilt the forts along the lower Rhine, while his son, Constantine I (306–337) perfected the strategy of defense in depth with a line of heavy fortifications along the river, guardposts at strategic locations, and a cavalry army held further back in readiness for a response. In 355–358, Julian defeated Frankish and Germanic tribal invasions and reclaimed Mainz which had fallen to the Alemanni. Walls were hurriedly rebuilt but the town fell again in 368. Rebuilding continued into the reign of Valentinian, who managed to retain control of the Rhine frontier with some new fortifications, but with the turn of the new century Rome slowly lost control over its northern provinces, which were increasingly overrun by tribes who themselves were remorselessly driven south by climate change and other tribes, accelerating the collapse of the empire in the west.

Stilicho—half Vandal—was the regent for Theodosius's son Honorius who came to the throne in 394. He kept the barbarians at bay for fourteen years, halting a number of invasions, but he did so by denuding the northern provinces. In December 406, a coalition of barbarian tribes flooded across the Rhine, defeated the Franks, and sacked Gaul. Constantine III set himself up as emperor in Britannia and, finally, Stilicho's opponents were able to bring him down. He was executed in 408. Without his expertise, two years later Alaric the Goth sacked Rome. Although the empire would hang on for another seventy years as mobile field armies played cat and mouse with different invaders, the death throes ended in 476 when the Germanic warlord Odoacer became first barbarian king of Italy. The western empire was no more.

ABOVE Lugdunum Batavorum (Katwijk, the Netherlands)
This bronze by artist Nicolas Dings is inspired by the story of how the Emperor Caligula made his men collect seashells as spoils of war against the sea gods.

BELOW Forum Hadriani (Voorburg, the Netherlands)
On the *Fossa Corbulonis*, named thus by the emperor in 121, the city—until abandoned in the late third century—was the most northerly in Germania.

Matilo and the *Fossa Corbulonis* (Leiden-Roomburg, the Netherlands)

Matilo was a vital fort on the Rhine at the head of the *Fossa Corbulonis*, named after Domitian's brother-in-law. The fort was constructed following the Batavian Revolt of 69 and underwent various upgrades with moats added and wooden buildings rebuilt in stone. Units attested: *cohors XV Voluntarium*; *cohors I Lucensium*; *Numerus Exploratorum Batavorum*. The photographs show the archaeological park—a national monument since 1976— its earth walls, gate towers, and a replica boat. Matilo still awaits a proper archaeological dig as it was decided to leave it unexplored until techniques were developed to allow the best analysis of the project.

Nigrum Pullum (Alphen-Zwammerdam, the Netherlands)

Nigrum Pullum was a small fort controlling the confluence of the river Meije with the Rhine, first erected in AD47 during the reorganization of the frontier by Corbulo. Destroyed in the Batavian revolt it was rebuilt some time after 80 and further upgraded in stone after 175, probably by men of *legio XXX Ulpia Victrix* from Castra Vetera (see p. 97). In excavations at its quay the remains of six ships were found. A reconstruction of one can be seen at Archeon in Alphen aan den Rijn, where it is hoped that the others will eventually be exhibited. These wonderful artist impressions by Stevie Heru show the fort and its nascent *vicus* (**ABOVE**) and the roofless *principia* (**BELOW**)—in which can be seen the *sacellum* where the unit's standards were kept.

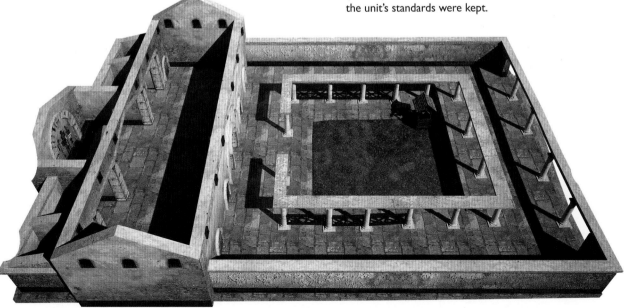

Hoge Woerd (Utrecht, the Netherlands)

The Hoge Woerd fort guarded the confluence of the small river Mare with the Rhine and was home to the naval unit *cohors I Classica Pia Fidelis*. It was occupied from about 47 to 270. Two large well-preserved barges have been found, one of them being completely excavated. It is housed in a museum on the site where the fort has been reconstructed. The other boat, the subject of a *Time Team* episode, was excavated sufficiently for it to be dated and its unusual building techniques identified. It seems to have been sunk deliberately in an attempt to stop the erosion of the riverbank, which carried the frontier road, as the Rhine changed course. The river was the principal highway for provisions and materiel from the south and was hugely important for the invasion of Britannia, and for supplying the province thereafter. Watchtowers and forts were important to guard the waterways from pirates, to police the border zone, and to help direct shipping.

ABOVE Under Utrecht cathedral square lies a Roman fort—Traiectum—that had a long history. First erected under Emperor Claudius in AD47, the original version was burnt during the Batavian revolt. It was rebuilt and manned for around 200 years by *cohors II Hispanorum*, an *auxilia* infantry unit.

ABOVE RIGHT AND BELOW Fectium (Vechten, the Netherlands)

Fectium was another cohort fort, this one guarding the confluence of the river Fectio (now Vecht) with the Rhine. Built at the turn of the first century AD by Tiberius, it was destroyed in the Batavaian Revolt and rebuilt around 138. It was eventually abandoned when silting made river access impossible some time after 275. Units attested: *cohors II Brittanorum*; *cohors I Flavia Hispanorum equitata*.

ABOVE Arnhem-Meinerswijk, the Netherlands
Another of Corbulo's auxiliary forts built around
AD47 on the lower Rhine, there is debate whether this
fort is Castra Herculis or Levefanum from the *Tabula
Peutingeriana*. Livius.org suggests the latter, and that
the name links the location to "a sanctuary (*fanum*).
Assuming that the map contains a spelling error, the
sanctuary may have been dedicated to the Batavian
goddess Haeva (*Haevae Fanum*)." Possibly dating to
Germanicus's campaigns in Germany, the original fort
was destroyed during the Batavian Revolt, rebuilt and
had a major upgrade under Hadrian. It was abandoned
after 274, when the emperor Aurelian reconquered
the breakaway Gallic part of the empire. Today's
reconstruction uses gabions to show the south gate
and main buildings.

OPPOSITE AND BELOW Castra Vetera and Colonia Ulpia Traiana (Xanten, Germany)

The history of the Vetera camps and the city of Xanten highlight much of the history of the northern limits of empire. The first camp was probably founded around 12BC by Drusus the elder, the Emperor Augustus's stepson, one of fifty he is said to have set up during the years he led attacks into Germania. The empire was still in its expansionist period, and knew no boundaries. By the time of the Batavian Revolt in 69–70, however, the Julio-Claudian dynasty was over and the Year of the Four Emperors saw revolt and civil war. The legionary base Vetera I—which had been rebuilt a number of times since its original construction—was pivotal in the revolt as the Batavians besieged and, after their surrender, killed the survivors of its defenders, *legio V Alaudae* and *XV Primigenia*. Vetera I was destroyed and was never used again, the new Vetera II being built to the east of the original. Units attested there were *legio VI Victrix* and after 275, *legio XXX Ulpia Victrix*. The course of the Rhine has changed over the years and obliterated Vetera II. What does remain, however, to the northwest of the forts is Colonia Ulpia Traiana, a city that dates back to 8BC, although people have lived at the confluence of Rhine and Lippe for centuries. Renamed after Emperor Trajan, the city succumbed to the Frankish invasion of 275, although it was revived under Constantius I Chlorus. Then named Tricensimae, it became Xanten later.

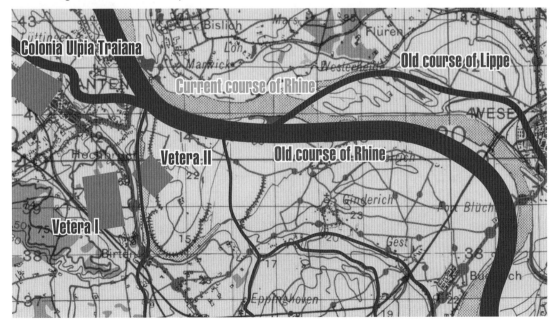

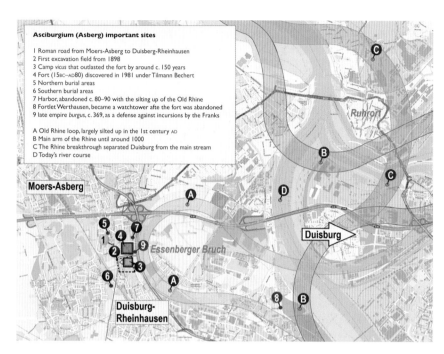

Asciburgium (Asberg) important sites

1 Roman road from Moers-Asberg to Duisberg-Rheinhausen
2 First excavation field from 1898
3 Camp *vicus* that outlasted the fort by around c. 150 years
4 Fort (15BC–AD80) discovered in 1981 under Tillmann Bechert
5 Northern burial areas
6 Southern burial areas
7 Harbor, abandoned c. 80–90 with the silting up of the Old Rhine
8 Fortlet Werthausen, became a watchtower afte the fort was abandoned
9 late empire *burgus*, c. 369, as a defense against incursions by the Franks

A Old Rhine loop, largely silted up in the 1st century AD
B Main arm of the Rhine until around 1000
C The Rhine breakthrough separated Duisburg from the main stream
D Today's river course

ABOVE Asciburgium (Moers-Asberg, Germany)

An auxiliary fort sited opposite the confluence of the Ruhr and the Rhine, Asciburgium was another fort originally built by Drusus. It was abandoned by the military in 83–85 when the Rhine changed its course, though it remained an important trading settlement. Later, Valentinian I (364–375) built a burgus on the site of the old fort. This map shows well the way that the Rhine's course has fluctuated over the years.

RIGHT Novaesium (Neuss, Germany)

One of the oldest Roman forts in Germania, Novaesium was a massive two-legion base built by Drusus before 16BC during his conquest of the fertile Lippe valley, at an important crossing point on the south bank of the Rhine and the Erft estuary. Surrendered and destroyed in the Batavian Revolt by *legio XVI Gallica*, which was consequently disbanded, it was rebuilt and occupied by *legio VI Victrix* until around 100. It was destoyed by the Franks in 275 and again rebuilt, its walls lasting until the ninth century. Units attested: *legiones V Alaudae, XX Valeria Victrix, XVI Gallica, VI Victrix, II Italica Pia*. Illustrated is one of the many Jupiter columns erected in Germania Inferior. Either representing Jupiter enthroned (as here) or, more frequently, Jupiter defeating a giant, the original seems to have been created in Mogontiacum (Mainz) around 65 to honor the Emperor Nero. Many can be found in Germania, particularly in Köln (Cologne), although none has been found intact. Most date to the second and third centuries AD.

Roman military units—*legiones, alae, cohortes*—carried honorifics as well as names. Thus *legio II Italica* was given the title *VII Pia VII Fidelis* (seven times faithful, seven times loyal) by Gallienus. *Auxilia* units which performed with extreme bravery were sometimes honored with citizenship—and earned the honorific *civium Romanorum*. The unit retained this although new recruits weren't allowed to enjoy the citizenship that the earlier unit had earned. Another was *cl*—although it's unclear what this means, with both *civium Latinorum* and *coram laudata* (publically praised) proposed.

Divitia (Köln/Cologne, Germany)

Situated at a vital bridging point on the Rhine, Divitia was another massive early base built to hold at least two legions. Its importance ensured continual expansion and after AD28 it became the capital of Germania Inferior. In AD50, it was renamed Colonia Claudia Ara Agrippinensium. Falling to Frankish invasions in the 260s and 270s, Constantius I Chlorus restored Divitia and his son Constantine I rebuilt the bridge in 310. Units attested: *legiones I Germanica*, *XX Valeria Victrix*, *VIII Augusta*, *numerus Exploratorum Divitiensium*.

ABOVE Divitia's walls were begun in the first century AD, and extend to some 2.5 miles in length with nine gates and nineteen round towers. These are the Roman Tower (**LEFT**) and the Helena Tower (**RIGHT**).

BELOW Köln's Roman sewers can be visited, as can the remains of the Roman governor's palace, the *praetorium*.

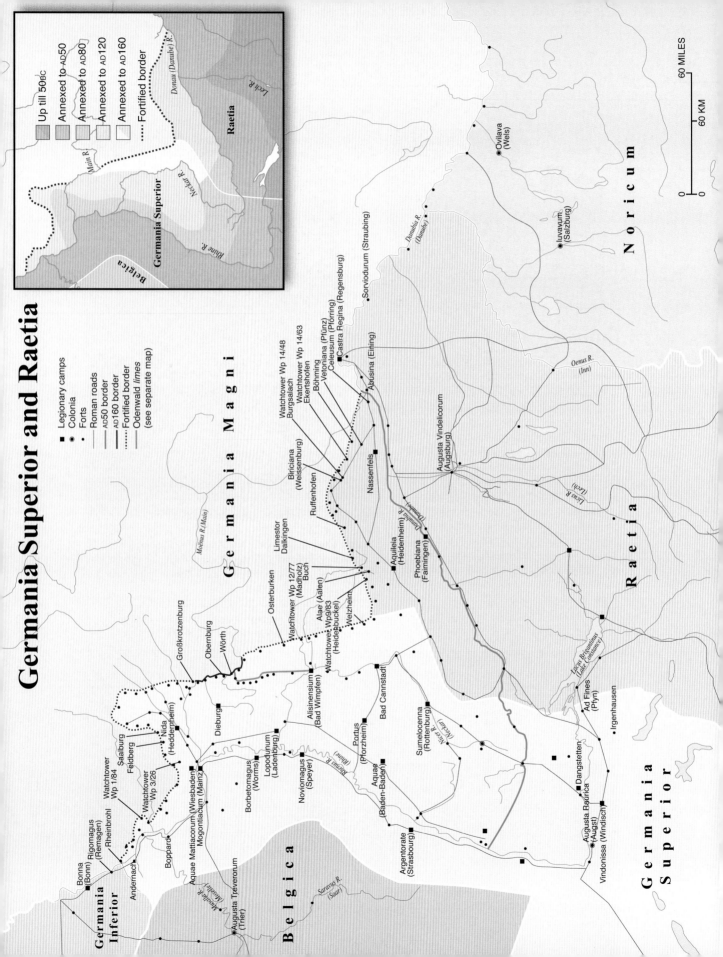

Germania Superior and Raetia

Legend:
- ■ Legionary camps
- ◉ Colonia
- • Forts
- — Roman roads
- AD50 border
- AD160 border
- Fortified border
- Odenwald *limes* (see separate map)

Inset legend:
- Up till 50 BC
- Annexed to AD50
- Annexed to AD80
- Annexed to AD120
- Annexed to AD160
- Fortified border

Donau (Danube) R.
Lech R.
Main R.
Neckar R.
Rhine R.
Belgica
Germania Superior
Raetia

60 MILES
60 KM

Ovilava (Wels)
Iuvavum (Salzburg)

N o r i c u m

Oenus R. (Inn)
Danuvia R. (Danube)
Sorviodurum (Straubing)
Celeusum (Pföring)
Castra Regina (Regensburg)
Abusina (Eining)
Vetoniana (Pfünz)
Böhming
Watchtower Wp 14/63
Watchtower Wp 14/48
Burgsalach
Ekertshofen
Biriciana (Weissenburg)
Ruffenhofen
Nassenfels
Augusta Vindelicorum (Augsburg)
Licus R. (Lech)
Aquileia (Heidenheim)
Phoebiana (Faimingen)
Danubii R. (Danube)
R a e t i a
Lacus Brigantinus (Lake Constance)
Ad Fines (Pfyn)
Irgenhausen
Augusta Raurica (Augst)
Vindonissa (Windisch)
Dangstetten

G e r m a n i a   M a g n i

Limestor Dalkingen
Osterburken
Watchtower Wp 12/77 (Madholz)
Buch
Alae (Aalen)
Watchtower Wp9/83 (Heidebuckel)
Welzheim
Maenus R. (Main)

Großkrotzenburg
Obernburg
Wörth
Dieburg
Nida (Heddernheim)
Saalburg
Feldberg
Watchtower Wp 1/84
Watchtower Wp 3/26
Rheinbrohl
Andernach
Bonna (Bonn)
Rigomagus (Remagen)
Boppard
Aquae Mattiacorum (Wiesbaden)
Mogontiacum (Mainz)
Borbetomagus (Worms)
Lopodunum (Ladenburg)
Noviomagus (Speyer)
Alisinensium (Bad Wimpfen)
Portus (Pforzheim)
Aquae (Baden-Baden)
Bad Cannstadt
Sumelocenna (Rottenburg)
Argentorate (Strasbourg)
Rhenus R. (Rhine)
Neckar (Neckar)

G e r m a n i a   I n f e r i o r
Mosella R. (Moselle)
Sarauus R. (Saar)
Augusta Treverorum (Trier)
B e l g i c a
G e r m a n i a   S u p e r i o r

OPPOSITE Just southeast of Remagen, where the River Vinxtbach joins the Rhine, Germania Inferior ends and the border crosses to the east bank of the Rhine. The *limes* of Germania Superior and Raetia initially ran along the Rhine and Danube, but during the 200 years from 50BC the empire pushed forward into the *Agri Decumates* and lost its natural riverine defensive line. A fortifed border was created. It's difficult to determine which element was first—although the Lautertal *limes* (the so-called *Sybillenspur* from the Neckar to the Schwabian Jura) was an early (c. end of first century AD) palisade and ditch system. The Odenwald *limes* (see pp. 102–103) was created in the 130s, and then the line moved further forward. The border stabilized around 160, running overland from the Rhine at Rheinbrohl to the Danube at Eining covering a distance of over 500km, with a section following the River Main from Großkreutzenburg to Miltenberg. There are 120 forts and 900 watchtowers; many were set up at the beginning or middle of the second century AD and existed until the end of the Roman occupation— 260/270 when the border once again reverted to the big rivers (see the Rhine–Iller–Danube *limes* on p. 118–119).

ABOVE Bonna (Bonn, Germany)
An auxiliary fort built by Drusus, Bonna sat opposite the confluence of the frontier river Rhine and one of its smaller tributaries, the Sieg, between AD13 and 16. Following the disaster of the Teutoburg Forest in AD9, a larger legionary base was built to the north of the original, becoming the home of *legio I Germanica*. After the Batavian Revolt, Bonna was rebuilt in stone and became the home base of *legio XXI Rapax* and then,

some time after 83, *legio I Minervia*. This plan (**ABOVE**) of the fort is near the foundation of the Dietkirche (which can be seen in the background). Except when called to serve in Trajan's Dacian War, this legion remained at Bonna until the end of the empire. With its massive walls the town survived attacks by the Franks in 275 and 355, but with the collapse of the western empire it and its inhabitants were soon entirely assimilated by the native population. Units attested: *legiones I Germanica, XXI Rapax, I Minervia, XXII Primigenia*. (See also p. 192.)

The Upper Germanic-Raetian *limes*

Section 1: Rheinbrohl–Bad Ems
Section 2: Bad Ems–Adolfseck near Bad Schwalbach
Section 3: Adolfseck near Bad Schwalbach–
    Köpperner Tal
Section 4: Köpperner–Marköbel
Section 5: Marköbel–Großkrotzenburg am Main
Section 6a: Hainstadt–Wörth am Main (older Main line)
Section 6b: Trennfurt–Miltenberg
Section 7: Miltenberg–Buchen-Hettingen (Rehberg)
Section 8: Buchen-Hettingen (Rehberg)–Jagsthausen
    (more recent Odenwald line)
Section 9: Jagsthausen–Alfdorf-Pfahlbronn (Haghof)
Section 10: Wörth am Main–Bad Wimpfen (older
    Odenwald line/Neckar–Odenwald *limes*)
Section 11: Bad Wimpfen–Köngen (Neckar line)
Section 12: Alfdorf-Pfahlbronn (Haghof)–Rotenbachtal
    near Schwäbisch Gmünd (end of the Upper
    Germanic *limes*, start of the Raetian *limes*–Stödtlen
Section 13: Mönchsroth–Gunzenhausen
Section 14: Gunzenhausen–Kipfenberg
Section 15: Kipfenberg–Eining

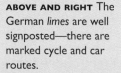

ABOVE AND RIGHT The German *limes* are well signposted—there are marked cycle and car routes.

LEFT Watchtower Wp10/15
The information boards show that this style of watchtower was quite common on the Odenwald *limes*. A dry stone ground floor supporting a two-floored timber structure above. The entrance was usually on the first floor, which was also the soldiers' living quarters while the second floor was the observatory, equipped with large windows (as on Wp10/37, **OPPOSITE, BELOW RIGHT**) or an outside gallery. Remnants of the lime mortar used show that the joints were painted red and exterior stone with inscriptions, indicating a degree of pride and prestige in their construction. Initially sited behind their own palisade, later the palisade was extended with a ditch and bank introduced.

OPPOSITE, TOP Buchen *villa rustica*
Once the *limes* had been pushed forward, settlers filled the country. This villa—as portrayed cleverly on a glass information board—is typical, a focal point for agricultural development that helped Romanize the newly conquered area. Excavations and other finds suggest that there were 1,200 manors on the right bank of the Rhine in today's Baden-Württemberg.

OPPOSITE, CENTER Watchtower Wp10/33
Building inscription dating to 146.

The Odenwald *limes*

The border in the *Agri Decumates* was in flux for 200 years between 50BC and AD160 when it stabilized for a century. The earlier Odenwald *limes* were set up from Wörth on the Main to the Neckar with wooden watchtowers that had a clear line of sight between them. They were linked by the frontier road and had frequent supporting forts. Antoninus Pius (emperor 138–61) decided to improve this, moving the original line in Germania Superior and Raetia to newly prepared forts and towers (the *Vorderer limes*). The move was between ten and twenty-five miles eastward and was efficiently performed and had the practical advantage of less distance between forts and towers, which were joined by a palisade and ditch. Today, the Odenwald *limes* boast a number of rebuilt towers and a wealth of museums and other sites.

Odenwald *limes*

ABOVE Mogontiacum (Mainz, Germany)

A massive two-legion base built by Drusus around 13BC, Mogontiacum's strategic position at the confluence of the Main and the Rhine made it an important city even when the border was advanced eastward. Its continued importance was cemented when it became the capital of the province Germania Superior c. 85. It had a bridge over the Rhine (twenty-one piers, 1,300ft in length), a base for the *classis Germanica*, and the weight of troops necessary to combat any incursion over the border by German tribes. The fortress was rebuilt in stone toward the end of the first century AD, possibly by Domitian who also ensured that it was supplied with water thanks to a nine-mile long aqueduct. Epigraphic attestations of units are many and varied, mostly based in pairs, but after the Saturninus rebellion (88–89) this was reduced to one: *legio XXII Primigenia* stayed for three centuries from 92. The provincial governor probably lived within the camp in a praetorium that expanded when the military contingent was reduced. Future emperor Trajan could have been governor here (he governed Germania Inferior under Nerva). A city grew around the fortress and walls were added in c. 259 following unrest. Sacked by the Alemanni in 368, it was rebuilt but fell to a confederation of Germanic tribes around 406, the Burgundians in 410, and Attila's Huns in 451. This is the theater, a large one whose stage is under the railroad lines.

LEFT The Drusus stone was originally covered in marble. It may be what remains of Drusus's cenotaph, the memorial to the stepson of Augustus and brother of Tiberius.

RIGHT Reconstructed arch of Dativius Victor who: "dedicated the arch with its decorations to Jupiter, the greatest and best of the gods, to honor the sacred imperial dynasty."

RIGHT Watchtower Wp I/I (Rheinbrohl, Germany)
At Rheinbrol a reconstructed watchtower (built 1973, and not a very accurate reconstruction) marks the beginning of the *limes Germanica* on the right bank of the River Rhine. It is built in stone with an all-round external wooden viewing platform at its top such as those built in the second century AD. Opposite Rheinbrohl, on the west bank, the River Vinxtbach—little more than a stream—marks the dividing line between Germania Inferior and Superior. It seems too small to provide such a division, but it may well have been a boundary between local tribes. Here the Southern German *limes* start on the east bank of the Rhine and walls and palisades take over from the riverine frontier. Nearby is a replica of a gravestone that was found there. It remembers a *signifer* (standard bearer). The inscription reads: "Pintaius, son of Pedilicus, from the fort Intercatia in Asturias, behind the mountain, standard-bearer of *cohors V Asturum*, thirty years old, seven years service."

BELOW Watchtower Wp I/84 (Stefansturm near Arzbach, Germany)
"Stefansturm" is another reconstructed watchtower, built in 1954 over the original stone foundations, beneath which were traces of the wooden original. It stands on a hill 1,388ft above sea level, to take advantage of the high ground—as the photograph shows. A few miles south, where the *limes* crosses the River Larm, section 2 of the German *Limeskommission*'s numbering system commences.

ABOVE Feldberg fort, Germany

Today surrounded by the wooded slopes of the Kleiner Feldberg, at 2,707ft just 175ft below the Großer Feldberg, this fort and nearby baths were the highest in the Taunus mountains. Probably built during Domitian's foray against the Chatti around 83, it was upgraded during the reign of Antoninus Pius (138–161) with a number of stone buildings, there is dendro-dating and coin evidence of around 160. It was an important location, defending a trade route and road over the nearby Feldberg pass "am Roten Kreuz" (of the Red Cross). Below the Taunus lies the fertile valley of the Main and there's a gold mine nearby, too. A *vicus* grew up around the fort, although not as large as that at Zugmantel some 12 miles away, where there was an amphitheater and what started as a *numerus*-sized fort

eventually was expanded to house a cohort—*cohors I Treverorum equitata* is attested. Feldberg fort fell into disuse as its garrison was moved west in the middle of the third century AD. An attested unit here was a *numerus* (about 160 men) of *Exploratio Halicanensium* (a semi-mounted reconnaissance unit from the Pannonian town of Halicanum (today Szerdahely in Hungary).

BELOW Watchtower Wp 3/26 (Idstein Dasbach, Germany)

This reconstructed watchtower in the Taunus mountains lies between Zugmantel and Feldberg. Built in 2002, it is one of the truest replicas—it has been plastered and painted white with red grout to simulate a regular stone pattern. Access to the tower was through a small hatch on the first floor.

Saalburg, Germany

Sited on the main ridge of the Taunus northwest of Bad Homburg, Saalburg is the most completely reconstructed Roman fort in Germany. Originally two enclosures used by troops fighting the Chatti, these were replaced by an earth and wood fort for a numerus c. 90, Under Hadrian mortared stone walls and ditches produced a cohort-sized fort that housed a mixed infantry/cavalry unit, *cohors II Raetorum civium Romanorum equitata* until c. 260. The garrison's baths were outside the main entrance in a *vicus* that grew up around it.

ABOVE RIGHT Antoninus Pius greets visitors to Saalburg. The inscription remembers Wilhelm II ("Kaiser Bill") who ordered the reconstruction.

CENTER RIGHT The reconstructed *horrea*.

BELOW RIGHT A 2020 aerial view. The palisade and ditch ran 330ft from the *porta decumana* hidden by trees at the bottom of the photo.

BELOW The red outline shows the footprint of the earlier fort and bath. The new fort's bath and *vicus* are outside the *porta praetoria*.

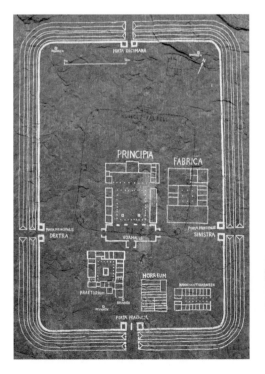

Großkrotzenburg, Germany

The River Wetter gives its name to today's Wetterau area of Hesse and also the Roman *limes* there—the bulge north of the River Main into Germania Magna. As the Romans advanced into the Taunus so they built forts and watchtowers along the important routes and passes; to facilitate trade and to control movement by the tribes. Starting with the Flavian emperors, Vespasian's push into this area was continued by Domitian and taken up by Trajan—by the time of Hadrian the advancing lines of forts and ditches had coalesced into a fixed border. The Großkrotzenburg cohort fort on the River Main was where the border followed the river down to Wörth, at which point the Odenwald *limes* began. Originally of wood and turf, Großkrotzenburg was rebuilt in stone during Trajan's tenure as a cohort fort. A bridge across the Rhine (**ABOVE**) was built around 140. A *vicus* built up around it and a *Mithraeum* has been discovered (relief **LEFT**) as has—within the fort—a tile factory that was set up by *cohors IIII Vindelicorum* around 193. Tiles with their stamp have been found at Mainz and elsewhere, transported not only down the River Main by barge but also the Nidda, Nidder, and Wetter.

Obernburg, Germany

South of Großkrotzenburg, Obernburg fort, now covered by the town of Oldenburg-am-Main, was rediscovered early in the eighteenth century, including a rich consecration district with many inscriptions. Originally built in 100/101, it was replaced in stone around 162 and was surrounded by a large *vicus*. It was at least partially destroyed around 233 during an Alemanni attack, but remained occupied until the *limes* was abandoned around 260–275. Units attested: *cohors I Germanorum*.

ABOVE LEFT This interesting altar, dated 207, in Obernburg museum refers to Jupiter Dolchiensus, a cult that found favor in the second and third centuries AD, especially in the legions, in this case a logging *vexillatio* of *legio XXII Primigenia*.

ABOVE CENTER This is the rider from a *Jupitergigantensäule*, a giant Jupiter column (see p. 98).

ABOVE RIGHT Dated to c. 189, this altar came from the *beneficiarii* station at Obernburg—there were probably others in this area at Miltenberg-Altstadt, Stockstadt, Seligenstadt, and Großkrotzenburg. The *beneficiarii* were senior soldiers who performed administrative

duties. A number—from thirty to as many as sixty—from a legion were attached to the provincial governor's staff (the *officium consularis*), which "assisted the governor in all his duties, administrative, judicial and military, and the beneficiarii were employed in a variety of roles, appearing in the sources as arresting officers, messengers, servants to the governor and general assistants. To indicate their status as officiales of the governor, they carried a decorated lance-symbol when operating away from the *officium*. In Britain and the two German provinces they were evidently outposted, apparently for periods of six months at a time, along the roads linking the provincial capitals with the frontiers, with neighboring provinces, and with Rome."

BELOW The building inscription from the Obernburg principia dates to 162.

ABOVE AND LEFT Osterburken, Germany

Osterburken was an unusual double fort at the southern edge of the Kirnau valley in Baden-Württemberg, some distance east of the Rhine. It is now built over, but famous for the UNESCO World Heritage Limes Römer-museum. The fort was built around 155 and had a substantial *vicus*. There were two bath complexes—perhaps one civilian and one military. A small irregular trapezoid annex fort was added sometime c. 185–192, for a *numerus*, an irregular auxiliary troop of about 120 men. Osterburken was attacked by the Alemanni in 233 but was partially restored, operating until the *limes* were abandoned. Units attested: *cohors III Aquitanorum equitata civium Romanorum*. The museum includes a large number of *beneficiarii* inscriptions—more than anywhere else in the empire. One was by a soldier from *legio VIII Augusta PFCC Antoniniana* in 212 which uniquely identifies that he was serving a *beneficiarii* station (**LEFT**).

OPPOSITE, ABOVE Welzheim, Germany

Around 160 the Romans founded a colony and built two cohort forts at Welzheim in the Swabian Forest, making it an important garrison town. The western fort has since vanished under modern building, but housed an *auxilia cohors equitata*—a mixed cavalry and infantry unit. The eastern fort is now Ostkastell, a UNESCO World Heritage Site archaeological park. Conserved are parts of the enclosure wall, a reconstruction of the west gate (as shown), and replicas of stone monuments and statuary. To the northeast the foundations of two watchtowers on the high ground nearby have been preserved and a third has been reconstructed in wood with a section of palisade.

RIGHT Freimühle, Germany
A small fort, Freimühle (C below) sat just back from the border close to where the boundary between Germania Superior and Raetia lay. It was at the provincial boundary that the hard border changed from palisade to stone as shown here. Archaeologists found some of the palisade timbers in 1977–83 and these were dated at 163/164.

BELOW RIGHT Kleindeinbach fort, Germany)
This landscape model shows the integrated defensive system that existed along the *limes* in the 160s. There's Cohort fort Schirenhof (**A**) and the small fort Freimühle about half a mile back from the *limes* (**B**); both these have bathhouses. The small fort Kleindeinbach (**C**)—designated Wp 12/22—is much closer to the palisade. Another cohort fort, Lorch, is about three miles away to the west. Kleindeinbach was built around 164 for 10–20 soldiers and was the easternmost fortification in Germania Superior, on the border with Raetia. This accounts for the density of Roman military bases in the local area. Schirenhof was built c. 165, abandoned c. 254, and garrisoned by *cohors I Raetorum*.

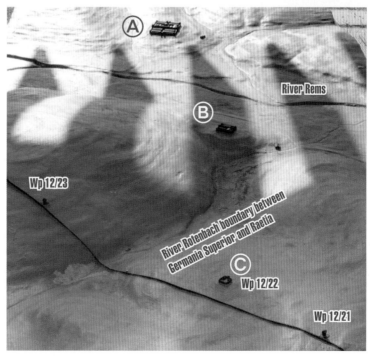

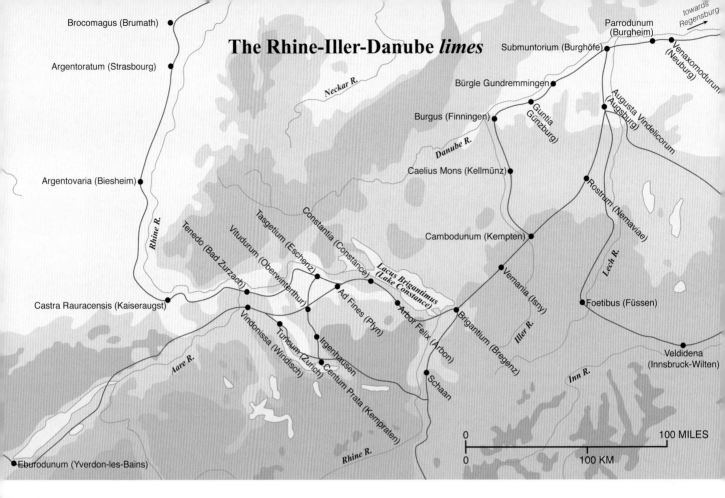

The Rhine-Iller-Danube *limes*

Brocomagus (Brumath)

Argentoratum (Strasbourg)

Argentovaria (Biesheim)

Neckar R.

Tasgetium (Eschenz)

Constantia (Constance)

Vitudurum (Oberwinterthur)

Tenedo (Bad Zurzach)

Rhine R.

Castra Rauracensis (Kaiseraugst)

Ad Fines (Pfyn)

Lacus Brigantinus (Lake Constance)

Arbor Felix (Arbon)

Vindonissa (Windisch)

Turicum (Zurich)

Centum Prata (Kempraten)

Irgenhausen

Schaan

Aare R.

Rhine R.

Eburodunum (Yverdon-les-Bains)

Submuntorium (Burghöfe)

Parrodunum (Burgheim)

towards Regensburg

Venaxomodurum (Neuburg)

Bürgle Gundremmingen

Burgus (Finningen)

Guntia (Günzburg)

Augusta Vindelicorum (Augsburg)

Danube R.

Caelius Mons (Kellmünz)

Rostrum (Nemaviae)

Cambodunum (Kempten)

Vemania (Isny)

Lech R.

Foetibus (Füssen)

Brigantium (Bregenz)

Iller R.

Veldidena (Innsbruck-Wilten)

Inn R.

0   100 MILES

0   100 KM

The Rhine–Iller–Danube *limes*

At Rheinbrohl (p. 105) the Upper German–Raetian *limes* diverge from the Rhine and follow the line of the Severan border that had been created as the empire pushed into Germania Magna. As we have seen, between 50 BC and AD 160 the border moved forward and a century of relative peace passed until the *Limesfall*—the complex series of events that led to the abandonment of the *Agri Decumates*, and all the rich farming lands and forest timber that the area possessed. Whether the reason for this was the incursions by the Alemanni, or simply the problems caused by the Imperial crisis of the third century—twenty-six emperors between 235 and 285—in about 260 the Romans retreated and the new border settled along the river lines: the Rhine to Lake Constance, then the Iller north to the Danube, and from the Danube to the Black Sea. Once again, the early settlements of Antunnacum, Baudobriga, Aquae Mattiacorum, Argentoratum, and Augusta Raurica were frontier towns.

LEFT Porta Antunnacum (Andernach, Germany)
Thirteen miles north of Koblenz, Antunnacum is one of the oldest Roman settlements in Germany, a harbor and cohort fort being built round AD 20. Here the Rhine narrows from both sides. The years after the Frankish invasion around 260 saw Antunnacum increasingly fortified, yet still it was destroyed by the Alemanni. The Emperor Julian rebuilt the fort—it had four gates and fourteen round towers—and it survived until falling to the Franks in the mid-fifth century. This famous gravestone remembers a soldier: Firmus, a Raetian cohort, who died in the mid-first century AD at the age of thirty-six after serving twelve (or more) years. Next to him is, possibly, his toga-wearing heir or son, and a headless figure, identified as Fuscus the slave, wearing a *cucullus* (hood) or *paenula* (cloak) over a tunic.

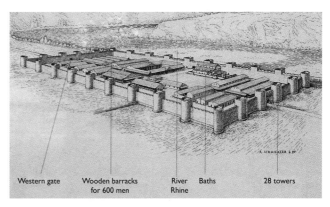

| Western gate | Wooden barracks for 600 men | River Rhine | Baths | 28 towers |

Baudobriga (Boppard, Germany)

Situated on a small plain the between mountains and the river in the Middle Rhine Valley, Baudobriga was first settled in the time of Claudius (AD41–54) who consolidated the local road network and built additional forts along the river. The remains visible today are of an impressive fourth-century late-Roman fort from around 360. It once had twenty-eight horseshoe-shaped towers and walls that were 8–10ft thick and 30ft high. Baudobriga was also a thriving civilian settlement and trading center that grew up around the fort. With the expansion of the borders the Middle Rhine lost its strategic importance until the mid-fourth century, when Julian defeated the Germanic tribes and the river became the empire's border once more. His successor, Valentinian I, built the final version of the fort, occupied until sometime in 404.

Aquae Mattiacorum (Wiesbaden, Germany)

The thermal springs at Wiesbaden were famous even before the bath-loving Romans arrived and called it Aquae Mattiacorum. A fort was built here in AD6, housing an auxiliary cavalry unit. Pliny the Elder extolled the benefits of the town's hot springs, even used in the therapeutic treatment of Roman army horses. Just across the river lies the provincial capital of Mogontiacum (see p. 104), connected by a prestigious and strongly fortified bridge. A coalition of Germanic Alemanni tribes captured the fort around 260. Later, in the 370s, when the Alemanni became *foederati*, they gained control of the Wiesbaden area and maintained its defense against other Germanic tribes.

ABOVE Wiesbaden's *Römertor* was made as a new road was cut through the *Heidenmauer*, the so-called pagan wall (**OPPOSITE, BELOW LEFT**) that dates to the second half of the fourth century.

LEFT At the Römertor there's a replica of the gravestone of Dolanus Bessus, son of Esbenius, rider of *cohors IIII Thracum*, who died age forty-six after twenty-four years of service. There were many Thracian units in the Roman army, both infantry and cavalry (as here). It's dated to around AD30–50.

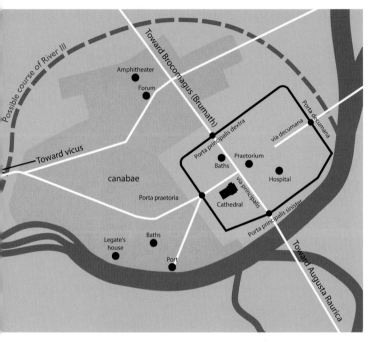

Argentoratum (Strasbourg, France)

First established as a Roman outpost in AD12, Argentoratum sat on the bank of the Ill river near the Rhine. The *canabae* that grew up around Argentoratum became the city of Strasbourg. From AD90 it was the home base of *legio VIII Augusta* and archaeological investigations have revealed the site was destroyed by fire six times in five centuries, in 70, 97, 235, 355, late 380s, and the early 400s. The critical battle of Argentoratum took place in 357, when Julian (then caesar in the west, later emperor) destroyed a huge Alemanni army. Little remains of the Roman city, although there is one interesting side story. In 1441 a new granary (**BELOW RIGHT**) made use of what remained of the Roman fort. It has been much modified over the centuries, but there are still some of the original Roman building materials apparent.

Augusta Raurica (Basel, Switzerland)

Founded on a high plateau just south of the Rhine following the Augustan conquest of the central Alps around 15BC, Augusta Raurica's remains are now an open-air museum located on the south bank of the river about twelve miles east of Basel, near the villages of Augst and Kaiseraugst. Famous and prosperous thanks to its pork exports, with a huge theater and amphitheater, in 250 the city was badly damaged by an earthquake and a decade later was stormed and burnt by the Alemanni. Maintaining a presence in the area, the Romans built a fortress, Castrum Rauracense, and resettled a small part of the original city. Today, there's an open-air museum.

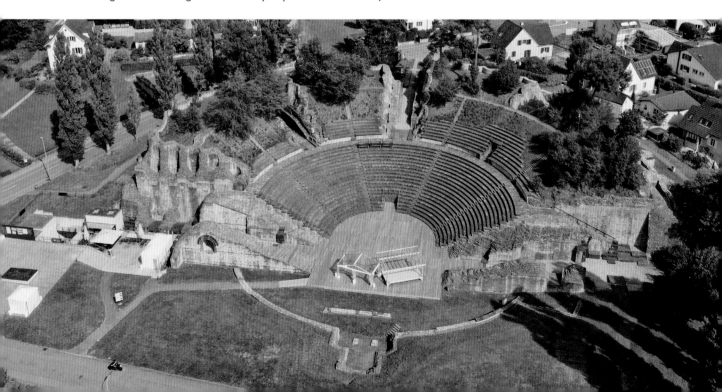

Vindonissa (Windisch, Switzerland)

The site at the confluence of the rivers Aare, Reuss, and Limmat, and the foot of a pass over the Jura, was a brilliant strategic position. A communications center, Vindonissa started as a small guard post established around 15BC. A legionary camp with its accompanying settlement was built around AD15 and a bath complex added around AD30. The aqueduct that brought water into the city was used until 1897. However, as the borders moved it lost military importance for a century, and by the beginning of the second century it had become a primarily civilian town. This changed in 260 as the Romans retreated and the city was refortified. Units attested: *legiones XIII Gemina, XXI Rapax, XI Claudia,* and various auxiliary cohorts. Photos show the modern impresssion of the Porta Praetoria (**ABOVE**) and what's left of the amphitheater (**BELOW**).

Raetia

With its provincial capital at Augusta Vindelicorum (Augsburg)—Vindelicia was added to the original Raetia province at the end of the first century AD—the Raetian *limes* ran from Lorch, at the border of Germania Superior, to Passau. The section between Lorch and Abusina (Eining) was one of the only parts of the European *limes* that was a "hard" border, with a stone wall and integral watchtowers. It was built in 205–206, replacing the palisade that had been there hitherto, much of it built by *legio III Italica* which was raised by Marcus Aurelius to fight the Marcomannic Wars of the 160s and stayed in Raetia after that. From the end of the 170s that was in Castra Regina, Regensburg. The *Notitia* records vexillations of the legion still in Regensburg in the fifth century. In around 260, when the *Agri Decumates* was given up, the Romans retreated from the northern border and the Raetian Wall, taking up a line from the Rhine along the River Iller to the Danube (see pp. 112–117).

ABOVE Alae (Aalen, Germany)
A major fort on a 15-acre footprint, Alae was built in the 160s under the expansion during Marcus Aurelius's reign. It housed 1,000 horsemen from *ala II Flavia milliaria Pia Fidelis*, making it the largest of its kind along the Raetian *limes*. It was occupied until about 260 when the Romans shortened their borders by moving back to the Rhine and Danube rivers, whereupon the Alemanni moved in. There was a civilian settlement of some 3,000 people nearby which continued in use for many years thereafter. Today, Aalen houses an important museum. Note the large *principia* with a huge exercise area that may have been 60ft high. An end of one of the twelve cavalry barrack blocks has been carefully reconstructed showing a two-story building divided into downstairs areas for the horses, equipment, grooms, and slaves with upstairs sleeping quarters for the cavalry. If accurate—and it looks it—then other locations will probably need to reconsider their approaches.

RIGHT Buch (on the Bucher Stausee, Germany)
With a similar history to the fort at Aalen, that at Rainau-Buch (**A**) is thought to have been occupied by *cohors III Thracum Veterana* (Thracian Veterans). Square rather than rectangular, outside the walls to the northeast (**B**) was a *mansio* (official resting point for couriers and officials) and a bathhouse, just uphill of a small river (since converted into a lake). Not much further away to the southeast was a *vicus* which is thought to have been inhabited by about 2,000 people. The fort was built around 165 and occupied until about 260; these days it is an open-air museum.

Limestor Dalkingen, Germany

Located between the villages of Schwabsberg and Dalkingen in the Ostalbkreis, Baden-Württemberg, near to the large cavalry fort at Aalen, is a triumphal monument that remembers the Emperor Caracalla's campaign against German tribes, the Alemanni and Chatti, in 213. The son of Septimius Severus who gained undivided control of the empire by having his brother murdered, Caracalla's expedition involved *legio II Traiana Fortis* who were themselves honored by the name Germania. Originally, the nearby palisade and watchtowers were built in the 160s and then reinforced in stone in the 180s by men of *legio III Italica*. The Limestor is on the top of an exposed hilltop and since 2010 has been encased in glass (**ABOVE**) for protection. Lying in the *Agri Decumates*, the Limestor ceased to be in Roman territory from 260 when the Alemanni pushed south.

ABOVE Biriciana (Weißenburg, Germany)

Located in Bavaria, covering over 12 acres, Biriciana had a *vicus* that stretched to over 75 acres. It is thought to have been built during Trajan's reign and to have acted as the base for *ala I Hispanorum Auriana*, whose troops may also have garrisoned local watchtowers as the fort is only big enough to house half of its twenty-four *turmae*. A second phase of construction work took place in about 130, and a third around 180. While most of the remains are still below ground level, the north gateway has been fully reconstructed. Note the white facing and red "grouting": this is how the buildings would have been finished. Extensive thermal baths were discovered in 1977—these now form part of a museum. On display are a series of votive items from a temple that were found buried near the site in 1979. The fort was destroyed in the mid-third century. A smaller fort nearby dating to the early part of the second century may have been garrisoned by *cohors IX Batavorum exploratorum milliaria equitata*.

BELOW Ruffenhofen, Germany

A Roman cavalry fort situated on flat ground giving commanding views across much of the local area, Ruffenhofen was garrisoned by a cohort of around 500 horsemen. It was probably built under Hadrian and may initially have been garrisoned by *cohors III Batavorum*. Between c. 119 and 250, the garrison was probably an unknown *ala quingenaria*. Covering nine acres, it was first built out of wood and earth, and then later reconstructed out of stone. Adjacent to the fort was a *vicus*. Most of the area—including the fort and some of the *vicus*—is now designated as an archaeological reserve that is open to the public interpreted by the adjoining Limeseum. Although a virtual reconstruction can be seen, the actual layout is marked by hedgerows.

ABOVE Burgsalach (in der Harlach, Germany)
On the road connecting Weißenburg and Pfünz forts, about a mile from the route of the *limes* wall, the building at Burgsalach in der Harlach is a mystery. Probably of two stories, its construction date is conjectural and usually placed in the reign of Caracalla (211–217). It was evacuated at the time of the *Limesfall* around 259/260. If it served a primarily military purpose, it could have been manned by a *centuria* of about eighty men. If that were the case, an argument has been made that it was built by men of *legio III Augusta*. The fort is similar to some in Africa and, after the legion had been disbanded in 238 by Gordian III (for siding with Emperor Maximinus and not his usurping uncles Gordian I and II), elements were sent to the Raetian *limes*. There are two other theories, both based on the building's proximity to the road.

The first, that it was a *beneficiarii* station to police the road, is plausible if unproven, as is the second, that it was a *mansio*. It has a courtyard surrounded by a covered walkway, rooms with brick fireplaces, and a cellar in the south.

BELOW Watchtowers 14/48 (LEFT Burgsalach, Germany) and 14/63 (RIGHT Ekertshofen, Germany)
Two reconstructed watchtowers on section 14 of the *limes* that runs through Bavaria from Gunzenhausen to the River Altmühl near the fort at Böhming in Kipfenberg (see p. 122). The Burgsalach watchtower was constructed before the *limes* wall, but was later integrated into the system. The reconstruction is historically inaccurate but gives an impression of the original. That at Ekertshofen is more recently made (1992) out of hand-cut limestone.

ABOVE Celeusum (Pförring, Germany)

A Roman cavalry outpost sited to protect an important crossing point of the Danube, Pförring was built in the reign of Trajan out of wood and turf. Iit was originally called Celeusum; a later phase saw it rebuilt in stone. It was occupied until at least 235 but possibly till 254. It had baths nearby (which were destroyed in 1823), temples, and a *vicus*. A high embankment is still in existence as well as remains of the eastern gate and the north corner tower. The imaginative reconstruction gives an idea of the scale of gatehouse. The garrison was *ala I Flavia singularium*.

BELOW Böhming, Germany

Probably built during Hadrian's reign, the *numerus*-sized fort is today under the church of St. John the Baptist (**A**), to the west of the village of Böhming in Bavaria. It was sited half a mile back from the border, north of the Altmühl but with direct line of sight to a number of watchtowers. It was destroyed during the Marcomannic wars and rebuilt in 181 before its final destruction by the Alemanni in the middle of the third century. A bathhouse (**B**) was located outside the walls beyond which to the south and southwest a sizable *vicus* was established. The garrison may have been some 200 men from *cohors I Breucorum* in Pfünz.

ABOVE Vetoniana (Pfünz, Germany)
Located on a hilly ridge, Vetoniana was built of wood and earth c. 90, later rebuilt in stone. It was protected by double ditches which were carved into the rock around the fort. It was the base for *cohors I Breucorum equitata civium Romanorum,* and is thought to have been occupied until around 230–240. Parts of the defensive walls are still visible, and some of the ditches and the road to the south are also still in evidence. A *mansio* was discovered nearby in 2010.

BELOW LEFT Watchtower 15/46 (Hienheim, Germany)
550km of wall ended at the Danube, making Hienheim and nearby Abusina important locations. This is a recent reconstruction (the 1975 version succumbed to arson).

BELOW RIGHT Abusina (Eining, Germany)
There was a small legionary fortress at nearby Eining-Unterfeld built by *legio III Italica* and in use c. 165–179 when the legion moved to Regensburg. Abusina was a small auxiliary fort on the Danube at Eining, about 30km southwest of Regensburg (Castra Regina). Built out of earth and timber by *cohors IV Gallorum* in 79–81, it was rebuilt in stone under Antoninus Pius when it was occupied by *cohors III Britannorum equitata.* A diploma of 147 attests a *vexillatio* from *cohors II Tungrorum* was in place between 120 and the mid-150s. Sacked by the Alemanni in 233, abandoned in c. 254, and reoccupied c. 280; in c.300 a new fortress was built in one corner and used until abandoned c. 410. Most of the fort was destroyed in a fire c. 430.

ABOVE Ad Fines (Pfyn, Switzerland)
Ad Fines—at the border—is a well-preserved late-era
auxiliary fort (built c. 300) set on a hilltop dominating the
Thur river and close to the Rhine. The red outline gives
a rough idea of the fort and its towers. The border in
question was that between Maxima Sequanorum (Gaul) in
the west and Raetia in the east. Ad Fines was garrisoned
by a *cohors equitata*—an *auxilia* mixed cavalry and infantry
unit—between the third and fifth centuries, overseeing
the road connecting the defense line between Arbon and
Oberwinterthur.

**LEFT AND BELOW Irgenhausen (near Cambodunum/
Kempten, Switzerland)**
Built to defend the road out of Raetia to Vitudurum
(Oberwinterthur) and thence to the Rhine at Tasgetium
(Eschenz), this restored fort was probably built on an
older *villa rustica*. The date for the fort's construction is
unknown and both Diocletian (284–305) and Valentinian II's
(375–392) reigns have been posited.

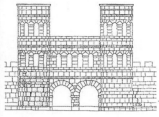

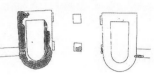

Castra Regina (Regensburg, Germany)

Regensburg's legionary fortress was constructed around 179 by *legio III Italica* where the River Regen joins the Danube. The original wooden barracks were rebuilt in stone in the first half of the third century AD. Protected by a sandstone wall that stood 16ft high (the southeast corner shown **BELOW LEFT**), with eighteen towers and four double-tower gates (the *porta praetoria* is shown **ABOVE** and **ABOVE LEFT**), it could not withstand the incursions of the third century, but *III Italica* was still in situ at the end of the fifth century (as attested by the *Notitia Dignitatum*. To the west of the fortress was an extensive *canabae* populated by civilians and tradesmen. To the southwest an auxiliary fort at was built by *cohors III Britannorum equitata*, who garrisoned there until 120. *Cohors II Aquitanorum* was there when the fort was destroyed during the Marcomannic wars.

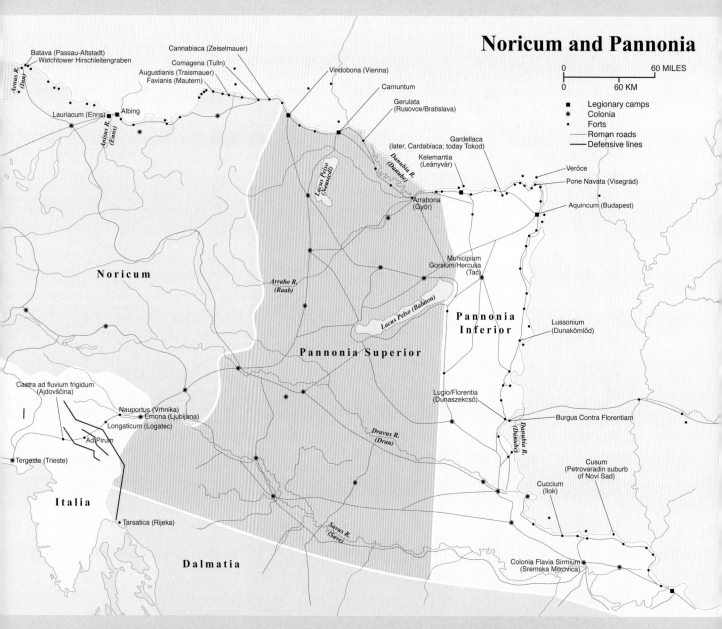

Noricum and Pannonia

■	Legionary camps
◉	Colonia
•	Forts
—	Roman roads
▬	Defensive lines

Map labels:

Batava (Passau-Altstadt)
Watchtower Hirschleitengraben
Cannabiaca (Zeiselmauer)
Comagena (Tulln)
Augustianis (Traismauer)
Favianis (Mautern)
Vindobona (Vienna)
Carnuntum
Gerulata (Rusovce/Bratislava)
Anisus R. (Enns)
Lauriacum (Enns)
Albing
Anisus R. (Enns)
Gardellaca (later, Cardabiaca; today Tokod)
Kelemantia (Leányvár)
Verőce
Pone Navata (Visegrád)
Aquincum (Budapest)
Danubia R. (Danube)
Arrabona (Győr)
Lacus Pelso (Venetia!)
Noricum
Municipium Gorsium/Herculia (Tác)
Pannonia Inferior
Lussonium (Dunakömlőd)
Arrabo R. (Raab)
Lacus Pelso (Balaton)
Pannonia Superior
Castra ad fluvium frigidum (Ajdovščina)
Nauportus (Vrhnika)
Emona (Ljubljana)
Longaticum (Logatec)
Ad Pirum
Tergeste (Trieste)
Lugio/Florentia (Dunaszekcső)
Burgus Contra Florentiam
Dravus R. (Drau)
Cusum (Petrovaradin suburb of Novi Sad)
Cuccium (Ilok)
Danubia R. (Danube)
Italia
Tarsatica (Rijeka)
Savus R. (Save)
Dalmatia
Colonia Flavia Sirmium (Sremska Mitrovica)

Noricum and Pannonia

The northeastern boundaries of the empire primarily followed the natural border of the Danube, Europe's second longest river, stretching for some 1,250 miles from the Black Forest to the Black Sea. The location of frontier installations was often dictated by the environment—high, steep banks in some parts, vast floodplains in others, and many tributary rivers flowing into it. The bigger legionary fortresses and auxiliary forts were regularly spaced and generally sited at the mouths of major tributaries, blocking access into the interior of the province. The border edged the provinces of Noricum, Pannonia, Dacia and Moesia; today's Germany, Austria, Slovakia, Hungary, Croatia, Serbia, Bulgaria, and Romania. Its strategic importance ensured comprehensive fortification, for one end of it was the shortest route to the Italian heartland and Rome itself, while the other marked the central axis of the empire between east and west.

River Danube

River Inn

River Ilz

Passau–Batavis (Passau-Altstadt, Germany); Boiodurum (Passau-Innstadt); Boiotro

Lying alongside the rivers Danube and Inn, Passau was an important strategic location for both military and toll/customs purposes. The forts on the peninsula were in Raetia; those on the south bank of the Inn were in Noricum. The cavalry fort at Passau-Altstadt was called Batava or Batavis (**A**) after its garrison, *cohors IX Batavorum exploratorum milliaria equitata*. Established in the first century AD, it was occupied until around 475 when it was destroyed by Alemanni and Thuringians, whereupon it was abandoned. The late-Roman Boiodurum (**B**) was built in the middle of the second century AD. After it was destroyed by invasion in the second half of the third century, another fort, upstream —Boiotro (**C**)—was built as a replacement under Valentinian I and lasted to the early fifth century. There were extensive *vici* around both Batavis and Boiodurum.

LEFT Lauriacum (Enns, Austria)
A legionary fortress, Lauriacum was built around 200 by *legio II Italica*. Located on the River Enns and surrounded by a large ditch system, an extensive *vicus* grew up on the north and western side of the fort. The site was probably occupied until around the end of the fourth century AD. Most of the stone used to construct the buildings was robbed from the medieval period onward and so all that is visible these days are the massive ditches.

CENTER LEFT Favianis (Mautern an der Donau, Austria)
A *castellum* built to protect a crossing point on the Danube, it was probably created toward the end of the first century AD. One of the units which occupied it during the second century was *cohors I Aelia Brittonum milliaria equitata* (with some 800 infantry and 240 cavalrymen); in the fourth century part of *legio I Noricorum* was stationed there. Parts of the outer wall around the *castellum* as well as two of its towers have been preserved.

BELOW LEFT Comagena (Tulln an der Donau, Austria)
Guarding another important fording point, the fort was built of earth and timber in the late first century AD and housed 500 cavalry troops from *ala I Commagenorum*. In the second century it was rebuilt in stone, and served until the fifth century. Toward the end of this period it expanded to become the base of a naval fleet as well as a cavalry regiment (*equites promoti Comagenis*). There were at least two *vici* associated with the fortress. Extensive parts of the Roman structures still survive, including the east gate, this substantial horseshoe tower of c. 300, and the foundations of another.

OPPOSITE Augustianis (Traismauer, Austria)
Although a castle was later constructed on the site, the original ground plan of the auxiliary fort is still discernible. As was typical of the era, the first fort was made from timber and earth, later replaced by stone. Probably occupied by Roman troops between the first and fifth centuries, a number of units are attested: *legio XIIII Gemina*, *ala I Hispanorum Auriana*, *ala I Augusta Thracum*, and the *equites Dalmatae*. To the east and south of the site was a large *vicus* with a bathhouse. Significant parts of the Roman structures still survive including elements of the *Römertor* gatehouse (shown here) although most have been incorporated into later phases of the castle.

Construction of a border started under Augustus. The border then consisted of a patrol road with wooden watchtowers and small auxiliary forts along the southern bank of the river, defended by ditches with earthen berms topped with palisades. Their density depended on local topography and the system relied upon the river's considerable width. The defenses were to monitor tribal movements, regulate trade, and collect customs fees, so the Romans cultivated local tribes with a strategy of trade and diplomacy alongside visible security to create a buffer zone.

There were two impressive fleets—*classis Pannonica* based at Arruntum, Mursa, and Florentia and *classis Moesica* at *Noviodunum,* Viminacium, and Aegetae in Dacia. (From around 75 both fleets gained the honorific *Flavia.*) These patrolled the river to ensure the smooth running of its vital trading and support capability. Under Trajan and Hadrian the wood and earth forts and watchtowers were rebuilt in more robust stone. Nevertheless, barbarian attacks were a constant threat, especially when the tribes confederated, achieving dangerous mass. Major trouble came first from the Dacians, who fought a series of wars with Rome after their raids into Moesia from 85 spurred a response. It took twenty years to subdue Dacia and the empire's frontier then changed markedly. Dacia was held for 160 years until Aurelian surrendered the territory north of the Danube.

In the late 160s the Marcomannic Wars saw the first major breach of the defense system, as confederations and coalitions of various tribes launched attacks along the Rhine (the Marcomanni, Quadi, and Franks) and Danube (Goths, Huns, Sarmatians, and Avars) in what was deemed a conspiracy because of its organization. In fact, the barbarians were learning from Rome and some of their leaders had served in its army.

Over the next decade the pressure on the northern frontier intensified, as a great climate change-driven migration pushed tribes south—up against each other and then the empire. Some were encouraged to settle and their sons were welcomed into the army. The treaty Commodus signed with the Germanic tribes at the end of the second century AD brought peace to the frontier for a few decades.

The instability of the crisis-ridden third century saw Rome's fragility exploited. In 275, Dacia north of the Danube was overrun by Goths, Huns, and Avars. In response, the fortifications on the southern bank of the river were restructured between Viminacium and Belene to once more assume frontier status. However, the Romans had learned that maintaining fixed border positions was no longer feasible. Northern provinces were subdivided into smaller areas of command, with manpower divided into mobile field armies (*comitatenses*) held in reserve, and stationary border troops (*limitanei*) guarding the border defenses.

The fourth century saw restructuring and rebuilding in stone from the reign of Constantine (who briefly reconquered Dacia) until Valentinian I. The *castra* were strengthened to be more like castles—walls were thickened and towers added at their corners. The density of intervening watchtowers increased and units of the Danube fleet were stationed at vulnerable points on the river. The barbarian raids persisted, but the eastern Moesian part of the line more or less survived the collapse of the western empire in the fifth century, was restored in the first half of the sixth, but then finally succumbed to the Avar and Slav invasion of the early seventh century.

ABOVE Cannabiaca (Zeiselmauer, Austria)

For many years, the fortifications at Zeiselmauer in Lower Austria were believed to be medieval. In fact they are Roman. Initially built of earth and timber in the Flavian period, the fort was later rebuilt in stone. The first stone camp was almost unchanged until the fourth century, when fan towers were placed in the corners, horseshoe towers added on the walls, and the gatehouses made significantly bigger. The fifth century saw a reduction in garrison numbers and more changes, with civilians allowed to live inside the walls. A smaller fort was constructed in the northwest.

A number of different units are thought to have operated out of the fort, including *legio II Italica*, *legio X Gemina*, *cohors I Asturum*, *cohors V Breucorum*, and *cohors II Thracum*. Cannabiaca was occupied until the fifth century when the Romans withdrew from the region. Illustrated are the medieval granary (**ABOVE LEFT**)—note the yellow line showing the remains of the archway of the former *porta principalis dextra*—and a replica second century gravestone. It's of Aelius Aemilius (from *cohors II Thracum*) and his wife Amuca (**ABOVE RIGHT**). She was probably a Celt and wears a Noric hood; he has a military scarf (*focale*). Dolphins are there to guide the souls of the deceased into the realm of the dead.

LEFT Vindobona (Vienna, Austria)

A military site was established at Vindobona at the end of the first century AD. It is believed that *ala I Flavia Augusta Britannica milliaria civium Romanorum* was the first unit to be based there. It was then superseded by *legio XIII Gemina* which arrived in around 98, having transferred from Poetovio (Ptuj, Slovenia). A legionary fortress was constructed sometime during this period, and various extensions and improvements were implemented throughout its occupation following Germanic raids or as the result of reconstruction phases. Vindobona was in two parts: the military, which covered about 50 acres and held about 6,000 men, and the *canabae*, which had somewhere between 15,000 and 20,000 inhabitants at its peak. It is thought the site was occupied until the fifth century when it was ceded to the Ostrogoths. Vindobana was in Pannonia, then Pannonia Superior after Trajan split the province. Finally, after Diocletian's reorganization, it came under Pannonia Prima.

Carnuntum (Austria)

First used as a Roman fort when Tiberius established it as the base for his campaigns in the area in AD6, in AD14 the fortifications were expanded when *legio XV Apollinaris* moved in as the local garrison. In 103, Trajan made Carnuntum the provincial capital of Pannonia Superior. From c. 63 *legio X Gemina* was based there before being transferred away again, replaced by *legio VII Gemina*, which was in turn superseded by *legio XIV Gemina*. This unit then stayed in place for three centuries until the Romans withdrew in 430. Carnuntum's position midway between Vienna and Bratislava on the banks of the Danube also made it the ideal location for the *classis Pannonica* which used it from AD50. Carnuntum was well placed to act as a trading center between the empire and northern Europe, and prospered greatly—especially as it was where the Amber Route crossed into imperial territory; at its height, the city had a population of around 50,000 people. Marcus Aurelius lived here for three years while he wrote the second book of his *Meditations*. Carnuntum was also the location of a famous meeting between retired emperors Diocletian and Maximian and the Tetrarchs on November 11, 308, as Licinius was elevated to Augustus. In 374 it was sacked by Germanic tribes, and thereafter Vindobona became more important. These days the remains, which include the *Heidentor* triumphal arch erected in the mid-fourth century to honor Constantius II (**BELOW LEFT**) as well as the reconstructed baths (**ABOVE**), are to be found in the Carnuntum Archaeological Park.

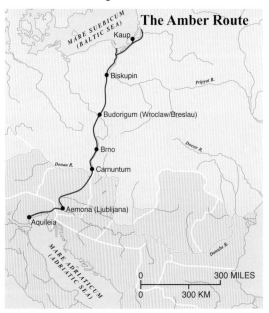

The Amber Route

LEFT Gerulata (Rusovce/Bratislava, Slovakia)
There was a Roman auxiliary fort at Gerulata, to the east of Carnuntum, established in the late first century AD, probably during Domitian's reign. Its exact location was only confirmed in 1967 after archaeological excavations found direct evidence. *Ala I Cannanefatum* arrived as a garrison in the early second century, its place taken by *cohors XVIII Voluntariorum civium Romanorum* when the former went to Africa. The fort was rebuilt in stone under the Antonines, and in the late third and early fourth centuries a smaller stone fort was built; later still, a *burgus* was erected in the corner. There was a large *vicus*, and evidence of substantial farmsteads to provision the fort.

BELOW Kelemantia (Leányvár, Slovakia)
Kelemantia or Celemantia was the site of a large fort which was built in the latter half of the first century AD and possibly garrisoned by *ala I Hispanorum et Aravacorum*. This area was hotly contested by the local Germanic tribes who probably sacked the site during the Marcomannic Wars (166–180). During Commodus's reign it was rebuilt in stone but was again fought over in the middle of the third century. Restored in the fourth and again during Valentinian's reign, it was occupied until the beginning of the fifth century when the region was abandoned. Its garrison was probably a *vexillatio* from *legio I Adiutrix* from the legionary fortress of Brigetio on the other side of the Danube. It was occupied by *I Adiutrix* from c. 86 to the fifth century.

Gardellaca (later, Cardabiaca; today Tokod, Hungary)
A late Roman fort located between Crumerum and
Solva on the site of what is present-day Tokod,
Gardellaca is positioned slightly away from the
Brigetio–Aquincum *limes*, but on the road to the latter.
The Danube lies about 1.5 miles to the north. Evidence
suggests that it was founded on top of an earlier first
century camp around the year 369–370. Built near to
a native settlement, it had two rectangular towers
guarding the single gate, together with towers at each
corner and along the sides; it was probably occupied
until the fifth century. Over a number of years
archaeological work on the site, which lies in open
grassland, has revealed many graves as well as a
bathhouse and a substantial collection of buildings. The
fort's outer walls as well as those of the main towers
and some interior structures are still visible.

Pone Navata (Visegrád, Hungary)

The Danube makes a sharp turn to the south between Visegrád and Budapest, and the Danube Bend—the Hungarian *Dunakanyar*—was a heavily protected section of the Pannonian *ripa*, particularly after Dacia was vacated. A Roman fort was established on Visegrád Sibrik Hill, to the north of Budapest. Located on the south bank of the Danube Bend, it was constructed under Constantine I, who was emperor in 306–337. The fortress was roughly triangular in form and measured 374ft by 426ft, and had a series of eleven horseshoe-shaped defensive towers built into the outer walls which were about 4ft thick. It was garrisoned by 300 troops—possibly from the *auxilia Ursarensia*—who accessed the fortress through a gate in the west wall. It was enlarged in the 360s and 380s, shortly before the Romans withdrew. Other elements of the *limes* in this area include—heading west from Pone Navata—*burgi* at Lepence, Steinbruch, and Donaufähre, a small fort at Visegrád-Gizellamajor built in the 330s, *burgi* at Dömös-Donaufähre, Köves-Bach, and Tófenék, and then Castra ad Herculem (Pilismarót) garrisoned by cavalry squadrons of the *equites Dalmatae* and auxiliary infantry (*auxilia Herculensia*).

Aquincum (Buda, Hungary)

The Romans established a fortress at Vizivarós, in present-day Buda somewhere between AD41 and 54. It was garrisoned by *ala I Hispanorum*, later *ala I Hispanorum Auriana*. Around 75 another fort was built at Óbuda by *ala I Tungrorum Frontoniana*. This fort was substantially enlarged by 89 with the arrival of 6,000 men from *legio II Adiutrix*. While that legion fought in Dacia and the east, its position was taken by *legio X Gemina*. As part of a major administrative reorganization, the fort became the capital of Pannonia Inferior in 106, holding that position for over a hundred years, during which time it was rebuilt in stone. This saw the civilian settlement expand into a city—with a population of at least 30,000 by the end of the second century. It later became a *municipium* under Hadrian, and then a *colonia* under Septimius Severus before being mostly destroyed by Germanic tribes in 350. There are two amphitheaters in Aquincum, a civilian one built 250–300 (**ABOVE RIGHT**) and a military one built in 145. The south and the west gates of the fortress, as well as the bathhouse and a mphitheater, are still visible above ground. There is a well laid-out museum with displays of artifacts, monuments, and other related items (**ABOVE LEFT AND BELOW**). Just over the river is another fort, Contra Aquincum, the foundation for the city of Pest. It may have been built after the Marcomannic wars, but the early fort was rebuilt during Constantine I's or Constantine II's reign.

ABOVE Verőce, Hungary

Established under Constantine II to watch over and defend an important crossing point on the Danube in Pest county, it was sited on the northern banks of the Danube. The main fortress was built from stone and brick, and measured 59ft x 75ft with walls that were 9ft thick. There was a substantial main building with multiple floors held up by a series of thick pillars and topped with a tiled roof. The outer walls were equipped with towers, and there was a dedicated landing area for boats and ships to dock and load/unload their cargoes. Situated close by were a number of supporting Roman strongpoints—several were on the large island of Szentendrei (St. Andrä) along with others on the south banks including a chain of watch-towers. Exactly what was there cannot be ascertained due to significant erosion by the river. Veróce was occupied by the Romans until the fifth century.

ABOVE RIGHT Lussonium (Dunakömlőd, Hungary)

Near Paks, a small town in Tolna county, on the right bank of the Danube about 60 miles south of Budapest in central Hungary, Lussonium was positioned on one of the hills that overlook the area. Its first phase was probably the middle of the first century AD, and it was occupied until the Romans withdrew from the region in the fifth century, with a stone fort replacing the wooden during the third century. Units attested at Lussonium are *cohors I Alpinorum equitata* and *cohors I Alpinorum peditata*. Part of an archaeological park, several of the buildings—including the north and south gates—have been reconstructed. (See also pp. 54–55.)

BELOW Lugio/Florentia (Dunaszekcső, Hungary)

A fortress built on the site of a Celtic settlement initially known as Lugio, by the fourth century this had changed to Florentia. Originally made out of timber and earth, the encampment was located on the right bank of the River Danube where it provided protection for an important river crossing point for the road linking Pannonia Inferior to Partiscum (Szeged) in Dacia Superior. The defenses, which measured 574ft x 246–426ft, were later upgraded to stone. It is believed that five main military units were based there over the years: *cohors I Alpinorum, cohors II Asturum et Callaecorum equitata, cohors I Noricorum, cohors VII Breucorum,* and a *vexillatio* of *legio II Adiutrix.* The Roman walls were used as foundations for later versions of the fort, especially during the medieval era.

Municipium Gorsium/Herculia (Tác, Hungary)

The Romans established a timber and earth fort on a Celtic site around 46–49 during the reign of Claudius. It was possibly first garrisoned by *ala I Scubulorum* (there are brick stamps) an *ala quingenaria* whose role was to protect a local river crossing. The temporary defenses were later replaced with substantial stone walls. By the beginning of the second century it was considered that the security situation was under control and that local patrolling was no longer required. This stimulated the creation of a new town, the first stages of which began around 103. At some date still to be determined, the town was accorded the status of *municipium*, and it grew to be an extremely important settlement from both a military and a civilian perspective, becoming one of the largest in Pannonia. This is borne out by the fact that the population there had Roman civil rights. At the peak of its existence, it covered 1,000 acres, and had such features as an amphitheater which could hold 20,000 people. It was the subject of many attacks by Germanic tribes. Much of it was set on fire by the Sarmatians during the Marcomannic Wars (c. 178), and it was sacked at least twice more by the Roxolani in 260. Toward the end of the third century, when Pannonia was split into four provinces, it became the seat of the governor of Valeria. The city was renamed Herculia in honor of Emperor Maximianus Herculius, but with increasing attacks its power began to decline, and it was abandoned in 430. These days there is a large archaeological park on the site and King St. Stephen's Museum. Photos show excavations in 1967 (**RIGHT**) and a more recent view of the site (**BELOW**).

TOP Burgus contra Florentiam (Dunafalva, Hungary)
This fort dates to the late fourth century and is typical of the *burgi* built under Valentinian. Burgus was situated on the eastern banks of the Danube opposite the hilltop fort of Florentia. It had the express purpose of securing the established river crossing where extensive marshy ground severely restricted the available routes. This was an important link on the road to Dacia, and it was garrisoned by the *equites sagittarii*—a unit of skilled horse archers. The fort itself measured 53ft x 72ft, and was constructed from stone. The fort's position on an island resulted in much of the site being eroded away by the river, and only the foundations of the southern corner tower are visible—and this only when the water level is low.

ABOVE Cuccium (Ilok, Croatia)
Built around the end of the first century AD above the right bank of the Danube on a steep hill, it was principally a cavalry fort, with the probable garrison units being the *cohors Lusitanorum*, the *equites sagittarii*, and the *cuneus equitum Promotorum*. Little is known of the exact nature of the encampment—it is likely that the first phase was built in timber and earth with later versions being constructed from stone. Due to the fortification's commanding position, there were excellent views across to the neighboring fort at Cornacum (present-day Sotin), giving good visual communication. None of the original structures are visible above ground these days as the site was built over when it became a medieval fortress.

ABOVE Cusum (Petrovaradin, Novi Sad, Serbia)
Established in lands which had previously belonged to the Celtic tribe of Scordisci, Cusum was an *auxilia* fort built on rocky ground that overlooks the southern banks of the Danube on the site of a prehistoric earthen fortification. Since it, in turn, was built over by the seventeenth-century fortress, it is difficult to know exactly what was there during the Roman era.

RIGHT AND BELOW Colonia Flavia Sirmium (Sremska Mitrovica, Serbia)
Sirmium is not directly part of the Danubian *limes*— it's nearly 50 miles down the River Sava on whose northern banks the city developed on the site of an existing Celtic settlement. However, it's one of Serbia's most important historic locations, has associations with many emperors—particularly the ten who took the purple in the third and fourth centuries—was the capital of the province of Pannonia Inferior, then Pannonia Secunda, and in 294, it was one of the four capitals of the Roman Empire under the Tetrarchy. Galerius, the eastern caesar, took it as his capital. Later still, in 375–379 it was the center of the praetorian prefecture of Illyricum. The exact size of Sirmium is hotly disputed, with estimates ranging from between 10,000 and 100,000 inhabitants. It is generally agreed that it was one of the biggest cities

of the time. It was with Sirmium as his HQ that Trajan planned his Dacian wars; Marcus Aurelius may have died here (or at Vindobona); and Licinius (who married a daughter of Constantine I and was emperor 308–324) created a royal palace here. It had a circus/hippodrome, a basilica, and water arrived by aqueduct. There was almost certainly a legionary fortress although no archaeology exists and fabricae of shields, Sirmium was taken by the Huns in 441 and the Avars in the late sixth century.

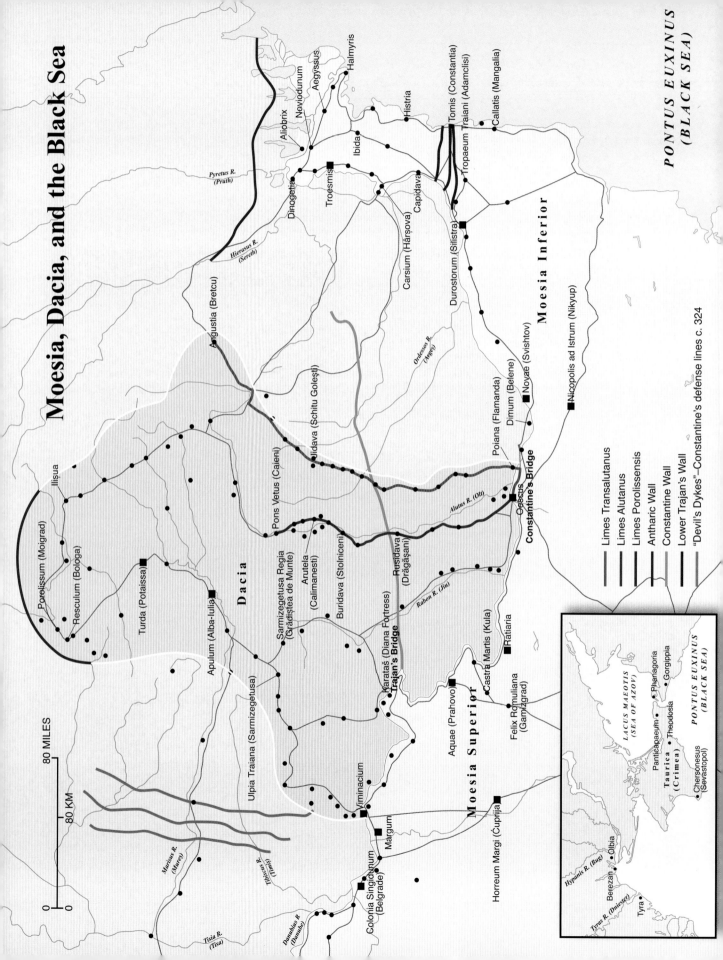

Moesia, Dacia, and the Black Sea

PONTUS EUXINUS (BLACK SEA)

Halmyris
Aegyssus
Noviodunum
Aliobrix
Ibida
Tomis (Constantia)
Histria
Tropaeum Traiani (Adamclisi)
Callatis (Mangalia)

Pyretus R. (Pruth)

Dinogetia
Troesmis
Capidava
Carsium (Hârşova)
Durostorum (Silistra)

Hierasus R. (Sereth)

Moesia Inferior

Nicopolis ad Istrum (Nikyup)

Augustia (Bretcu)

Ordessos R. (Argeş)

Sucidava (Schitu Goleşti)
Novae (Svishtov)
Poiana (Flamanda)
Dimum (Belene)

Ilişua

Pons Vetus (Caieni)

Alutus R. (Olt)

Constantine's Bridge
Oescus

Porolissum (Moigrad)
Resculum (Bologa)

Dacia

Sarmizegetusa Regia (Grădiştea de Munte)
Arutela (Calimanesti)
Buridava (Stolniceni)
Rusidava (Drăgăşani)

Rabon R. (Jiu)

Castra Martis (Kula)
Ratiaria

Turda (Potaissa)

Apulum (Alba-Iulia)

Karataş (Diana Fortress)
Trajan's Bridge

Aquae (Prahovo)

Felix Romuliana (Gamzigrad)

Ulpia Traiana (Sarmizegetusa)

Moesia Superior

—— Limes Transalutanus
—— Limes Alutanus
—— Limes Porolissensis
—— Antharic Wall
—— Constantine Wall
—— Lower Trajan's Wall
—— "Devil's Dykes"–Constantine's defense lines c. 324

80 MILES

Marisus R. (Mureş)
Tibiscus R. (Timiş)

Viminacium

Horreum Margi (Ćuprija)
Margum
Colonia Singidunum (Belgrade)

Tisia R. (Tisa)
Danubius R. (Danube)

80 KM

LACUS MAEOTIS (SEA OF AZOV)

Phanagoria
Panticapaeum
Gorgippia
Taurica (Crimea)
Theodosia
Chersonesus (Sevastopol)

PONTUS EUXINUS (BLACK SEA)

Hypanis R. (Bug)
Olbia
Berezan
Tyra
Tyras R. (Dniester)

Moesia, Dacia, and the Black Sea

Made famous by Trajan's column in Rome, the conquest of Dacia brought a century of peace to the Danube gorge area of Moesia Superior, curtailing the cross-river raids. However, it soon became clear that Trajan's province could not be kept intact and Hadrian was forced to return some territory to the Roxolani. The Romans flooded the area with settlers, but more trouble in the Marcomannic Wars (161–193) saw reorganization and many defensive walls and forts. The Goths attacked in 250 and killed Emperor Decius at Abritus. Paid to stay away, in 267 they invaded again by sea but were smashed at Naissus in 268 or 269. In the 270s, Aurelian abandoned Dacia and the Danube became a frontier once again. Moesia was reorganized and then, under Diocletian, reorganized again into four provinces: Moesia Prime and Dardania from what had been Superior; Secunda and Scythia Minor from Inferior. In the late 360s the Goths invaded again by sea and defeated and killed the Emperor Valens at Adrianople in 378. Moesia was finally invaded by the Slavs and Avars in the sixth century.

ABOVE RIGHT Apulum (Alba-Iulia, Romania)
There were valuable gold reserves in the mountains and to make the area even more desirable, the plains along the Marisus river were extremely fertile, enabling large garrisons to be provisioned at low financial and logistical cost. The main unit based there, from the initial conquest right through to the Aurelian withdrawal, was *legio XIII Gemina*. The legion had a stone fortress situated in a huge camp that covered 70 acres. A *vicus* was established to the south, becoming the *municipium Aurelium Apulense* under Marcus Aurelius, and the *colonia Aurelia Apulensis* under Commodus. There was also a second town to the north and eastern sides of the fort: *colonia nova Apulensis*. There's not a great deal to see as it was robbed of construction materials in the medieval period.

BELOW RIGHT Colonia Ulpia Traiana Augusta Dacica Sarmizegetusa, Romania
Ulpia Traiana grew out of the camp of *legio V Macedonica*, which was located a few miles from Tapae, a key pass between the Banat and Iron Gates of Transylvania. The "Sarmizegetusa" element of the name came from the erstwhile capital of Dacia some 25 miles away (see p. 143) destroyed in the conquest. The exact date of *colonia Ulpia Traiana*'s establishment is not known, but it is believed to have been shortly after the conquest. It took the title *colonia* from the beginning, and soon covered an area of about 82 acres, the incoming population largely made up of 25,000 veterans of the Dacian wars. It became the capital and the largest city in Roman Dacia, latterly identified as a metropolis. The city was eventually overrun by the Goths who then destroyed it. These days, large numbers of the remains can still be seen, including the amphitheater (**CENTER RIGHT**) with Temple of Nemesis (**A**) and gladiator school (**B**).

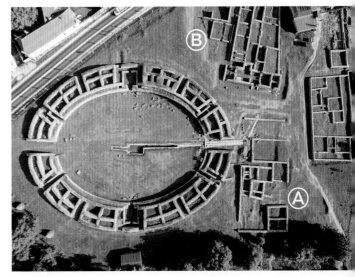

ABOVE AND BELOW Porolissum (Moigrad, Romania)
The defense of northwest Dacia was of paramount importance to the Romans, because it was a key access point for the tribes and just to the north of the gold mines. Porolissum became the lynchpin of a deep defensive system of three lines, established by Trajan after the second war (105–106) and finished in the first quarter of the second century to protect the main routes through the mountains to the interior of the province. The strategically placed main fort was initially made from timber on a stone base. It was big enough to garrison 5,000 *auxilia* brought in from Spain, Gaul, Britain, Thrace, and Syria—although their identities are harder to specify. There are many tile stamps, and the authority on the subject, C.H. Oprean, suggests that the garrison was *cohors I Brittonum* and *cohors V Lingonum*, with *numerus Palmyrenorum Porolissensium* at first in a smaller nearby fort on Citera Hill before moving into the main camp. As time went on, the fortifications were enlarged and the timber parts were replaced with stone. A *vicus* grew up to the south and east, and in 124, Hadrian created the province Dacia Porolissensis. It became a significant trading center, and either under Emperor Severus or his son Caracalla, Porolissensis was awarded *municipium* status, which conferred significant mercantile and administrative benefits on the 25,000 or so occupants. Unfortunately, the days of "*Dacia Felix*" (happy or fertile Dacia) were numbered. The Romans began leaving the region in the 260s and finally withdrew around 271.

OPPOSITE, ABOVE Sarmizegetusa Regia, Romania
The Dacian capital before the Romans invaded, Sarmizegetusa was one of six Dacian mountaintop fortresses in the Orastie Mountains. It was the center of the Dacians' religious life, too, and this photograph shows the great circular sanctuary (**A**), a temple (**B**), and a solar disk (**C**). On a plateau at 4,000ft, the Romans probably stormed the fortress—there's some debate as to whether the Dacians destroyed it themselves—in 106, although the Dacian king, Decebalus escaped. He later killed himself to avoid capture. The battle was undertaken by *legiones II Adiutrix, IV Flavia Felix*, and a *vexillatio* of *legio VI Ferrata*. *IV Flavia Felix* then moved to Berzobia (Berzobis) where it created a fort which was abandoned around 117 when the legion moved to Singidunum in Moesia Superior; *legio XIII Gemina* was placed at Apulum which became capital of Dacia Superior after the reorganization of 120–123. Additionally, as has already been mentioned, many *auxilia* units were based in Dacia.

BELOW Resculum (Bologa, Romania)

An auxiliary fort built from timber and earth on a high piece of ground where it had good views across the neighboring terrain including the confluence of the rivers Secuieu and Cris, Resculum's role was to defend the southwestern section of the *limes Porolissensis* and control passage along the route through the Ciuceam Pass. The first garrison and builders was probably *cohors I Ulpia Brittonum*, who arrived 110–114. Later enlarged, *cohors II Hispanorum Scutata equitata* stayed until the third century, but in the meantime they were joined by specialist javelin throwers from *cohors I Aelia Gaesatorum milliaria*, who also stayed to the end.

BELOW Arutela (Calimanesti, Romania)

The *limes Alutanus* ran north from the Danube along the west side of the River Alutus (Olt). It consisted of a road, a ditch, and an earth berm with regular forts (at least seven and possibly twice that number). The first was created during the Dacian wars, but their importance was accentuated after 117–118 when the land to the east of the river was abandoned. New fortifications were started, such as Arutela, whose *porta praetoria* has been reconstructed. It was built by a unit of Syrian archers (the *surii sagittarii*) around 138. Other brick stamps indicate *legio V Macedonica* and *cohors I Hispanorum veterana equitata* may have been garrisoned.

ABOVE Buridava (Stolniceni, Moldova)
Another fort on the *limes Alutanus* that was located on the banks of what was then called the River Alutus (now the River Olt), the site was roughly midway between Pons Aluti (Ionestii Govorii) and Castra Traiana (Sîmbotin). It is thought that it may well have been constructed under Hadrian by the *cohors I milliaria Brittonum*. Stamping marks on bricks discovered there show that a number of different military units had been present, including *legiones I Italica, V Macedonica*, and *XI Claudia* as well as auxiliaries from *cohors II Flavia Bessorum, cohors IX Batavorum*, and *pedites singulares*. The outlines of the town that grew up to the north of the military camp have recently been worked out showing that it was over half a mile long and about 300yd wide. This became a trading center which mostly dealt with salt and sheep farming. Among the many structures uncovered

so far—most of which were built of stone and terra-cotta—a large bathhouse has been identified in which a life-size bronze statue of an emperor was found. It is thought that the civilian settlement continued to be used long after the Romans left in 271.

BELOW Jidava (Schitu Golesti, Romania)
Built between 190 and 211 by *cohors Prima Flavia Commagenorum*, Jidava was the most important of the strongpoints on the *limes Transalutanus*, a line set up further east than the *limes Alutanus* under Commodus. Strongly constructed from stone and brick, its purpose was to defend and control the strategically important route through the Bran Pass which gave access to Wallachia. Garrisoned by between 200 and 400 troops, these days the camp is one of the best preserved in Romania, with various reconstructions, walls which still stand up to six feet high, and many substantial structures.

ABOVE Colonia Singidunum (Belgrade, Serbia)
Located where the Sava River joins the Danube,
Singidunum later developed into present-day Belgrade.
As part of the fortifications of the Danubian *limes*, it
not only helped defend the empire's border against the
Dacian tribes but also protected the *via Militaris*. The
first fort on the site was built from timber and earth,
but this was later rebuilt in white limestone. A medieval
fortress was later built over the top of it and today
only small sections of the original structure can still be
seen. The first Roman garrison—from 46 to 69—was
probably *legio VIII Augusta*. In 86 Domitian placed *legio IV
Flavia Felix* there. One of its tasks was to build a
pontoon bridge across the Sava so that his forces could
respond quickly if required in or around Taurunum, a
settlement on the opposite bank. *IV Flavia* took part in
Trajan's invasion of Dacia and the battle at the capital,
Sarmizegetusa. Afterward, the legion—or a large part of
it—remained in Dacia, but it's likely that some returned
to Singidunum, especially after *legio VII Claudia* left
Viminacium for Parthia around 114. The adjacent *vicus*
was partly populated by retired legionary veterans,
and as a result quickly grew in size. As part of this, it
was first awarded *municipium* status, and then later it
became a full *colonia*. It enjoyed all the usual features
of the period: a forum, large baths, warehouses, shops,
temples, etc. Roman control began to wane toward
the end of the second century, and after Dacia was
eventually abandoned between 256 and 270 as the
result of an invasion by the Goths, Singidunum returned
to the forefront of the *limes*, an important border control point and legionary center.

BELOW The *via Militaris*
There were two major Roman roads into the Balkans
from Aquileia, the transport node at the head of the
Adriatic: the *via Flavia* along Dalmatia to Dyrrhachium
where it became the *via Egnatia* to Byzantium; and the
via Pannonia to Sirmium, then by the *via Militaris* through
Singidunum to Byzantium. Sirmium was the capital of
Pannonia Inferior and, after 294, one of the four capital
cities of the Tetrarchy. The *via Militaris* passed through
Viminacium (Kostolac, Serbia), Naissus (Nis, Serbia),
Philippopolis (Plovdid, Bulgaria), and Hadrianopolis
(Edime, Turkey) on its way to Byzantium and proved
durable enough to act as a route for the Ottoman
Turks in the fourteenth and fifteenth centuries. This
section is at Castra Rubra in Turkey near a Roman road
station.

Viminacium (near Kostolac, Serbia)

Capital of Moesia Superior, at its peak home to 40,000, Viminacium was strategically important for the defense of the borders but also a prosperous trading center. The first fort was Augustan, probably the work of *legio V Macedonica* who may have been here in AD 10–58. Their timber fort was replaced in stone by *legio VII Claudia Pia Fidelis,* attested here first around 52. It was *legio VII Claudia* and *IV Flavia* that did so much of the preparatory work for Trajan's wars, creating the towpath road through the Danube gorge. Viminacium became a city in 117, after Trajan had used it as his HQ during the Dacian wars—*Municipium Viminacium Aelium Hadrianum*—and a *colonia* in 239. It was an important port: the *classis Pannonica* was based here. Today, although far from completely excavated, the archaeological park includes reconstructions (such as the amphitheater **ABOVE** and Roman villa **BELOW**) and reenactments.

ABOVE Karataš (later, Diana Fortress, Serbia)
Built in Claudian times on cliffs above the Danube near what is now Kladovo, Karataš was rebuilt by the Flavian emperors, destroyed by a Dacian attack in 85–86 and subsequently was strongly constructed from stone by Trajan around 100. One of its functions was to protect the bypass canal that avoided the cataracts on the Danube built by Trajan in preparation for his Dacian invasion. One of the largest *auxilia* forts, it was later significantly reinforced at the end of the third century as the result of threats from barbarian tribes across the frontier. These improvements included the addition of extra towers on the side which fronted the Danube. Despite this, it was badly damaged by the Huns in the mid-fourth century, and Justinian ordered its rebuilding in 530.

Various units are attested: *vexillationes* from *legiones V Macedonica, VII Claudia, IV Flavia*, and *XIII Gemina*; auxiliary troops—*cohors VI Thracum* and *V Gallorum*.

BELOW Trajan's Bridge (near Kladovo, Serbia)
Designed by Apollodorus of Damascus, the 4,000ft bridge between Pontes and Drobeta was built by the legions, particularly *legio VII Claudia* stationed at Pontes and other forts. Near to the bridge were large *horrea* and a logistics center. Only a few of the bridge pillars remain but there are detailed descriptions of it in Dio Cassius's *Historia Romana*. Dio also notes that the wooden elements were taken down in Hadrian's reign to reduce the likelihood of an enemy using the bridge.

Felix Romuliana (Gamzigrad, near Zajecar, Serbia)
Emperor Galerius built Felix Romuliana, an Imperial palace, to celebrate his place of birth. Begun in 298, it was named after his mother, Romula, and located south of the Danube in Dacia Ripensis, the area of Moesia Inferior that was renamed after Dacia was abandoned in 275 by Aurelian. It's a huge, eleven-acre complex of palace buildings and temples that had a fortified outer wall with twenty defensive towers. It was built by *legio V Macedonica*. On a hill outside were two mausoleums—for Galerius and his mother. As well as these, there were many sculptures and fine mosaics and pilasters which featured notable Roman emperors. Coins found on the site show that the complex was used until the Huns sacked it and the city around it in the mid-fifth century.

RIGHT Colonia Ulpia Traiana Ratiaria (Archar, Bulgaria)

A vital location on the Danubian *limes*, a legionary fortress and naval base, Rataria is one of only a few locations with a name that directly relates to sailing: *ratis* means raft. Originally established by the Moesians in the fourth century BC, the earliest Roman presence in the area came about in the first century BC. Thrace south of the Danube became Roman in AD46; forty years later Vespasian created the two provinces of Moesia Superior and Inferior. The first wooden fort was constructed by *legio IV Flavia Felix* during this period, and it became the home base for the *classis Moesica*. It is likely that the city obtained much of its wealth from its gold mine, together with the associated trade derived from the work of its goldsmiths. When Dacia was eventually subdued the defensive needs of the location lessened and it became a *colonia*. In this form the city was a significant trading and customs port. It was also one of the arsenal locations where arms were built for the legions. After Dacia was abandoned, it was once more in the front line and the forts were brought back into use and there was rebuilding and larger walls were constructed. *Legio XIII Gemina* was garrisoned there from around 272. T he Huns sacked the city in 440 or 441, after which it was rebuilt under Anastasius I who also renamed it Anastasiana Ratiaria. It was sacked again by the Avars in 586. Unfortunately, since the 1980s it has been sacked again: by treasure hunters. Where once there were walls and one of Bulgaria's archaeological jewels, today there are craters and pits where thieves have used heavyweight digging equipment. This is not an isolated problem in Bulgaria where all too many sites are being ruined by greed.

BELOW Ulpia Oescus (Gigen, Bulgaria)

Another important legionary fortress on the banks of the Danube in Moesia, Oescus was the site of one of the world's best-known ancient bridges, famous for being the longest stone bridge across the Danube.

Known as Constantine's Bridge, it linked Oescus with the city of Sucidava (modern-day Corabia, Romania). Nearly 8,000ft long, it was completed in 328 and was used for some decades after. Whether it was destroyed by an enemy, or was destroyed to stop an enemy using it is unknown. The fortress was the base for *legio V Macedonica* who garrisoned it intermittently from 10 to 101, with spells in Armenia and Egypt in between. When it was decided that reinforcements were needed, *legio IV Scythica* joined them. At its peak, the city—which by then had reached the status of a *colonia*, covered around 70 acres and had a population of about 100,000. The city was left in ruins after the Huns sacked it in 411, and although it was rebuilt under Justinian the Avars destroyed it again in 585/586. These days some parts of the outer wall are still in place and various other features can also be discerned including the remains of a necropolis.

ABOVE Dimum (Belene, Bulgaria)

Another *limes* fort on the banks of the Danube, Dimum started as little more than a temporary camp, but gained importance when it became a customs post linked to imports for nearby Novae and exports of wheat. During its history, the site was attacked, destroyed and rebuilt several times, but little can be seen today as the site's situation next to the Danube has led to much of it being washed away. Some of the original outer walls, which were 11ft thick, are still visible when the water level is low. Various parts of the site's walls have recently been restored, and there is a visitors' center in the Persina Nature Park alongside. The *cuneus equitum Solensium* garrisoned in the second and third centuries.

BELOW Novae (Svishtov, Bulgaria)

Novae was a legionary fortress that was built first in timber in about AD45 by *legio VIII Augusta* on uneven sloping ground high above the southern banks of the Danube. Some twenty-five years later, in 69, *legio I Italica* replaced *VIII Augusta* and set about reconstructing the fort in a more substantial manner using stone, partly because King Decebalus of Dacia was becoming a major threat to the area. War started in 85, and it took twenty years to overcome the Dacians. As a result of this, the civilian settlements were able to expand and prosper, and further trade resulted when a road was built linking the site to Nicopolis and Augusta Traiana. During the third century, Novae was destroyed but restored, the legionary fortress used for stone. The legion left around 441 but the city continued to prosper—it was well known for its glassware—and it became a bishopric, the cathedral built over the fort. Walls were constructed but they couldn't stop the Avars and Slavs finally destroying the city in the late sixth century.

ABOVE Nicopolis ad Istrum (Nikyup, Bulgaria)
Established by Trajan around 102—the name means "Town of the Victory at the Danube"—where the Iatrus (Yantra) and the Rositsa rivers met, it prospered through the years of the Hadrian, Antonine, and Severan dynasties. The city was sacked in 170–171 by the Costoboci from what is today's Ukraine. This spurred the city's authorities to build fortified walls around most of the buildings, which once again allowed the population to thrive. The Goths under Cniva attacked in 250, but they were defeated at Nicopolis ad Istrum by the Emperor Decius. After this, the city grew once more under Diocletian, and it is probable that around this time it became a major logistical supply base for the military units stationed in the region. There were all the usual trappings of a successful Roman city, including at least three aqueducts, as well as a forum, public baths, temples, shops, walkways, and so on. The Huns under Attila destroyed the town in 447. It was rebuilt but was finally razed by the Avars and Slavs.

BELOW Durostorum (Silistra, Bulgaria)
An important legionary fortress and river port located in Moesia Inferior, the first fort was built in 29BC. It retained the original name of an earlier Thracian settlement on the site. At some stage before 114, *legio XI Claudia* was moved in to garrison the base, which before long became the center of military activity in the province of Moesia. This prosperity saw the adjacent civilian town grow into a city by the time of Marcus Aurelius, and it also became a focus of Christianity in the region. Durostorum became a *municipium* in 167. When the Roman Empire was split, it joined the Eastern (Byzantine) Empire, and continued to flourish until well into the sixth century when it was finally taken over by the Slavs. These days, many ruins of the fortress, its towers, a gate, and parts of the Roman settlement are still visible in Silistra's main park.

Tropaeum Traiani (Adamclisi, Romania)

Erected in Civitas Tropaensium to commemorate Trajan's triumph over the Dacians at the battle of Adamclisi, the monument was built in 109 in place of an altar which listed the 3,000 legionaries and auxiliary troops who had died in action. Made with a concrete core, the circular structure had limestone faces and featured fifty-four metopes (rectangular panels with carved reliefs—see p. 21) depicting Roman legions fighting their enemies. At the base were nine steps, and at the top was a conical roof on top of which was a trophy sculpted in the form of a tree trunk which had prisoners bound to it. The monument was intended primarily as a form of propaganda to warn the local tribes not to resist Roman rule. The monument that stands today (**ABOVE**) is a 1977 reconstruction as the original was more or less destroyed. Today forty-nine of the original metopes survive, with one in Istanbul and the rest in the nearby museum (**BELOW**) which also displays many archaeological finds from the site.

ABOVE Capidava, Romania

Capidava was a square-shaped fortress that was constructed on the right bank of the Danube high on a rock formation overlooking the river and surrounding area. Its main purpose was to protect a strategically important fording point. Built as part of Trajan's preparations for his upcoming war with the Dacians, the actual work was carried out by *legio V Macedonica* of Troesmis and *legio XI Claudia*. Once completed, it was garrisoned by *cohors I Ubiorum* until 243, when the troops were replaced by those of *cohors I Germanorum civium Romanorum*, who remained there until the late third century. The fort itself had substantial outer walls and seven towers which reached over 30ft in height. On the southwest side a gateway gave access to the adjoining port which was used as a fleet station by the *classis Flavia Moesica*.

Capidava was well positioned on the local road network and this made it an important administrative center for the region. It was also popular with legionary veterans who chose to settle there, and as a consequence the adjacent *vicus* quickly expanded. It was equipped with the usual facilities, such as storage warehouses, public baths, and cemeteries. The fort and settlement were destroyed by the Goths in the third century, but they were later rebuilt and the site was in constant use until it was finally abandoned in 559 after an invasion by the Avars. These days, extensive remains are still visible above ground, with the bases of most of the walls, towers, and buildings still in place.

BELOW Carsium (Hârsova, Romania)

Located on the right bank of the Danube to protect an important fording point, the auxiliary fort of Carsium was built in 103. It was positioned on the *limes* between Capidava and Troesmis to which it was linked by road at a point where significant amounts of trade crossed between Histria and the Wallachian plain. Much of the trade traveled to the area on boats along the Jalomitza river which joined the Danube opposite Carsium. Attested units were *legio I Italica*, *ala II Hispanorum et Aravacorum*, and *milites Scythici*, the latter during Diocletian's rule. The extra military presence in the area encouraged several civilian settlements to become established, such as the *vici* Verobrittiani and Carporum. Nothing remains from the site itself, so no details of the shape or size of the fort are known.

ABOVE Troesmis (Iglita-Turcoaia, Romania)
A legionary fortress in Moesia Inferior, the area was taken from its Getae population between 29BC and AD15 by Pomponius Flaccus. The garrison between 107 and 161 was *legio V Macedonica* and later in its history—between 337 and 361—*legio II Herculia*. At some stage it is thought that *legio I Iovia* was also stationed there. Much of the stone from the fortresses' walls and buildings was robbed and sold off in the late nineteenth century, and as a result, apart from a few ruins, only the outlines of the rest of the camp can still be seen.

BELOW Dinogetia (Bisericuta-Garvan, Romania)
Located on the southern banks of the Danube, close to where the River Siret joins it, Dinogetia was in a strategically important location near the mouth of the Danube on a good crossing point in a marshy area. It endured periods of major unrest that increased after

Dacia was abandoned and various barbarian tribes began attacking the region. Originally in Moesia Inferior, later reorganized by Diocletian as Scythia Minor, it was eventually overrun by the Avars in 559 following which the site was abandoned by the Romans. Archaeological evidence shows that underneath later structures there had been an earlier fort and ditch. The final Roman fort had substantial fourth-century walls—up to 10ft thick and with fourteen horseshoe-shaped towers arranged along their length—and baths outside. Brick stampings show that *legio I Iovia* was stationed there at that time. Other units attested: *Milites Scythici*, as well as *legio V Macedonica*, *legio I Italica*, *cohors I Cilicum*, *cohors I Mattiacorum*, and the *classis Flavia Moesica*.

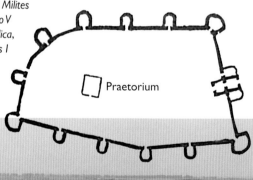

Praetorium

ABOVE Halmyris (Cetatea, Romania)

Occupied long before the Romans conquered the region, the area was populated by the Getae who traded with the Greek trading posts in the Danube delta. Marcus Licinius Crassus incorporated these lands into the empire around 27BC. A fort was established on the site which formed an important component in the *limes* border fortification system. Alongside the fortress, which lay on a rocky outcrop at the end of the Dunavat peninsula just above the marshes around the mouth of the Danube Delta, was also a naval port and a civilian settlement. The local geography lent itself to a defensive stance, with the delta to the north and east, the Tulcea hills to the west, and Razelm lake to the south. The first *castrum* was constructed in the usual way from timber and earth, however, this was replaced by a more substantial stone version under Trajan—built by *legiones I Italica* and *VI Claudia*. Further improvement took place in 270–285. The fort was rebuilt as an irregular polygon with fifteen towers and two strongly built gatehouses. Within the walls were a number of barracks, as well as a basilica and a bathhouse. Being strategically positioned at the mouth of the Black Sea, the port was of vital significance to the Roman fleet, and a *vicus classicorum*—a seaman's village—soon grew up alongside. The Roman fort was attacked in 294, 314, and winter 384/385 when the Danube froze over, allowing the barbarian tribes to cross and attack, and in 390 the Huns took the fort briefly. They came back in 408 and destroyed it. Finally, the Byzantines left for good in the seventh century. A number of powerful earthquakes in the fourth century changed the course of the river, and not long afterward the port began to silt up decreasing the importance of the site. Today the Danube runs just over a mile further north.

BELOW Olbia (Parutyne, Ukraine)

The Greek city located on the banks of the Bug, Olbia was founded in the seventh century BC and proved a great success until largely destroyed by the Getae in the first century BC. It was rebuilt on a smaller scale and became part of the province of Lower Moesia when the Romans established themselves in the region. A garrison was installed in the mid-second century, but Goths overran the city, burnt it on two occasions, and it was abandoned in the fourth century.

ABOVE Charax, Crimea

Taurica—the Roman Crimea—was only partially under Roman control save for a brief period under Nero, as it was controlled by a client state, the Bosporan Kingdom. Charax was a Roman fortified camp that was founded under Vespasian and located at the western end of a rocky peninsula near the Cape of Ai-Todor. It was surrounded by a defensive wall that was around 1,300ft long. Its role was to provide protection to the region's trade as well as to secure access to the area's military bases in the face of Scythian threats. These grew so bad, however, that the Roman troops stationed there were withdrawn by the end of the first century. Some years later, the site was reoccupied and rebuilt by a *vexillatio* of *legio I Italica*, and then part of *legio XI Claudia* took it over toward the end of the second century. The Roman presence became increasingly precarious as time went on, and they once again abandoned the camp somewhere around the middle of the third century under pressure from the Goths. The exact details of what was at Charax are not yet known—it is possible that there was also a city alongside it, and there is the possibility that the Romans dismantled the fort themselves before leaving. Archaeological work continues at the site. Thus far baths, an aqueduct, a gymnasium, and a sanctuary have been discovered.

OPPOSITE, BELOW AND THIS PAGE Chersonesus (Sevastopol, Crimea)

It means peninsula in Greek, and Chersonesus was positioned on the coast of the Black Sea on the Crimean Peninsula. Lying in the outer parts of what is present day Sevastopol, it was the Romans' main naval base in the region and probably manned by a division of the Pontic fleet as well as by ground troops. The port became very prosperous since it was also much used for mercantile trade, especially in the main products that were shipped out from there: wheat, clothing, wine, and slaves. Despite all the commerce and their having significant forces garrisoned there, Rome never held full control of the area with large parts of the interior beyond their grasp, and on occasion—such as in 250 when the Goths conquered the whole area—they lost it completely, albeit only temporarily. These instances aside, the Roman presence, largely represented by a series of client kings, ran from 47BC to around AD340. Their influence gradually diminished, however, as the Goths established themselves in many of the local territories. The Huns then took over fully when they moved in around 375/376. As the photos show, the remains are substantial. It is possible to walk along the original streets among the marble columns and ruins of villas, public squares, a basilica, an underground temple-mausoleum, a theater, various workshops, and a mint as well as the remains of fortified towers and defensive walls.

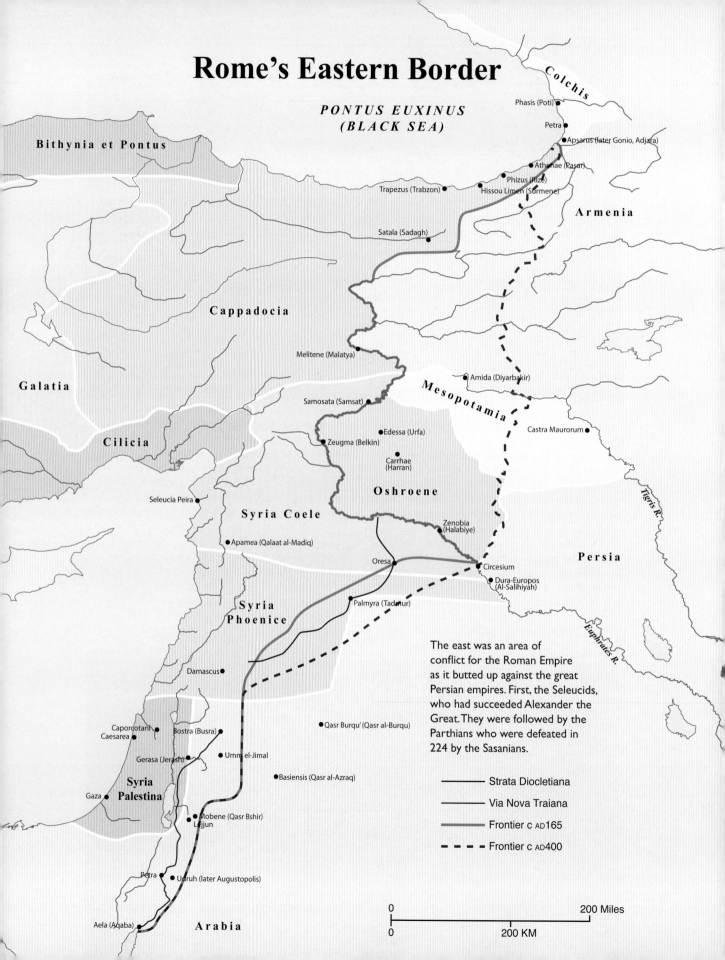

Rome's Eastern Border

PONTUS EUXINUS
(BLACK SEA)

Bithynia et Pontus

Colchis

Phasis (Poti)

Petra

Apsarus (later Gonio, Adjara)

Athenae (Pasar)

Phizus (Rize)

Trapezus (Trabzon)

Hissou Limen (Sürmene)

Armenia

Satala (Sadagh)

Cappadocia

Melitene (Malatya)

Amida (Diyarbakir)

Mesopotamia

Galatia

Samosata (Samsat)

Edessa (Urfa)

Castra Maurorum

Zeugma (Belkin)

Carrhae
(Harran)

Cilicia

Oshroene

Seleucia Peira

Tigris R.

Syria Coele

Zenobia
(Halabiye)

Apamea (Qalaat al-Madiq)

Persia

Oresa

Circesium

Dura-Europos
(Al-Salihiyah)

**Syria
Phoenice**

Palmyra (Tadmur)

Euphrates R.

Damascus

The east was an area of
conflict for the Roman Empire
as it butted up against the great
Persian empires. First, the Seleucids,
who had succeeded Alexander the
Great. They were followed by the
Parthians who were defeated in
224 by the Sasanians.

Caporcotani

Qasr Burqu' (Qasr al-Burqu)

Caesarea

Bostra (Busra)

Gerasa (Jerash)

Umm el-Jimal

Basiensis (Qasr al-Azraq)

**Syria
Palestina**

Gaza

Mobene (Qasr Bshir)
Lejjun

———	Strata Diocletiana
———	Via Nova Traiana
———	Frontier c AD165
- - -	Frontier c AD400

Petra

Udruh (later Augustopolis)

Aela (Aqaba)

Arabia

0 ———————— 200 Miles

0 ———————— 200 KM

Rome's Eastern Border

Stretching from the Caucasus Mountains and the Black Sea to the Sinai Desert and the Red Sea, the eastern frontier of the empire passed through a varied landscape of mountains, plains, and desert, with a few major rivers that were key to life and commerce. Beyond Asia Minor were the lands of a different kind of highly mobile combat, centered on horse armies of lightly armored bowmen and heavily armored cataphracts, not that of heavy infantry. Here there were older working states and empires already in existence with which Rome had to come to terms. The nearest, largest, and richest was Parthia, an Iranian empire that stretched far into present-day Afghanistan and Pakistan.

Rome's first hostile contact with this major regional power came during the final days of the Republic and the scar of the disastrous battle of Carrhae (53BC) ran deep thereafter in the Roman psyche, ensuring that they were usually the more aggressive in the wars that sparked into life from time to time over the next 300 years. But although there was rivalry and combat, for the most part it was easier to deal with another organized entity rather than a conglomeration of unruly tribes. Instead there were times of cold war, fought by proxies—buffer states caught between the two rivals, who became client states as control over them oscillated.

The chief of these unfortunate in-between countries was Armenia, whose geographical position made it the site of all the main altercations between Rome and Parthia. These wars yielded mixed results but ultimately ended in stalemate. The Sassanid Persians who superseded the Parthians in 224–226 had the zeal of a fresh start and therefore proved much more aggressive foes. The Augustan policy had set the Euphrates as the natural boundary of the empire and although Roman expansion had reached much deeper into Mesopotamia, it never progressed more than temporarily beyond it. The Flavian emperors began the establishment of a more solid eastern frontier when they resettled the legions along the river and began systematically upgrading and linking its fortifications. Though Roman control of northern Mesopotamia ran considerably beyond this boundary, the

BELOW Apsarus (later Gonio, Adjara, Georgia)
The eastern Black Sea coast was important to the Romans who used client kingdoms to counter the Parthian/Sasanian threats. The coast remained Roman, the rest was fought over. The sizeable fort at Apsarus was part of Nero's Pontic *limes*—he had ambitious plans to connect the empire with India. Arrian talks about five *cohortes* being stationed here, one of which seems to have been *cohors II Claudiana quingenaria peditata*.

BELOW Trapezus (Trabzon, Turkey)
On the Black Sea, Trapezus was an important hub linking by sea the *limes* along the Rhine and the Danube to the *limes* along the Euphrates. This made it an important supply base for campaigns in the area, especially during the reigns of Nero and later Vespasian. Emperor Hadrian improved the port and probably visited it in 129. It was sacked by the Goths in 257 and Persians in 258. It only recovered in the sixth century under Justinian.

ABOVE Apamea (Qalaat al-Madiq, Syria)
A former citadel of Seleucid kings, Apamea was captured by Pompey in 64BC. It was targeted as a useful crossroads on a plateau overlooking the valley of the Orontes and became part of the Roman province of Syria. *Legio II Parthica* had its winter quarters here in the early third century and there are interesting tombstones. It is particularly notable for its near 1.2-mile long colonnade between its northern and southern gates.

BELOW Zenobia (Halabiye, Syria)
The Euphrates was the shortest route between the Persian and Roman empires, and Zenobia stood at a vital choke point where it flows through a narrow gap. Captured in 273 by the Romans in the battles against Zenobia, Queen of Palmyra, it was refortified as part of the *limes Arabicus* against the Persians. The remains of Zenobia mostly date to Justinian's refortification in the sixth century.

ancient city states there had client status and so only their administrations were changed and a smattering of troops stationed. The Euphrates was the vital artery of trade and communication linking the Parthian capital of Seleucia-Ctesiphon with the main Roman cities of the Near East by river and then road through Palmyra as the hub. The main crossing point and a site of critical strategic importance was Zeugma (modern Bitlis), home of a Roman legionary base. Other major bases were spaced upriver on the border with Armenia at Meltene, Satala, and Samosata, with cavalry and cohort forts between them linked by road.

Elsewhere in the east, client kingdoms in Colchis and the Crimea Commagene, Osrhoene, Judea, Arabia, and Palmyra, buffered the empire, although most were eventually absorbed by the Romans between the first and third centuries. To the south the deserts were a natural barrier, but it was crossed by roads that allowed caravans to negotiate the burning heat to trade. The path from Bostra to the Red Sea was renewed with the *via nova Traiana*, with fortified caravanserai, water stations, and border posts to monitor and control the traders.

The fertile coastal and river strips formed an important economic basis for development and were significant producers for the empire. After the western empire fell, the eastern (Byzantine) half continued in its fruitless and resource-consuming wars against the Persians until the Arab Muslim conquests of the seventh century.

ABOVE Cepha (Hasankeyf, Turkey)
Located on the left bank of the Tigris, this ancient
settlement and its bridge have recently been
overwhelmed by the Ilisu Dam project, despite being one
of the oldest continuously inhabited settlements in the
world. The Romans built bridges near here, although this
one dates from the thirteenth century. In 363 Emperor
Jovian and King Shapur II of the Sasanian Empire agreed
a peace treaty in which the border between the two
empires was drawn along the rivers Nymphius (about
25 miles west) and this stretch of the Tigris. Cepha then
became one of Rome's easternmost legionary fortresses.
In 330 when the Roman empire split, the city's name
changed to became Kiphas. The *Notitia* identifies the
garrison as *legio II Parthica* under the *Dux Mesopotamiae*.

BELOW Dura-Europos (near Al-Salihiyah, Syria)
Sitting at the intersection of the major east–west trade
route, Dura-Europos was a strategic gem. Flanked by
two deep wadis and only open on the desert side, it
commanded a steep escarpment of the eastern bank
near a bend of the Euphrates. After Emperor Lucius
Verus in person captured the city in 165, he put in a
Roman garrison to defend the border and southern
hinterlands against the encroaching Parthians. The
Roman Army took over a "military quarter" in the city,
rather than building an encampment, although they did
build a *principia* and small amphitheater. Up to 2,000 men
included *dromedarii* (camel troops) and *cohors XX
Palmyrenorum* were stationed there. The city was
destroyed by the Sasanians in 265 and never rebuilt.

LEFT Nova Traiana Bostra (Bosra, Syria)
A early capital city of the Nabataeans, Bostra was captured by Trajan in 106. He made it the capital of the province of Arabia Petraea and the home of *legio III Cyrenaica*. An important trading city, Bostra was the junction of a leg of the Incense Route with the *via nova Traiana*—built around 109 by Trajan out of his own pocket to connect Damascus to the Red Sea. The Incense Route was an ancient network that brought frankincense from Oman and Yemen. Here, **A** is the Roman reservoir; **B** the Hippodrome; **C** the theater, converted into a fortress in the eleventh century.

CENTER LEFT Palmyra (Tadmur, Syria)
Founded on a fertile natural oasis in the Tadmorean Desert, Palmyra is one of the oldest inhabited places in the area. Its wealth came not just from its fertile surrounding lands, but also as the meeting point of two major trade routes: the overland Silk Road from the Mediterranean all the way to China over 9,000 miles away; and the sea route that started in India and went to the head of the Persian Gulf at Spasinou Charax, then overland to Babylon (on the Euphrates) or Seleucia (on the Tigris), then west across the desert to Palmyra. When the Roman Republic conquered the Seleucid Empire in 64BC, it didn't immediately take Palmyra whose trade benefited from being the inter-mediaries between the Romans and Parthians. During Tiberius's reign, the city became part of the empire and it continued to grow. In 260, after thirty years of Roman succession problems, when Valerian was defeated by the Sasanians at Edessa, Palmyrene King Odaenathus defeated the Sasanians and imposed his rule on Rome's eastern provinces. He was careful to keep good relations with Rome, but after his assassination in 267, his queen, Zenobia, was less circumspect. In 272 she declared herself empress and her son emperor. The Palmyrene Empire reached its high point when her army invaded and took Egypt. In 272 Aurelian reconquered the area and took Palmyra, which he spared, although another rebellion in 273 saw harsher treatment.

BELOW LEFT Qasr Burqu' (Al-Qasr, Jordan)
In the remote Umayyad desert about 2,000ft above sea level, the desert castle of Qasr Burqu' started as a small, Roman fort built in AD3 to protect and control a valuable seasonal freshwater lake. The fort was later increased in size by the Arabs.

ABOVE Umm el-Jimal, Jordan
One of the furthest outposts of Rome, this ancient frontier village in the north Jordan desert existed largely thanks to Nabataean traders journeying between Petra and Damascus. The area became part of the province of Arabia in 106 when Trajan incorporated these lands into the Roman Empire. Umm el-Jimal became part of the *limes Arabicus* and grew into an important military base. After the rebellion of Queen Zenobia of Palmyra, a huge fort for a military garrison was constructed under emperors Diocletian and Constantine. The photo shows the "barracks," a later, Byzantine, building.

BELOW Gerasa (Jerash, Jordan)
Thanks to its location in a fertile valley and wealth from the iron ore mines in the northern Ajloun mountains, the city of Gerasa was prosperous before the Romans arrived. Inevitably, it was subsumed into the province of Syria after the Roman conquest of the area by Pompey the Great. For a time the city was one of the Decapolis group of ten autonomous city-states, a buffer on the empire's eastern frontier, but when Rome annexed the Nabataean kingdom in 106, Gerasa was absorbed into the province of Arabia. Emperor Hadrian stayed here in 129 and it became a *colonia* under Marcus Aurelius. Illustrated is the Oval Plaza built at the beginning of the second century AD.

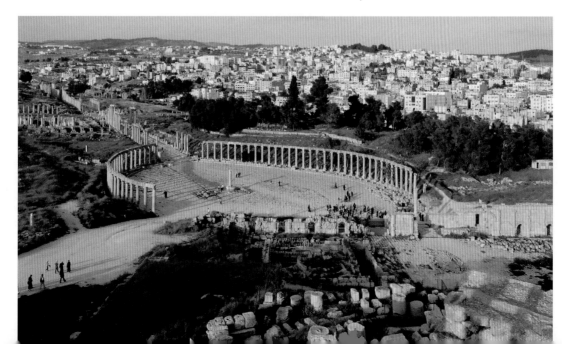

ABOVE Mobene (Qasr Bshir, Jordan)

On the far southeastern fringe of empire the Romans built the defensive *limes Arabicus*. Located on a wide, stony plain, Mobene is one of a chain of forts and watchtowers constructed along the desert fringe as first-line defense to protect the province of Arabia against raiding and pillaging desert nomads. Despite being built in a shallow depression, the *castellum* dominates the surrounding broad, wadi-cut plain. These irregular watercourses all drain west into the vast Wadi Mujib, which in turn drains into the Dead Sea. The fort was built over an earlier Nabataean stronghold. Dated by inscriptions to 293–305, Mobene remained in use throughout the fourth century. It does not appear to have been big enough to garrison a full-strength unit (normally 120–150 men), so it's been speculated that it was used by the provincial governor when he had business with the local tribes.

BELOW Basienis (Qasr el-Azraq, Jordan)

The Romans valued Basienis for its strategic location near the only fresh water oasis (Azraq) in the vast Jordanian desert. This made it an invaluable watering-hole on the Wadi Sirhan trade route. The wadi was also on the route that Arab nomadic tribes used to attack the Romans after they took Nabataea. In about 200, Emperor Septimius Severus decided to thwart the attacks by building three forts about nine miles apart, along the route. Basienis was one of them; it remained in use until the fourth century.

Petra, Jordan

Surrounded by mountains, the city of Petra lies at the eastern end of the Arabah valley that runs from the Dead Sea to the Gulf of Aqaba. Established by nomadic Arabs, at one time it was the capital of the Nabataean kingdom and an important halt and regional trading hub. Its viability relied on an elaborate system of numerous underground tunnels, cisterns, and wells to collect and contain rainwater. The wealth of Nabataean Petra was known across the Levant and was a significant factor in Rome's eventual annexation. In 1 BC the Nabataeans became a client state of the Roman Empire; many years later, in AD 106, Emperor Trajan annexed Nabataea—apparently peacefully—and made it part of the province of Arabia Petraea. Apart from its wealth and water, Trajan wanted Petra as a base for consolidating his control over this huge desert area before moving across the Tigris and attacking Mesopotamia. He built the *via nova Traiana* to link Bostra, the provincial capital, to the port of Aqaba, for easy access and control across the province. Petra was located in the center between Bostra and Aqaba. (See caption p. 166.) Roman rule lasted for 250 years until the middle of the fourth century when an earthquake struck. Today Petra is an important tourism site.

ABOVE AND CENTER RIGHT Ad Deir—the monastery— probably carved in the mid-first century AD, is typical of Petra's beautiful carved rock tombs and temples.

BELOW This panorama shows the Great Temple (**A**), the Temple of Dushares (**B**), Winged Lion Temple (**C**), and Blue Chapel (**D**).

Limes Arabicus

Fortifications were begun by Trajan after his annexation of Nabataea to protect the ancient but still vital trade route connecting Asia to the Arabian peninsula. His new road was called the *via nova Traiana* and ran some 270 miles from Bostra, the capital of the new Roman province of Arabia Petraea, to the port of Aela (Aqaba) on the Red Sea. It was constructed in segments and protected by a system of watchtowers and over 100 small forts, with major legionary fortresses at Bostra, Petra, and Aela. Begun by Trajan, it was completed around 114 by Hadrian, who also shrank the size of the province in his empire-wide restructuring program. Before the end of the century Septimius Severus expanded it again and strengthened the frontier defenses, constructing several forts at the northwest end of the Wadi Sirhan. Diocletian divided the Arabian province in half, assigning the southern part to the province of Palaestina. He then undertook a major military upgrade of the region (284–305), adding new small forts, extra watchtowers, and fortresses along the fringe of the desert just east of the *via nova*. This was extended into and connected with the series of fortifications and roads in the northern Negev, running from Rafah on the Mediterranean to the Dead Sea. The empire's growing manpower shortage led to Roman troops gradually being replaced with native Arab *foederati*, chiefly recruited from the friendly Ghassanids. The *limes Arabicus* disappeared as a discrete entity following the Muslim Arab conquest early in the seventh century, though individual forts, sited in strategically important places, remained in use.

ABOVE Udruh, later Augustopolis (Adhruh, Jordan)
There are few contemporary Roman references to Udruh. It was previously a Nabataean settlement but became Roman on the fall of their kingdom. The fort was built c. 303/304 by *legio VI Ferrata* beside the *via nova Traiana* where it had panoramic views over a large fertile plain. Remnants of watchtowers on nearby high hilltops seem to be linked and indicate communication with Petra (4.5 miles east) through line of sight.

LEFT *via nova Traiana*, Jordan
The *via nova Traiana* started in the north at Nova Traiana (Bostra) and from there went across plains and deserts to Umm el-Jimal, Philadelphia (Amman), Umm ar-Rasas, Kerak, Tafilah, Shoubak, Petra, Sadaqa, Humayma and finally finished at Aela (Aqaba) on the Red Sea. In 64BC the Romans took the Nabataean port of Elath and named it Aela. Thanks to its location on the coast at the northeastern tip of the Red Sea where Africa meets Asia, it was a thriving port and center of commerce. From here travelers could head south along the road leading to Paralia and Roman Egypt or join the *via nova Traiana*.

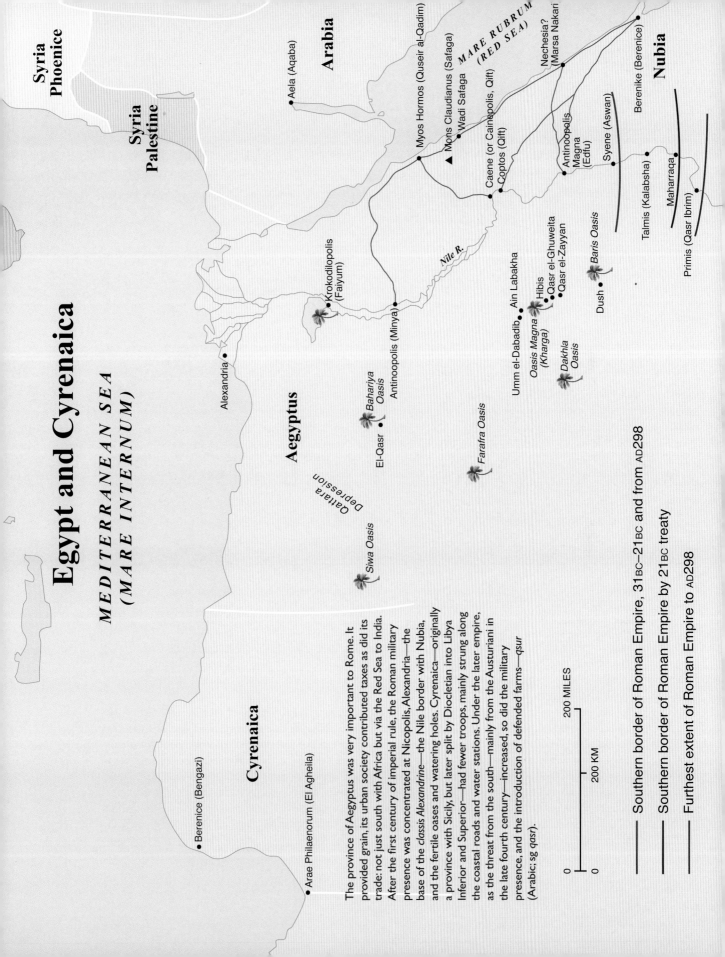

Egypt and Cyrenaica

MEDITERRANEAN SEA
(MARE INTERNUM)

Cyrenaica

Aegyptus

Syria Phoenice

Syria Palestine

Arabia

Nubia

MARE RUBRUM
(RED SEA)

Nile R.

Qattara Depression

Berenice (Bengazi) •

Arae Philaenorum (El Agheila) •

Alexandria •

Siwa Oasis

Krokodilopolis (Faiyum) •

Bahariya Oasis

El-Qasr •

Antinoopolis (Minya) •

Farafra Oasis

Umm el-Dabadib •
Ain Labakha •

Hibis •
Qasr el-Ghuweita •
Oasis Magna (Kharga)
Qasr el-Zayyan •

Dakhla Oasis

Dush •

Baris Oasis

Aela (Aqaba) •

Myos Hormos (Queiser al-Qadim) •

Wadi Safaga •

▲ Mons Claudianus (Safaga)

Caene (or Cainepolis, Qift) •
Coptos (Qift) •

Nechesia? (Marsa Nakari) •

Berenike (Berenice) •

Antinoopolis Magna (Edfu) •

Syene (Aswan) •

Talmis (Kalabsha) •

Maharraqa •

Primis (Qasr Ibrim) •

The province of Aegyptus was very important to Rome. It provided grain, its urban society contributed taxes as did its trade: not just south with Africa but via the Red Sea to India. After the first century of imperial rule, the Roman military presence was concentrated at Nicopolis, Alexandria—the base of the *classis Alexandrine*—the Nile border with Nubia, and the fertile oases and watering holes. Cyrenaica—originally a province with Sicily, but later split by Diocletian into Libya Inferior and Superior—had fewer troops, mainly strung along the coastal roads and water stations. Under the later empire, as the threat from the south—mainly from the Austuriani in the late fourth century—increased, so did the military presence, and the introduction of defended farms—*qsur* (Arabic; sg *qasr*).

	0		200 MILES
	0	200 KM	

——— Southern border of Roman Empire, 31BC–21BC and from AD298

——— Southern border of Roman Empire by 21BC treaty

——— Furthest extent of Roman Empire to AD298

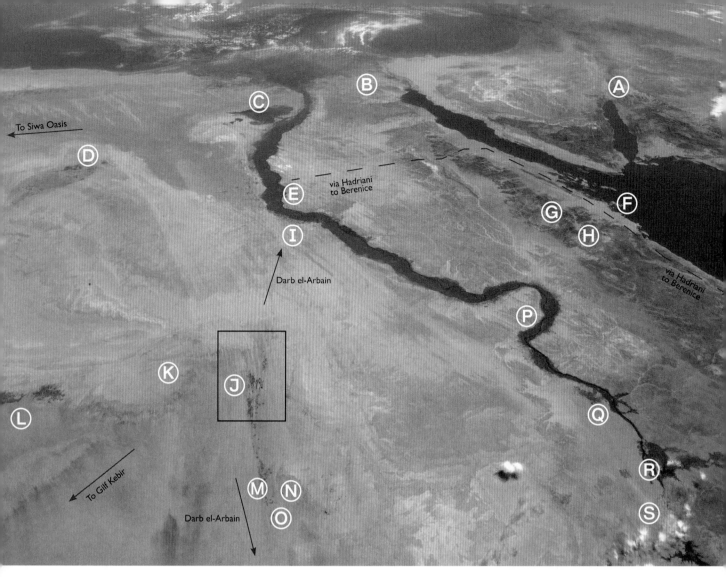

To Siwa Oasis

via Hadriani
to Berenice

Darb el-Arbain

via Hadriani
to Berenice

To Gilf Kebir

Darb el-Arbain

ABOVE

A Aela (Aqaba)

B Location of canal from Great Bitter Lakes to Nile

C The Faiyum

D Bahariya Oasis

E Antinoopolis (Sheikh Ebada)

F Hurghada, a port

G Mons Porphyrites

H Mons Claudianus

I Lycopolis (Asyut)

J Kharga Oasis (Oasis Magna): see detail p. 170

K Ain Amur

L Dakhla Oasis

M el-Qosseir

N Qasr Dush

O Qasr Baris

P Luxor

Q Edfu

R Kom Umbu

S Syene (Aswan)

Egypt and Cyrenaica

The empire's borders here were delineated mainly by the hostility of the Sahara desert, the extreme fertility of the areas along the Nile and the oases, and the Red Sea highway for trade. The proliferation of Roman forts—as far afield as the Farasan Islands—serves to emphasize the importance of trade routes that stretched to India and beyond. An insight into Roman long-distance trade is glimpsed from the *Periplus Maris Erythrae*i: a first-hand account by an unknown Egyptian merchant, dating from about AD60. It's a guide to the places and peoples as well as the navigation and trading between Egypt, particularly Berenice and the Horn of Africa, to the Persian Gulf, the Arabian Sea, and across the Indian Ocean to the southwest coast of India. Listing ports and coastal landmarks, it describes the journeys, noting safe anchorage and what goods are traded to and from each port. It also refers to trading across to China for silk, as well as down the east coast of Africa. Some historians theorize that it gives a misleading impression of the amount of trade between the Roman Empire and distant lands, while others consider

that the fact it's written as a guide shows that trade and travel around the Indian Ocean was well established. The same qualification can be made of the route of the Darb al-Arbein (Path of forty [days]), south from the Kharga Oasis. It is possible that it only became important in the late third century after the Blemmyes occupied Lower Nubia and cut off the thriving river trade up and down the Nile Valley; certainly, there was a Roman military presence at Kharga but the *Notitia* refers only to the *ala I Abasgorum*—a presence at a level that suggests monitoring, surveillance, and perhaps, a control over the main water sources rather than any great defensive options.

The army in Egypt under Augustus initially had three legions, but by AD23 there were only *legiones III Cyrenaica* and *XXII Deiotariana* at Nicopolis. In 119, *III Cyrenaica* left the province and in 127/8, *II Traiana* arrived and stayed for the next 200 years. With them in the province were auxiliaries (as attested by diplomas): three to four *alae* and about seven to ten *cohortes*, of which *ala Apriana* is attested 37/40–268/70, and *cohors II Ituraerorum equitata* from 39 to the *Notitia*. The main military centers were the legion(s) near Alexandria—to provide assistance to the provincial governor—units at the oases, and *auxilia* on the Nile at Syene (modern Aswan) and Maharraqa to guard against a southerly attack. The Kushites had attacked in this region c. 23BC and the Romans kept a garrison first at Qasr Ibrim and then Maharraqa. The main threat in later years were the Blemmyes and Nobatae, the latter were paid off but the Blemmyes grew in power and by the third century the border was regularly under threat with major attacks in 250, 253, 265, and 279–280. Diocletian created the provinces of Thebais Superior and Inferior and placed there *comitatensis* troops—*legiones I Maximiana Thebanorum* and *II Flavia Constantia*, although the Thebans moved to Thrace by 354 as Diocletian made peace with the tribes, moved the border back to Philae and paid them an annual stipend. The fact that the local gold mines had also declined reduced Roman interest in Nubia.

Another important mining area that required military attention was the quarrying operation at Mons Claudianus for granite and Mons Porphyrites for porphry (see p. 26). The army protected and helped the workers there as well as policing the *via Hadriani* down the Red Sea to Berenice.

ABOVE AND RIGHT Mons Claudianus, Egypt
Just under 400 miles south of Cairo, 2,296ft above sea level, lies the quarry complex of Mons Claudianus. Exploited from the first century AD until the mid-third century, Mons Claudianus quarry lies north of Luxor in the arid eastern desert of Upper Egypt. It's the source of an igneous granite-like stone called granodiorite that the Romans routinely shipped to Rome for use in imperial buildings—Hadrian's Villa at Tivoli, the Basilica Ulpia, and the columns of the Pantheon among many other projects. The Romans appear to have founded the settlement of Mons Claudianus (**ABOVE**) where an estimated thousand people lived. Many of the men worked in the quarry, they were not slaves but well-paid skilled and unskilled men and their families. The administration, however, was entirely Roman. Tool marks and wedge holes proved that the workers used iron tools and the area is still littered with abandoned columns (such as this **RIGHT**), pedestals, and basins. After quarrying, the stone was at least partially dressed, then moved by cart on a minimum five-day journey to the Nile, stopping at guarded way stations overnight, before shipping across the Mediterranean, barged up the Tiber, and then taken to Rome.

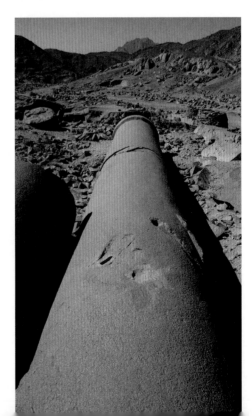

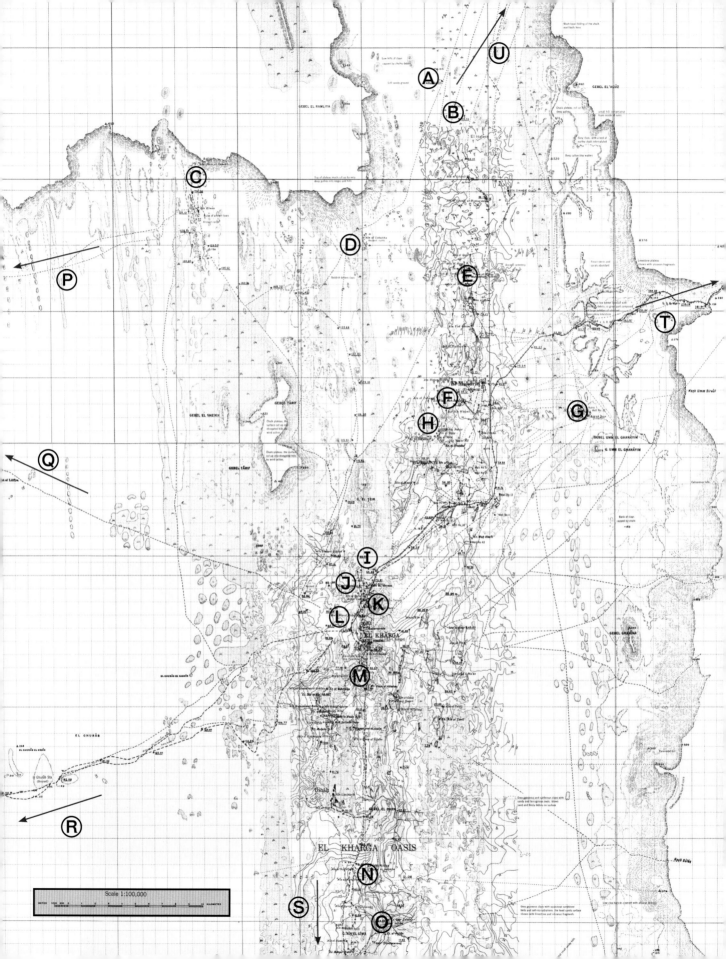

Oasis Magna (El-Kharga, Egypt)

One of the largest oases in the vastness of the Western Desert it consists of two depressions—the Kharga and Dakhla. It has been a vital transit point for desert caravans since ancient times. Kharga sits in a depression over 115 miles long north to south, and between 12 and 20 miles wide. To the west lies Dakhla, which runs for 60 miles east to west, 10 to 15 miles wide. It's the meeting point of a number of trans-Saharan caravan routes, in particular the Darb el-Arbain that connected Ancient Egypt to the interior of Africa and countries to the south.

A Qasr el-Gib/Ain Gib—fort
B Qasr el-Sumeira/Someira/Sumayra—fort
C Ain Umm ad Dabadib/el-Dabadib (**ABOVE RIGHT**)
D Qasr al Labakha/Labeka/Ain el-Lebekha (**RIGHT**)
E Ain Tauleib (p. 172)
F Ain el-Tarakwa—Roman settlement
G Deir el-Munira (El-Deir/Al-Deir) (p. 172)
H Ain el-Dabashiya—Roman settlement
I Deir Mustafa Kashef (monastery built over Roman fortress) (p. 172)
J Temple of Hibis (and **ABOVE**)
K Temple of Nadura
L Qasr el-Baramuni/Baramoudy—settlement and fort
M Qasr el-Nasima/Qasr el-Nessima—settlement and fort
N Qasr el-Ghuweita (p. 172)
O Qasr el-Zayyan—Greek temple; Roman fort
P Darb Ain Amur—path to Ain Amur and thence to Dakhla, the Inner Oasis. Kharga was the Outer Oasis: in Roman times the two were grouped together as Oasis Magna (Great Oasis)
Q Darb el-Ghubbari (Dust road)
R To Gilf Kebir
S Darb el-Arbain—the "Path of forty days"—said to be the duration of the path, but that depends where you're heading. (The path is 1,700 miles long.) To el-Qosseir, Qasr Baris, Dush, Upper Egypt, and Sudan
T Path to Abydos, Farshut, Dendera, and Luxor
U Darb el-Arbain north to Asyut and Middle Egypt

TOP Temple of Hibis (El-Kharga, Egypt)
Built under Persian emperor Darius I in the sixth century BC, the Romans added to this, the best preserved temple in the oasis.

ABOVE CENTER Umm el-Dabadib (El-Kharga, Egypt)
Fourth century AD Roman fort built with a commanding view of the southern plain. It is surrounded by a settlement laid out in a grid pattern and has subterranean aqueducts and wells. Sadly this site was badly damaged by looters in 2004.

ABOVE Ain El Labakha (El-Kharga, Egypt)
One of the chain of late Roman fortified settlements in the oasis, possibly part of Diocletian's reorganization of the southern frontier to control and benefit from the important trans-Saharan caravan routes and the mining and agricultural potential of the oasis.

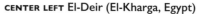

ABOVE LEFT Ain Tauleib (El-Kharga, Egypt)
Another Roman fort in the Oasis Magna. By the fourth century the waters had been so exploited that it ran dry in many areas. A number of sites were abandoned in the fifth century and much of the oasis became desert.

ABOVE Qasr el-Ghuweita (El-Kharga, Egypt)
The hilltop mud-brick fortress and temple was built on top of a much earlier settlement. Little is known about the Roman occupation, but troops could have been garrisoned here to guard the desert caravan trade routes. It also appears to have been a thriving agricultural community particularly celebrated for its vineyards and prized wines. An extensive Roman town surrounded the fort.

CENTER LEFT El-Deir (El-Kharga, Egypt)
This is one of the most impressive Roman fortresses in the oasis. It sits at the terminus of the caravan trail from the Nile Valley. Built by Diocletian, it had twelve towers. The Roman genius for water management saw them develop a deep-water well located in the central courtyard from where three tunnels fed water to the outlying buildings and fields via a system of gates and sluices. Trenches were covered by large flat stones to help prevent evaporation.

LEFT Deir Mustafa Kashef (El-Kharga, Egypt)
This remote place was a refuge for early Egyptian Copts (Christians) fleeing from Roman oppression in the third and fourth centuries. Dissident Christians were also banished to the oasis by the Roman authorities. Mustafa Kashef contains a sixth-century Coptic monastery built over the footings of a third-century Roman fortress.

ABOVE Qasr Dush, Egypt
South of the Kharga Oasis lies the first-century Domitian-era mud-brick fortress of el-Qasr. Overlooking the wide desert plain, this border fort would have housed a small garrison, possibly to control the southern end of the busy Darb el-Arbain. Herodotus described it as a route "traversed … in forty days." The Temple of Qasr Dush is dedicated to the goddess Isis and the god Serapis. The main gate (**ABOVE**) has an inscription dedicated by Trajan dated to 116. Dush's wells dried up in the fourth century and the town was abandoned.

BELOW AND RIGHT Ammon (Siwa Oasis, Egypt)
Ammon lies between the Qattara Depression and the Great Sand Sea in the Western Desert. Emperor Augustus banished political prisoners to distant Siwa, home of the temple and oracle to the ancient Libyan deity Ammon, although the Romans discouraged the god's worship. Roman tombs in the area indicate considerable wealth in the first and second centuries. It is probable that the Romans built a mud brick fort here and the remains of a Roman temple have recently been found dating to the reign of Emperor Antoninus Pius.

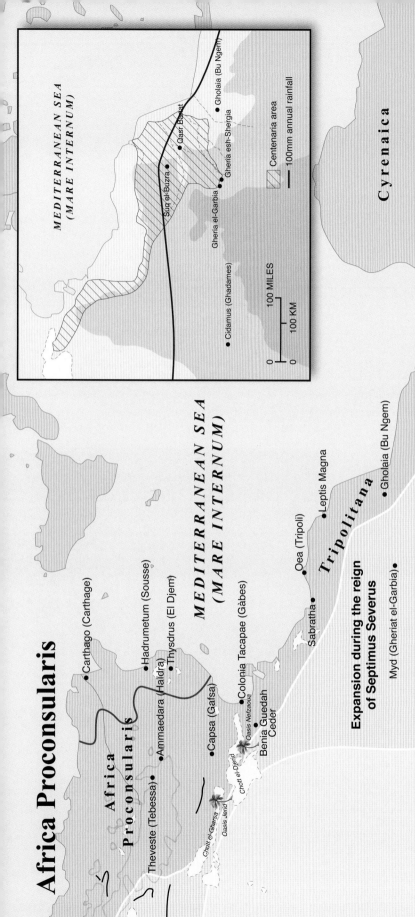

Africa Proconsularis

Africa Proconsularis

MEDITERRANEAN SEA (MARE INTERNUM)

- Carthago (Carthage)
- Hadrumetum (Sousse)
- Thysdrus (El Djem)
- Ammaedara (Haïdra)
- Theveste (Tebessa)
- Capsa (Gafsa)
- Colonia Tacapae (Gàbes)
- Benia Guedah Ceder
- Oasis Nefzaoua
- Oasis Jérid
- Chott el-Djérid
- Chott el-Gharsa
- Sabratha
- Oea (Tripoli)
- Leptis Magna

Tripolitana

- Myd (Gheriat el-Garbia)
- Gholaia (Bu Ngem)
- Cidamus (Ghadames)
- Garama (Germa)

Garamantes

Cyrenaica

- Arae Philaenorum (El Agheila)

Expansion during the reign of Septimus Severus

Brief military presence AD 203

After Carthage fell, the first Roman province on a new continent was formed: Africa. There were various reorganizations over the years, finally Diocletian split it into three: Africa Zeugitana/Byzacena/Tripolitania. The Vandals took it from Rome in 439 and held the area until Justinian's General Belisarius regained North Africa for the Eastern Empire in 533. The Byzantines held it until the Muslim conquest of 698.

—— Fossa Regia

—— Fossatum Africae

The first linear border in Africa was the *fossa Regia* that was constructed by Scipio Aemilianus after the capture of Carthage in 146BC. Pliny tells of "Africa is divided into two provinces, the old and the new, separated by a ditch." It wasn't military but administrative and an indication to the king of Numidia where Roman administration started. The later *limes Tripolitanus* were primarily concerned with control, taxes, and customs duties. Walls blocked unrestricted movement and channeled it through controlled gates. As the security position worsened, and the number of troops on the ground reduced—so *centenaria* fortified farms similar to the *qsur* in Cyrenaica, sprang up.

0 — 200 MILES

0 — 200 KM

Inset map

MEDITERRANEAN SEA (MARE INTERNUM)

- Cidamus (Ghadames)
- Súq el-Buzra
- Qasr Bshir
- Gheria el-Garbia
- Gheria esh-Shergia
- Gholaia (Bu Ngem)

Centenaria area

—— 100mm annual rainfall

0 — 100 MILES

0 — 100 KM

Africa Proconsularis

To the west of Egypt lay the coastal strip inherited from the conquest of the Carthaginians, bordering the land of the Berber Garamantes (today's southern Tunisia and Libya). A tranche of fortifications, known as the *limes Tripolitanus*, was constructed to deal with their raiding into the provinces of Tripolitana and Africa Proconsularis. The culture of the Garamantes was sophisticated, their wealth based on farming and trading. Their irrigation systems, which allowed cultivation of areas that are desert today, were, however, based on fossil water maintained by a large slave population, and when the water ran out, couldn't be sustained. Their track record of raiding went back to the Republic's civil wars. They had fought for the Numidian Jugurtha and the Mauretanian Juba. Their targets were the rich cities of Leptis Magna, Sabrathra, and Oea. After their coastal raid of 69, the Garamantes were conquered and turned into a client state, but there were always rogue tribes and nomads that continued to try their luck, so a first defense line of forts was begun in 75. These were linked with additional watchtowers and the forts upgraded with more substantial defenses by Hadrian.

Emperor Septimius Severus was born in Leptis and so paid particular attention to this part of the empire, improving the desert fortifications and pushing the borders southward. In 202–203 *legio III Augusta* campaigned against the Garamantes, capturing several towns and their capital Garama nearly 400 miles inland, deep in the Fezzan. This combination of a strengthened defense network of watchtowers and fortlets and an attack that penetrated to the very heart of the kingdom taught the Garamantes that they could no longer raid with impunity. Roman hegemony was substantially increased in the Fezzan and neighboring Numidia. Desert and mountain raiders could never be entirely subdued, but just as the geography of North Africa limited Roman expansion, it also limited the threats. This is evinced by the strength of the army for the whole region: a single legion and its auxiliary units widely spread out, and only very occasionally were extra troops brought in to help. The threat of raiders wasn't the only reason for the barriers. Taxation, movement control, and customs dues were also significant. However, *legio III Augusta*'s battles of the third century and the threats posed, for example, by the Austurians in the 360s, led to the construction of *centenaria*—fortified farms, possibly inhabited by veterans or military contingents. There is much debate about this and whether there are direct military connections, although frequently locations near other elements of the *limes* (watchtowers, *clausurae* walls to block defiles) are more likely to have a military purpose.

Sabratha (Sabratah, Libya)

The ancient coastal Phoenician trading port of Sabratha was annexed by Rome in 105BC during the reign of Julius Caesar to become part of the province of Africa Nova. The Romans greatly developed the city to become the westernmost of the ancient three cities of Regio Tripolitania, alongside Leptis Magna and Oea (modern Tripoli). Much of its wealth came through the trans-Saharan trade route from the African interior via Cidamus (the oasis of Ghadames, the Pearl of the Desert)—particularly ivory. Sabratha was sacked in the fourth century—probably by the Asturians—before being taken by the Vandals. Sabratha's decline, except for a brief resurgance after Justinian's reconquest, was completed under the Arabs, who moved the market to Tripoli.

ABOVE Myd (Gheriat el-Garbia, Libya)
The Romans knew that in the desert, if you controlled the oasis, you controlled trade. In 201 under Septimius Severus, a fort was built at Gheriat el-Garbia to guard the oasis, control the caravan route from the south, and to form part of the *limes Tripolitanus* to protect from raids by nomadic tribes. It was built on a hilltop near the Wadi Zemzem by soldiers of the *legio III Augusta* who then garrisoned the fort.

BELOW Qasr Banat, Libya
Qasr Banat was a *centenarium*, a third-century fortified farm, built along the *limes Tripolitanus* when *legio III Augusta* disbanded and the locals had to defend themselves. *Centenaria* were built to a standard design—a square plan with watchtowers, they were located so as to be able to communicate by line of sight with each other. This one was built on a steep hill along the Wadi Nefud and remained inhabited for centuries. It is possible that veteran soldiers were settled near such defenses given land to farm and defend. Built on fertile soil, they grew grain, olives, dates, and vegetables and farmed cows, goats, and dromedaries. This way they helped to green up the arid desert by building cisterns and dams to manage the waters. The remains of over 2,000 *centenaria* have been found in North Africa.

RIGHT Bani Walid, Libya
Tripolitania was already an important agricultural area before the Romans arrived, but they seem to have regulated and ordered it by improving the systems of water management and hence the viability of crop growing. They built dams, barriers, cisterns, embankments, and terrace walls to collect and retain every drop of the valuable seasonal rains that fell in this arid land. They grew drought-resistant species of crops which were then sent to market in Leptis Magna from where they were exported to Rome. Many monuments and pottery remains show agricultural motifs such as palm trees heavy with dates (as here) and dromedaries plowing the soil. Adept water technology was not just a Roman preserve, however, as was shown by the Garamantes and their remarkable system of water collection and usage. Unfortunately for them, it was fossil water and a finite commodity. Once it was used, it could not be replaced and the civilization struggled and did not survive in its original form.

RIGHT Suq al-Awty, Libya

The complex of buildings around Wadi Buzra include four *centenaria* (of which this is the northernmost, built on a northern spur), water cisterns, and a Byzantine church. This farming community—and the *centenaria* are sizable—survived into the seventh century, probably to the time of the Muslim takeover. The sophisticated water technology shows how farmers were able to make the desert bloom. Pottery finds show that it predated construction of the *limes Tripolitanus* that was promoted by Septimius Severus.

CENTER RIGHT AND BELOW Golaia (Bu Njem, Libya)

Dating to 253–259, *ostraca* found here detail daily duty reports by a *vexillatio* of *legio III Augusta*. They refer to the garrison doing surveillance operations and what can best be described as passport control. This further indicates that Roman intentions in North Africa were primarily financial: control of the people and trade, not one of expansion (with Septimius Severus being the exception to the rule). *III Augusta* served in the area from Augustan times but endured a rocky period in the third century when it fought on the wrong side, against the supporters of the two Gordians and for Maximinus Thrax. After the latter died and Gordian III acceded, the legion was disbanded around 218. It was reconstituted in 253 by Emperor Valerian using troops from Raetia and Noricum.

It's impossible to be precise about the garrison for the province but David Mattingly suggests in his monumental work, *Tripolitania*, that in Severan times, as well as *III Augusta*, it probably included two *cohortes*, *II Flavia Afrorum equitata* and *I Syrorum Sagittariorum* (initially *quinquenaria*, later *milliaria*—possibly after the legion was disbanded—probably *equitata*) and a *numerus Collatus* all of which are attested to have been present, as was *cohors VIII Fida* from the 250s.

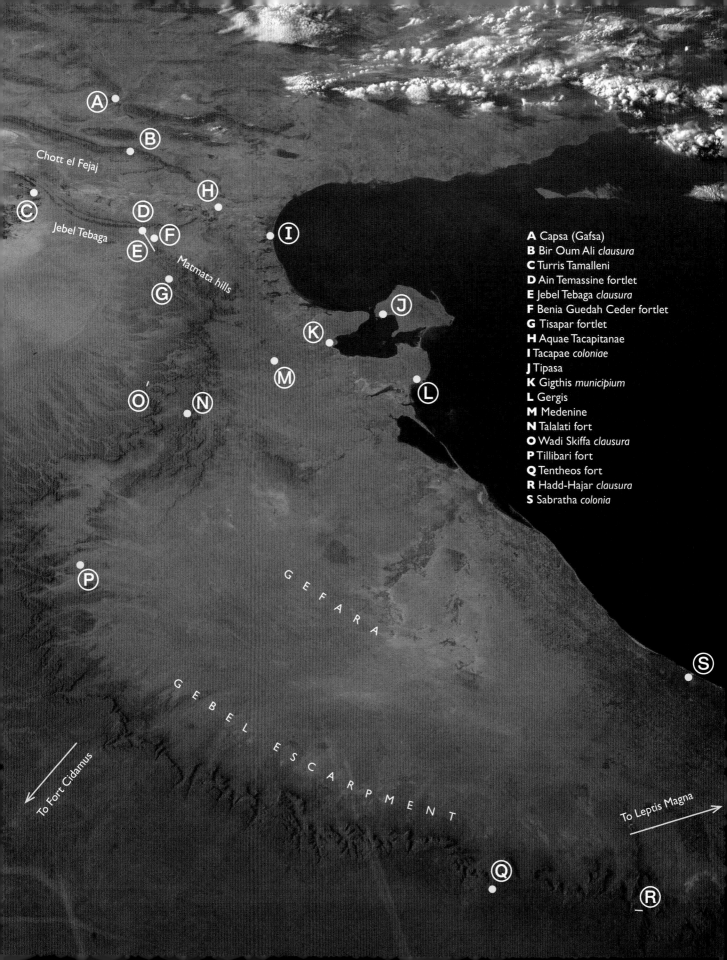

Chott el Fejaj

Jebel Tebaga

Matmata hills

A Capsa (Gafsa)
B Bir Oum Ali *clausura*
C Turris Tamalleni
D Ain Temassine fortlet
E Jebel Tebaga *clausura*
F Benia Guedah Ceder fortlet
G Tisapar fortlet
H Aquae Tacapitanae
I Tacapae *coloniae*
J Tipasa
K Gigthis *municipium*
L Gergis
M Medenine
N Talalati fort
O Wadi Skiffa *clausura*
P Tillibari fort
Q Tentheos fort
R Hadd-Hajar *clausura*
S Sabratha *colonia*

GEFARA

GEBEL ESCARPMENT

To Fort Cidamus

To Leptis Magna

OPPOSITE Africa proconsularis

Today's Tunisia is fertile in the north and east, mountainous in the northwest and southeast, with huge saltpans (*chotts*) in the southwest. The Gebel escarpment runs to the sea at Leptis Magna, it encloses the Gefara—today a shifting sea of sand-dunes—and while there is evidence of this encroaching Sabratha in antiquity it's possible that over-exploitation in classical times made it worse. There has been little, if any, climate change. The Romans built *clausurae*—walls to close off passes, wadis, and defiles as opposed to the long linear walls associated with Hadrian's Wall—which helped them control the movement of the pastoral nomads who practiced transhumance farming (movement of livestock between summer and winter pastures) as well as supplying some protection from raids from the south. Examples identified on the map are the *clausurae*: **B** at Bir Oum Ali (see also **ABOVE**); **E** in the Tebega Gap; **O** at Wadi Skiffa (see also p. 180); and **R** at Hadd-Hajar. Other than attacks from raiders—the most damaging

being the Asturians in the 360s—Africa proconsularis was reasonably peaceful in Roman times, until the civil war of the late 420s and the arrival of the Vandals. They had crossed over the Rhine at the end of 406 (so says Prosper of Aquitaine, although some argue for 405) and advanced along with the Alans through the empire leaving a swathe of destruction behind them. Defeated by the Visigoths, in 417/8 what was left of the Vandals and Alans crossed to North Africa and by 430 were at the gates of Hippo Regius. In 439 they took Carthage and cut off Rome's grain supply—a disaster from which the empire never recovered.

ABOVE Bir Oum Ali *clausura*, Tunisia

Nearly 20ft high and 4.5ft wide, the *clausura* at Bir Oum Ali was a substantial wall. The channel visible at **A** has aroused some discussion. Could be a walkway? It's a bit thin. Could it be a water channel? If so, it needs to be linked to a cistern. The channel was topped with inverted v-shaped capstones (**B**).

ABOVE Fort Benia Guedah Ceder, Tunisia
Beyond the *limes Tripolitanus* is a late Roman small square fort on the south side of Tebaga Gap that guarded the only passage through the Matmata hills. Running broadly north–south, it gives access from the hostile southern desert to the green and fertile coastal plains to the north and east. To control the pass, the Romans built the Jebel Tebaga *clausura*, a 10.5-mile linear earthwork from Jebel Tebaga to the foothills of the Jebel Melab. Passing close by the fort, it consisted of walls on the scarps of the jebels, watchtowers, and a ditch and bank across the valley floor. The southern end of the wall is at the foot of the mountains on Jebel Melab, the northern end on the ridge of Jebel Tebaga.

LEFT Wadi Skiffa *clausura*, Tunisia
Modern roadworks allowed a section of the wall of the Wadi Skiffa *clausura* to be identified—as shown here. It's 25ft wide.

Thysdrus (El Djem, Tunisia)

The Roman amphitheater at Thysdrus was built around 238 as a symbol of the town's prosperity and importance. Built of stone blocks, it had an estimated capacity of 35,000. It is thought to have been ordered by the local proconsul Gordian, who later (briefly) became emperor Gordian III. The amphitheater was used mainly for gladiator shows and chariot races. It was the third largest Roman amphitheater ever built but was possibly never finished. The city was founded by Julius Caesar in 46BC as Thysdrus, following the Punic wars. There was already a third-century BC Punic settlement at the site. As the center of an important olive growing region, Thysdrus became the leading provider of olive oil in North Africa. The town had an estimated population of between 20–30,000 and became very wealthy—that wealth went into both public and private buildings. In 238 (as the amphitheater was under construction) Rome imposed a tax on olive oil. This sparked a North-Africa wide rebellion and the murder of the imperial procurator. The Romans ruthlessly repressed the rebellion and Thysdrus was sacked by soldiers loyal to emperor Maximinus Thrax. The city never fully recovered. As the borders crumbled in 695, Queen Kahina made her final stand against the Muslim conquerors here.

Mauretania and Numidia

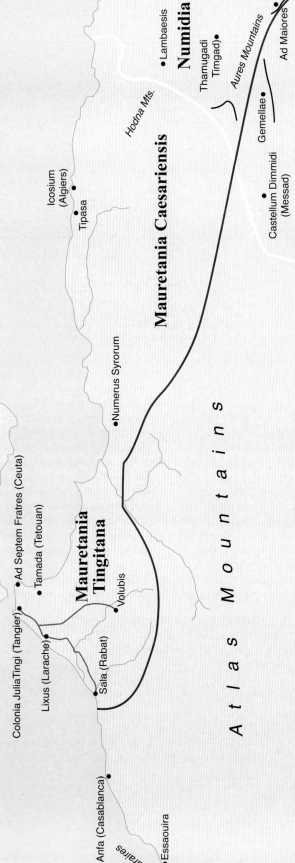

Baetica

*MEDITERRANEAN SEA
(MARE INTERNUM)*

Mauretania Tingitana

Colonia Julia Tingi (Tangier) •
• Ad Septem Fratres (Ceuta)
• Tamada (Tetouan)
Lixus (Larache) •
• Volubis
Sala (Rabat) •

Anfa (Casablanca) •
• Essaouira
Îles Purpuraires

A t l a s   M o u n t a i n s

• Numerus Syrorum

Mauretania Caesariensis

Icosium
(Algiers) •
• Tipasa

Hodna Mts.

Numidia

• Lambaesis
Thamugadi
(Timgad) •
Aures Mountains
• Ad Maiores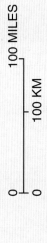

Castellum Dimmidi
(Messad) •
• Gemellae

The Atlantic coast of Africa was a long way from Rome, but the reach of empire enfolded it in the first century AD. The Phoenicians had, of course, got there first and there was already some trade down the west coast. The Romans turned Sala into a port whose most important cargoes were from Essaouira, Anfa, and Mogador in the Îles Purpuraires, where Tyrian purple dye was made. It's possible that traders went fuurther south into the Gulf of Guinea. The two provinces of Mauretania Tingitana and Caesariensis were set up in AD 44, and parts survived under Roman rule until the Vandals arrived in 429. The two provinces were linked by sea rather than road because of distance—but also because the tribes were never subdued completely.

—— Furthest extent of Roman power

—— *Fossatum Africae*

100 MILES
0   100 KM

Lambaesis, Algeria

Legio III Augusta was founded in 30BC and immediately went to Africa. It stayed there until the late fourth century, surviving a decimation in AD18 and being disbanded in 238 for choosing the wrong side in a civil war. It did a lot of building: its main bases were Haedra to AD14, Ammaedara until 75, and Theveste (Tebessa) until 128 when it moved to Lambaesis where it stayed until it was disbanded. Emperor Hadrian visited that year during his African tour and inspected the legion. A rare monument records parts of his *adlocutio,* inscribed on the base of an honorific column on the parade ground outside the fort. It describes a soldier's duties and how he should perform them. In it he reprimanded *cohors II Hispanorum* for being too reckless, but praised *legio III Augusta*'s horsemen, "…You performed the most difficult task, throwing the javelin in full armor … I also approve your spirit." He also praised the *principes* after an exercise in fortification building, "What others would take several days to finish, you completed in one day. You have built a wall, a lengthy construction … with large, heavy and irregular stones. You have cut a ditch in a straight line through hard and rough gravel and have leveled it smooth." Most of *III Augusta*'s strength stayed in Mauretania although *vexillationes* were used to garrison forts and fortlets along the *limes*. While the legion's main duties would be control of the border, North Africa was certainly not always peaceful. The best-known conflicts (outside the regular emperor/usurper issues) were in 15–24 when they resisted the Tacfarinas rebellion led by ex-soldiers; the war against the Moors in Antoninus Pius's reign; the war against the Berber "Five Peoples" that caused the legion to be refounded in 253. That war lasted till 260 before flaring up again in 289–297. The legion also was involved in fighting elsewhere—Parthia, during the Marcommanic Wars, and Judaea during Jewish revolts. Photos show the Arch of Commodus (**LEFT**) and the fort's *principia*.

Mauretania and Numidia

The final part of the 2,500-mile long African border, the *limes Mauretaniae* and *Numidiae* wasn't a continuous line, but a collection of defenses that catered for the more complicated geography at the end of the continent. This included the mountains and valleys of the Atlas and the Rif, peopled by hostile tribes, as well as the Atlantic and Mediterranean coasts, the hunting grounds of pirate raiders. The Rif and the Atlas were never permanently occupied by Rome, whose presence was originally limited to the fertile coastal region in the east based closely around Carthage and the Bagrada Valley, relying upon older client state links with local inland tribes.

The year AD17 saw an invasion of Numidia by desert tribes (Musulamii, Mauri, and Garamantes) commanded by Tacfarinas, a Numidian who had been a Roman auxiliary. *Legio III Augusta* could not cope by itself and another legion (*IX Hispania*) was brought in to tip the balance. By 24 Tacfarinas had been killed and the revolt ended.

Colonia Marciana Ulpia Traiana Thamugadi (Timgad, Algeria)

Trajan planted a military colony at Thamugadi in 100 as part of his objective to encircle the Aurès mountain massif that harbored a continuing source of resistance to Roman rule. In turn they were connected by road to the Flavian outposts on their northern flank. This defense doesn't seem to have been extended in Hadrian's time, but the encirclement was (probably) completed in 145 under Antoninus Pius when the road to Lambaesis was extended to Vescera and completed the encirclement.

In the west, Augustus had supported King Juba II as a client in Mauretania. Juba had grown up in Rome and had been on campaign with the then Octavian. He and his successor, his son Ptolemy, were loyal to Rome. Then Caligula had Ptolemy assassinated in 40 while on a visit to the capital and the kingdom rebeled. It took four years and many casualties to reassert Rome's control, and Claudius ended Mauretania's client kingdom status in 44, annexing it to make two provinces: Mauretania Tingitana (northern Morocco) with its capital at Tingis (Tangiers) and Mauretania Caesariensis (central and western Algeria), with its capital at Caesarea (Cherchell). The River Malva and the Rif mountains served as the border between them, but the Rif's bulk prevented land communications between Caesarea and Tingis, so they were normally maintained by sea.

The Mauretanian coastal cities grew extremely rich providing Rome with grain, olive oil, fruit, and salted fish—there are many *cetariae*, artifical ponds used in the salting of fish and in the production of fish sauce, as well as some evidence of kilns making the salazón amphora in which they were transported, although many also came from Baetica on the Iberian peninsuls. The area also supplied exotic African animals for the amphitheater.

All along the North African coast, the cities thrived. Carthage became the largest and richest city in the western empire after Rome; hundreds of new colonies were founded in the first and second centuries, intensifying land use, as North Africa became Rome's major supplier for grain and oil. Colonies on higher farmland inland (Dougga, Djémila, Timgad, Volubilis, and El Djem) became successful commercial cities.

All these developments were incentives for resentful local tribes who were squeezed out, and untamed mountain ones looking for a raiding opportunity. (Mauretanian light cavalry were appreciated by the Romans, who recruited them for the *auxilia*.) There were sporadic revolts and raids, so the defenses were gradually built to monitor and cope with these occasional problems.

The work of Colonel Jean Baradez in the immediate postwar period suggested that there were long linear boundaries, the *Fossatum Africae*. It is in Mauretania and Numidia that the main sections of this have been identified, despite the inevitable fast erosion in the mountains. The Hodna or Bou Taleb section runs for about 60 miles, enclosing the eastern end of the Hodna mountains for the defense of Cellas and Macri. The Tobna section is about 30 miles long and encloses part of the Awras and Zab mountains, defending Mesarfelta. Running for some

Tipasa (Tipaza, Algeria)

Originally an important ancient Punic trading port and market, Tipasa was built on three small hills directly overlooking the Mediterranean. Following emperor Claudius's conquest of the kingdoms of Mauretania, it became a Roman *colonia* in Mauretania Caesariensis and the emperor granted its residents *Jus Latii*—the rights of fellow Roman citizens. Rome used Tipasa as a strategic base for its military campaigns. At some point the town was surrounded by a defensive wall just over a mile long, built to repel invaders. Tipasa reached its peak during the reign of Emperor Septimius Severus by which time it was important and wealthy enough to become a *municipium*. As Christianity made inroads into Roman life, increasing numbers of Christian buildings appeared, although the majority of inhabitants were not Christian. In around 372 the Vandals raided Tipasa and imposed Christian rule, causing many inhabitants to flee to Spain to avoid persecution. Soon after, the city's wealth declined and it disappeared in the sixth century.

40 miles, the Gemellae section was the most southerly of the Roman defenses—at the tip of the Sahara—with the important and impressive legionary castra at Gemellae at its center, protecting the city of Vescera.

While a number of longer lengths have been identified, more recent research has shown that the borders were more nuanced than this—and certainly less structured than Hadrian's Wall or the Germanic–Raetian *limes*. The distances involved and the desert environment precluded long linear barriers with the requisite garrisons. Indeed, *III Augusta* was the only legion in the area and even with *auxilia* units would have been spread too thinly to do this. This doesn't mean that the frontiers were disorganized. The fortifications consisted of various sizes and combinations of ditch and embankment, stone or mud-brick walls and forts, interspaced with watchtowers, usually within sight of each other. As has been discussed earlier, there were two different types of wall, the longer *fossata* and the shorter *clausurae*. The Romans were sensible enough to know that they could not produce a cordon sanitaire and their troops—and the *auxilia*—were trained for rapid response, but some places were blocked to channel travelers through gates that could be controlled.

An example of the short blocking walls is provided south of Sala (Rabat). It started out as a ditch and earthwork system at the end of the first century AD running some 7 miles from Seguia Faraoun, on the Atlantic coast to Dar Daqios, on the River Bouregreg. There were watchtowers either end and nearby the fort Exploratio Ad Mercurios. The wall was rebuilt in stone in the second century.

Tingitana had to be heavily defended. Eleven inscriptions dated between 170 and 280 identify agreements made between Rome and various tribes of the highlands, such as the unreliable Baquates. All to no avail. The province kept contracting in the face of regular raids and in spite of a significant influx of troops. Save for the walled port of Sala, the big cities were abandoned by the military in the 280s, although places like Volubis and Lixus still had populations a century later.

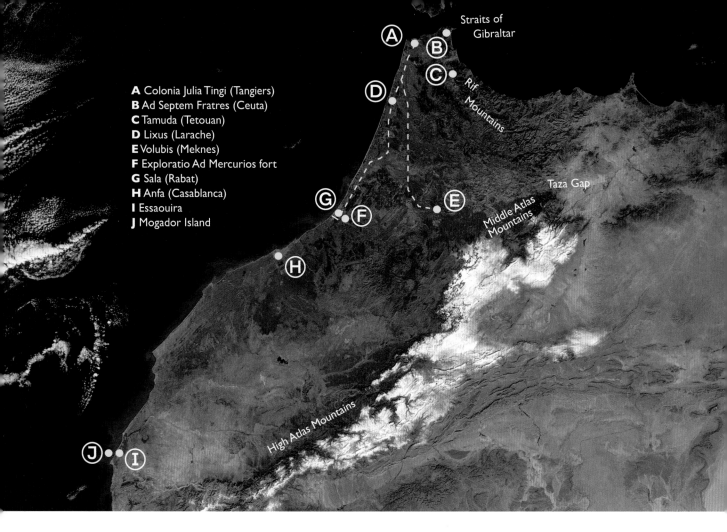

A Colonia Julia Tingi (Tangiers)
B Ad Septem Fratres (Ceuta)
C Tamuda (Tetouan)
D Lixus (Larache)
E Volubis (Meknes)
F Exploratio Ad Mercurios fort
G Sala (Rabat)
H Anfa (Casablanca)
I Essaouira
J Mogador Island

ABOVE Mauretania Tingitana. Note the *clausura* at Sala (below **G**). To date there is no indication of land links with Mauretania Caesarea through the Tebega Gap. The tribes in this area were happy to sign treaties, but they didn't hold to them. The Romans brought in troops and built forts—especially around Volubis but this couldn't stop the contraction of Roman territory to enclaves around Tingi and Sala.

By the time of the *Notitia*, Tingitana had a *comitatenses* legion (*II Flavia Constantia*) and possibly one *pseudocomitatenses* (*Constantiaci*). The Vandals occupied part of the country when they crossed from Spain in 426; they returned in 533 after having been expelled from Carthage by Belisarius, but were defeated again. The Visigoths moved into Tingitana in the 540s before being pushed out of the country by Byzantine troops. The peace was kept by the *dux et praeses provinciae Mauretaniae et Caesariensis* until the Umayyeds took the area in 709.

Auxilia units attested in Mauretania Tingitana (end first/early second centuries AD)

Cohortes
peditata
I Asturum et Callaecorum civium Romanorum
I Ituraeorum civium Romanorum
I Lemavorum civium Romanorum
II Hispana Vasconum civium Romanorum
II Hispanorum civium Romanorum
III Gallorum felix
V Delmatarum civium Romanorum

Cohortes
equitata
II Syrorum sagittaria milliaria
III Asturum Pia Fidelis civium Romanorum
IV Gallorum civium Romanorum
IV Tungrorum (vexillatio)

Alae
I Augusta Gallorum Gemelliana
I (Flavia) Gallorum Tauriana Victrix
III Asturum Pia Fidelis civium Romanorum
I Hamiorum Syrorum sagittaria

Source M. Roxan (1973)

ABOVE Tamuda (Tetouan, Morocco)
The ancient Berber/Phoenician city was destroyed by the Romans c. AD40–41 and in the next century a fort was erected. Growth ensued thanks to industry (there's a possibility that the Romans even processed whales here) and the largesse of Trajan and Severus. The fort gained exterior, semicircular towers. The *Notitia* places an *ala Herculea* here at the end of the fourth century.

BELOW Sala (Rabat, Morocco)
The Romans improved Sala's Phoenician port from which they reached the Îles Purpuraires. Here, in a factory on Mogador, they made from sea snails Tyrian purple, the dye used to provide the stripes on senatorial togas. At Sala, Exploratio Ad Mercurios fort and a seven-mile defensive structure made up of ditch, *clausura* wall, and watchtowers were built to block tribes moving down the coastal road (which went to Anfa). Sala continued as an enclave until the fifth century.

5

Border Life

Almost every Roman fortification or camp, whatever the size, had its camp followers. From courtesans to slavers, the military provided business opportunities that ensured a *vicus* grew up immediately beyond the fort's ditches—and in some cases seems to have been allowed for during the fort's construction. This was the civilian settlement for people—often not Romans—who supplied and serviced the military for much of their leisure and personal needs. A *vicus* (plural *vici*) was usually extant during the occupation of an auxiliary fort and disappeared when the garrison left. *Canabae* were usually associated with a legionary fortress and was accordingly bigger, with more status. These sometimes grew into the towns we know today.

Outside a fort, there were areas that were essential for the conducting of military matters: parade grounds, and fields and meadows for grazing animals (particularly necessary for auxiliary cavalry units). There would be other important structures such as bathhouses, temples, and cemeteries that were closely linked to army life.

Not as much is known about the *vici* as one might expect—partly because of their generally temporary nature—but their footprints have been found (athough not necessarily excavated) around many Roman fortifications. Historical and contemporary descriptions of *vici* were described as "frustratingly ambiguous" by Robin Birley, hence the considerable speculation as to their nature and cultural makeup. Often the size of the *vicus* was much greater than the extent of its associated fort, but they varied enormously. They grew and flourished with the importance of their accompanying fort and declined when the fort ceased occupation and the garrison withdrew. The secondary *vicus* Ad Legionem at León was in use from the middle to late first century AD to around 260 when it was abandoned. That date, of course, rings an immediate bell: the start of Procopius's Gallic Empire. It is noticeable that not all *vici* were abandoned when garrisons left. Some larger *vici* survived the withdrawal of the Roman military establishment to become *civitas*: examples include Nida (Frankfurt-Heddernheim), Isca Dumnoniorum (Exeter), and Viroconium (Wroxeter). This may have been helped by outside factors—their involvement with local tribes or importance on trade routes.

The majority of border military *vici* seem to have started as street settlements built on open ground on the "safe" Roman side of the frontier, alongside the main access road (*via principalis*) in front of the main gate (*porta praetoria*) to the fort—although there are plenty of exceptions to this rule. Over time they usually developed random street patterns and networks of paths and alleys. Only very occasionally a *vicus* grew within the annex of a fort. The commonest type of structure appears to have been long, narrow strip buildings lying at right angles to the street (well illustrated in the aerial view of Vindolanda, **RIGHT**). These had a continuous roof and

usually a narrow open front and a porticus (reminiscent of the street vendors in Pompeii). The open front could probably be closed and faced the street where customers were served. They seem to have had a dual purpose for both commercial and domestic use that was flexible enough to be changeable. In the front section were taverns, shops, and kitchens, living quarters, and storage areas. At the back were the latrines, stables, any workshops and outhouses, rubbish pits, and ideally, a well for water. Very occasionally these buildings had cellars. Larger settlements had squares directly in front of the gates where military and civilians could do business. In a very few places such as Noviomagus (Nijmegen), Carnuntum (Bad Deutsch-Altenburg), and Vindonissa (Brugg-Windisch), forum-like remains have been unearthed but their purpose is unknown. It's possible that they served as marketplaces. There's no doubt that some *vici* were less salubrious than others. Not all could benefit from stone foundations. More temporary structures made of turf, mud, and wood have left little to no trace and certainly would have been present in numbers.

Three main types of *vicus* are generally agreed, although some developed elements of each other. The first, and commonest, is the linear type already described which accreted around the principal access road to the main gate. The second is known as a ring-type *vicus* and was aligned on the side facing away from the fort beside a circular bypass around the camp. This type appears to have developed outside the surrounding ditches and road of a fort garrisoning a mounted cohort. Examples of places include Celeusum (Pförring) and Niederbieber. Archaeologists speculate that such large elongated open spaces were needed to drill and exercise the horses and their riders.

The third and least common form of *vicus* is known as tangent-type and these seem to have been built where the fort itself lies in an exposed location so the *vicus* is a short distance away on safer ground. One such is at Sulz where the fort lies on a spur on top of steep slopes about 100yd above the River Neckar. For this type, the buildings of the *vicus* are aligned along the highway, but facing away from the fort to which it is connected by a short length of road.

Many legionary fortresses in border areas have a second *vicus*, c. 1.5 miles away. In Spain, *legio VII Gemina*'s camp at León has one, on the other side of the River Torio, referred to as Ad Legionem. Archaeological investigations showed the presence of buildings that open onto the street—probably shops or *tabernae*. These are not strip buildings as in the Housesteads *vicus*, but what are termed "complex" buildings, with peristyle-like courtyards. Similar constructions have been found in other locations: at Ladenburg (Lopodunum), Wimpfen, and elsewhere. Some of the buildings have porches or porticus to protect pedestrians from rain or excessive sun. In one medical and surgical instruments may identify a doctor's accommodation. Cirdan (2017) suggests that this was "established at an important communication hub and functioning as a *mansio*." The reason for the distance from the fortress is because of legal restrictions on tenants or land ownership close to the legionary fortress. The distance of 1.5 miles meant that the *vicus* or *canaba* was on non-military ground where land could be bought and sold. Here camp followers, traders, and retired servicemen could form their own legal authorities to control the settlement, and in time try to acquire rights to become a *municipium*.

Military *vici* are almost exclusively found in the frontier regions of the Roman empire, notably in Britain along the northern frontier and Hadrian's Wall, where fewer than sixty recorded examples have been found. There are 192 known *vici* discovered in what was Gaul. All of them vary considerably in purpose, layout, and size, but they are all associated with a fort or fortress.

In northern Britain and Germany archaeologists have studied the existence of the *vicus* and concluded, broadly, that they offered localized trade and manufacturing to the garrison, particularly when the unit needed supplies and resources that the military establishment was not necessarily able to easily source. So the *vici* were closely associated with military business as well as pleasure. Because of the temporary nature of the *vici* and the perishability of the building materials, archaeologists have found few remains on which to speculate as to how the *vicus* actually worked. The evidence that has been found indicates that non-local people lived in the *vicus* including foreign merchants and traders who brought in produce and goods from much further afield.

Initially, a *vicus* was made up of camp followers—*lixae* (sutlers) and an assorted collection of people selling various services to the garrison: "Traders, merchants, craftsmen, tavern keepers, musicians, prostitutes, actresses, physicians, priests, soothsayers, along with the soldiers' wives, concubines, children, veterans, servants and slaves." (Morillo 2012) The latter selection—wives, families, servants, and slaves, are groups of camp-followers often played down when discussing the Roman Army. Slaves and servants were also a part of army life and while many of these may have been involved directly in camp, there would have been many who had to use the *vicus*. And there were a lot of servants. Tacitus may have been exaggerating when he said that in AD69 Vitellius's 60,000 army was accompanied by "still greater was the number of camp-followers" (*Histories* 2:87) or of Antonius's army at Cremona that "Forty thousand armed men burst into the town; the number of camp-followers and servants was even greater" (*Histories* 3:33). The proximity of the *vici* to the fort (as at Vindolanda) shows that the community was closely involved.

A Roman soldier's life was a harsh one—constant training, parades, marching, building, digging (lots of digging), and occasionally fighting. He was provided with adequate sustenance, lodgings, and kit. Any little extras, let alone luxuries, he had to buy for himself from his wages. Often billeted miles from civilization, the only place he could spend his money was in the *vicus*—so the enterprising locals were only too pleased to provide the extras that soldiers wanted. The *vicus* was where the serving Roman soldier went to relax and play. Outside the strict confines of the fort or military encampment he could eat and drink, bathe, worship, gamble, consort with women, barter for items of kit or equipment, or even sometimes, it seems that the odd entrepreneurial soldier could start growing a small sideline of his own by going into business with a local dealer or trader.

A successful *vicus* quickly developed temples, a bathhouse (unlike the legionary fortresses)—always outside the fortress because of the danger of fire—bakery (ditto), and cemetery alongside the numerous drinking establishments, food vendors, gambling houses, and brothels. Evidence of taverns has been found at Caersws and Housesteads, where gaming counters and dice were discovered as well. Kilns for the making of local pottery production were also common. Archaeological finds show that metal working existed in *vici* and even that military equipment was made and maintained by local craftsmen. Pottery kilns have been found, as well as brickworks, glass-making, bronze-making and bone-working facilities. Prostitutes (*scorta*) would have been around, possibly in dedicated brothels, although no definite evidence has been found for this.

Prostitutes followed the army and on a famous occasion Scipio Aemilianus expelled 2,000 of them from the camp at Numantia in 134BC. That was an army on campaign. Garrisons were different. As *vici* developed they would have provided access to prostitutes, but also to families. This is from a famous Pompeiian brothel.

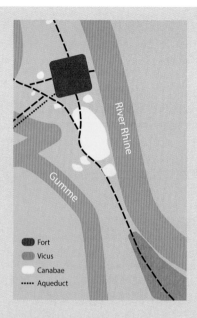

ABOVE *Vicus Bonnensis* developed between the Rhine and the watery marshlands of the Gumme—the remnant of an old oxbow bend of the river. Note the aqueduct entering the fortress from springs near Hardtberg.

RIGHT Gladiator carving on show in the Bonn Haus der Geschichte.

Castra Bonnensia (Bonn, Germany)

This legionary base developed from a small Augustan auxiliary fort built around 16–13BC, opposite the confluence of the Rhine and the much smaller River Sieg. The legionary fortress was erected in wood for *legio I Germanica* around 35. This was later replaced in stone for *legio XXI Rapax*, which stayed until c. 82, and *I Minervia* that was still in situ into the middle of the fourth century. During this time a significant *vicus Bonnensis* grew up a mile or so to the south, home to as many as 10,000 people. Well placed on the road and river transport link, Bonn thrived and public buildings were constructed: a Gallo-Roman temple, baths and public latrinae, and a public square—probably a forum and marketplace. There seems to have been a busy port.

Typical long strip houses lined paved streets. With shops at the front and workshops and living quarters at the back, archaeology has revealed bakery ovens, pottery kilns, and gardens.

Unlike the *vici* that developed near auxiliary forts—such as those on Hadrian's Wall, for example—those that developed around legionary fortresses often survived through the centuries and formed the basis for modern cities. Bonn survived incursions by the Franks, before the inhabitants moved into the fort for protection.

Most Romans were deeply religious—or at least superstitious—and would worship at temples and cult buildings. The soldiers' favorite was Mithras, and many a camp had its own Mithraeum. Such temples were often found in or near the *vicus*, and would often include temples for local gods as well. Inscriptions at Lambaesis identify gods and goddesses worshiped there: Rome's big three, Jupiter, Juno, and Minerva; other Roman divinities—Aesculapius, Apollo, Ceres, Diana, Janus, Hercules, Mars, Mercury, Neptune, Pluto, Salus, and Venus; foreign gods—Jupiter Depulsor, Dolichenus, or Heliopolitanus, Cybele, Iorhobol, Isis, Liber and Libera, Malagbel, Medauros, or Mithra, Serapis; and the African gods—the dii Mauri, Caelestis, Africa, and especially, Saturn.

There is evidence of *vici* around many of the desert forts, and of veterans congregating near to where they had served. At Gholaia there was a large local *vicus* north of the *porta principalis sinistra* that sprawled to almost entirely surround the fort. Unfortunately there is very little hard evidence about it, although it has been estimated to contain about 500 villagers, many of which were probably veterans. The Gholaia *ostraca* mention a temple for Ammon, as well as other temples, and a dromedary station. To sustain the villagers and the garrison, the Romans developed dams and dykes to collect and contain the regular if unpredictable rains. This meant that the locals could grow olives for oil and grain for bread, so the garrison did not have to depend on distant supplies for food. From the *ostraca* found in the fort it appears that the Garamantes and the Romans had a tacit agreement that the former would help them capture runaway slaves and return them to the embrace of empire.

Veterans

The idea that a veteran should end his service with a golden handshake was not a time-honored right. It was the veterans of Gaius Marius, Julius Caesar, and Pompey who pushed for land grants at the end of their service. It became a necessity under Augustus, who set up the *aerarium militare* (military treasury) to provide pensions (*praemia*). During the Principate some received cash rather than land, but many veterans' colonies were introduced—sometimes with the ulterior motive of having soldier supporters in strategic locations. Large numbers of veterans were settled by Julius Caesar—15,000 between 47 and 44BC—but it was after Philippi and Actium and when Augustus reduced the number of legions from over fifty to twenty-eight that significant numbers were settled: 44,000 in 41BC, 10–15,000 in 36BC, and after Actium, 50,000 more were settled around 30BC. In total he identifies in Res Gestae that he settled 300,000 veterans either in colonies or sent home with land or money. Initially, he was able to find land for them cheaply or by appropriation. As time went on, this became more difficult and he had to resort to payments rather than land.

The number of veterans discharged was much smaller thereafter. If a full-strength legion of 6,000 men served for twenty-five years, each legion would relese 240 veterans a year, but epigraphic evidence suggests that the proportion was actually less than half: J. C. Mann quotes a dedication at Viminacium recording that of the men recruited to *legio VII Claudia* in AD134–135, the number discharged (probably in AD160) was 239–120 a year. The others would presumably have died from action or natural causes. Other epigraphic evidence gives smaller numbers. From thirty legions, if the number was 100 from each, 3,000 veterans would have been discharged each year.

After the conquests of the Augustan period up to the reign of Hadrian, these men would often be given land in recently conquered territory or areas that needed populating. However, it seems that most veterans just didn't want to move: they prefered to retire near to where they served, and Hadrian was the last emperor to found such colonies. In later years the legions became less mobile and Diocletian's reforms saw fixed *limitanei* take over the protection of the borders. This tied the veterans even more to a location.

Ironically, after so many centuries that Roman soldiers hadn't been allowed to marry, in the second century recruitment began to depend on sons of serving soldiers or veterans—in Africa as early as Hadrian's reign. The alternative was *peregrini*. By the third century hereditary service by veterans' sons became obligatory if a veteran was to receive his *praemia*. Legionaries always had formed relationships and sired children—as is amply attested by discharge diplomas and funerary inscriptions. The families almost certainly lived locally and would have packed up their goods and chattels and followed the legion or cohort whenever it was relocated, moving and following time and again as the military marched to new camps.

Today's army brats know that feeling only too well!

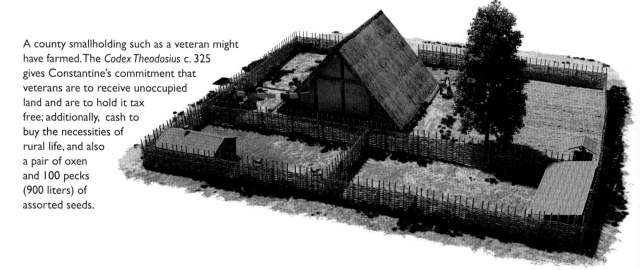

A county smallholding such as a veteran might have farmed. The *Codex Theodosius* c. 325 gives Constantine's commitment that veterans are to receive unoccupied land and are to hold it tax free; additionally, cash to buy the necessities of rural life, and also a pair of oxen and 100 pecks (900 liters) of assorted seeds.

Glossary

Lixus, on the River Loukkos in Morocco, was one of the main cities in Mauretania Tingitana. It was abandoned as late as the seventh century.

aerarium militare Military treasury in Rome that paid army pensions (*praemia*).

Agri Decumates Area at boundary of Germania Superior and Raetia. See p. 101.

ala pl *alae* Cavalry wing made up of *turmae*. See p. 42.

auxilia Troops from the empire who were not Roman citizens fighting in the Roman Army. See p. 40.

barbaricum Northern tribal areas not controlled by Rome.

beneficiarii A soldier on special assignment; *B. consularis*, soldier attached to staff of a provincial governor.

bucellari The escort retinues of important people.

burgus pl *burgi* Late empire watchtowers. See p. 59.

calo pl *calones* Slaves—in a legion, usually servants/grooms etc.

canaba pl *canabae* The civilian areas that grew up around legionary fortresses. See also *vicus*.

castellum pl *castella* Fortlet, also used for watchtower.

castrum pl *castra* Fort. *C. aestiva/hiberna* = summer/winter quarters.

centenarium pl *centenaria* Fortified farm (mainly in Tripolitania: see pp. 176–177.

classis Fleet as in *classis Britannica*.

clausura pl *clausurae* The walls built to close defiles or wadis; not to be confused with *fossata*.

cohors pl *cohortes* The building block of the legions, a unit of 400–800 men either on foot (*peditata*) or a mixture of infantry and cavalry (*equitata*).

colonia The highest rank of city, usually peopled by citizens (often retired veterans), sometimes converted from legionary fortresses. See also *municipium*.

comitatenses The late empire units that composed field armies as opposed to the fixed *limitanei* (qv).

contubernium The men sharing a tent—usually ten of whom eight were soldiers (including the *decanus*) and two servants.

decanus Commander of *contubernium*.

decurio Cavalry commander of a *turma*.

Dominate Term used to mean the empire from the Tetrarchy (qv). See also Principate.

dux pl *duces* Diocletian reorganizations led to more but smaller provinces. The military forces in place (*limitanei*) there were headed by a *dux*.

fabrica pl *fabricae* Workshop, also armaments factory.

foederati Non-citizen, usually Italian, soldiers in the early days of the Republic. Under treaty, they agreed to fight for Rome. In the late empire the *foederati* were "barbarians" and the treaty agreed the duration—and payment—for their service.

fossa Ditch. There were various types, such as *fastigata* (= V-shaped); also used to mean canal.

fossata pl *fossata* From *fosso* (to dig), the long linear fortifications in Africa. See also *clausura*.

horreum pl *horrea* Granary/warehouse.

hydreuma pl *hydreumata* Enclosed and often fortified watering station.

immunes Soldiers with skills/seniority which excused them from the general labors of a *miles gregarius* (ordinary soldier).

laeti Gauls and Franks allowed to settle in the empire in the late third century in return for military service.

legatus pl *legati* Legate. From Augustan times senatorial legionary commander (*legatus legionis*); from Septimius Severus, prefects or others—later still *praepositi*—were used in place of senatorial legates. The *legati Augusti pro praetore* ran imperial provinces.

legio pl *legiones* Legion. From the word levy, the c. 30–33 legions of the Principate were around 5,000-strong. After Diocletian the number of legions rose and their manpower decreased.

liburna pl *liburnae* Originally a small galley, came to mean any military vessel.

limes pl *limites* Originally a path or line separating fields, used in geographical terms: *limes Raetia*. They used other words, too: *praetentura* or, if the frontier were along a river, *ripa*. We use the word to mean the border and its defenses and it is incorporated into a number of German words such as *Limesfall* (qv).

limitanei In late-empire parlance, these were fixed frontier units as opposed to the *comitatenses*.

Limesfall (German) The period when the empire pulled back from its fixed border in the *Agri Decumates* (qv) and established the frontier on the Rhine–Iller–Danube *limes* (see pp. 112–117).

lixa pl *lixae* or *mercator(es)* Sutler.

magister Master. A late empire title: *M. equitum* master of the horse, *M. peditum* master of the infantry, etc.

mansio Roadside resting places for people on official business.

milliaria 1,000—nominally the strength of the larger of the two forms of *auxilia* unit (the smaller was *quingenaria* = 500). See p. 42.

missio Released from service; *M. agraria*, with a grant of land; *M. nummaria*, with a grant of money.

municipium Second-rank Roman town. Unlike a *colonia* (qv), the inhabitants were not all Roman citizens; often formed from tribal centers, run by elected officials.

navis Ship. *N. actuaria* or *oneraria* transport vessel; *N. lusoria* troopship.

Notitia Dignitatum List of offices. Late empire (end 4th and early 5th century) listing of titles, positions, and military units.

numerus pl *numeri* Originally, a military unit that was composed of barbarians not in the *auxilia*; later, a c. 300-strong *Limitanei* unit.

officium consularis A governor's administration staff which included, among others, *speculatores* (originally spies, latterly a rank) and *beneficiarii*.

origo castris From the camp. Children of veterans who enlisted, See p. 193.

ostracon pl *ostraca* Sherds of pottery that have been written on.

paenula Cloak. Originally just worn by soldiers, latterly more widespread use.

palatini The top troops of the *Comitatenses*, both legions and *auxilia*.

peregrinus pl *peregrini* Foreigners, but free subjects of the empire.

Pia Fidelis Loyal and faithful—legion honorific awarded by a thankful emperor.

praefecti legionum Gallienus and Septimius Severus replaced the senatorial *legati legionum* with equestrian *praefecti legionum*.

praesidium Guard post or garrison.

praemium Army discharge benefits (usually cash or land).

praetorium The CO's building in a fort or camp.

Principate The empire from Augustus to Diocletian.

principia The HQ building in a fort or camp.

quingenaria See *milliaria*.

qsar pl *qsur* Similar to *centenarium*; a fortified farm.

ripa River bank; a *riparius* was a *limitanei* soldier on a river front in a *riparenses* unit.

sacellum The location in the *principia* where a unit's colors were kept.

sagittarius Archer or arrow-maker.

Tabula Peutingeriana A medieval copy of a Roman atlas showing their road network.

Tetrarchy Diocletian's attempt to reorganize the control of the empire into two augustus and two caesar.

turma pl *turmae* Cavalry unit made up of *alae* (qv).

vallum Entrenchment—particularly the ditches and berms along Hadrian's Wall.

vexillatio pl *vexillationes* Legion detachment; later, *V. comitatensis* or *V. palatina* field army cavalry units.

via Road as in *via Militaris* (see p. 145) or *V. decumana* /*praetoria* in forts (see p. 53).

vicus pl *vici* Civilian encampment next to a fort.

villa rustica Country villa, usually a farm.

Bibliography

The fourth-century fort of Mobene—Qasr Bashir in Jordan—was part of the *limes Arabicus*.

Bishop, M.C.: *Handbook to Roman Legionary Fortresses*; Pen & Sword, 2012.

Bishop, M.C., and Coulston, J.C.N.: *Roman Military Equipment*; Oxbow Books, 2006.

Bowman, Alan K.: *The Cambridge Ancient History Vol XII The Crisis of Empire AD193–337*; CUP, 2008.

Breeze, David et al: *Frontiers of the Roman Empire: Slovakia*; UNESCO, 2008.

Breeze, David: "The Value of Studying Roman Frontiers"; *Theoretical Roman Archaeology Journal*, 1(1): 1, pp. 1–17 (via *doi.org/10.16995/traj.212*).

Campbell, Brian: *The Roman Army 31BC–AD336—A Sourcebook*; Routledge, 2000.

Campbell, Duncan B.: *Fortress 83 Roman Auxiliary Forts 27BC–AD378*; Osprey, 2009.

Collins, Rob, Symonds, Matthew, and Weber, Meike: *Roman Military Architecture on the Frontiers*; Oxbow Books, 2015.

Cupcea, George: "The Evolution of Roman Frontier Concept and Policy"; *Journal of Ancient History and Archeology*, No. 2.1, 2015.

D'Amato, Raffaele: *New Vanguard 231 Imperial Roman Warships 27BC–197AD*; Osprey, 2016.

D'Amato, Raffaele: *New Vanguard 244 Imperial Roman Warships 193–565AD*; Osprey, 2017.

Dinter, Marieke van: *Living along the Limes*; Utrecht Studies in Earth Sciences, 2017.

Dyczek, Piotr: *Frontiers of the Roman Empire: The Lower Danube Limes in Bulgaria*; UNESCO, 2008.

Erdkamp, Paul (ed): *A Companion to the Roman Army*; Wiley-Blackwell, 2011.

Fields, Nic: *Fortress 31 Rome's Northern Frontier AD70–235*; Osprey, 2005.

Flynt, Shannon Rogers: *The Military Vici of Noricum*; Thesis, University of Missouri-Columbia, 2005 (via *mospace.umsystem.edu/*).

Gaiu, Corneliu: "The Beneficiarius Spearhead from Arcobadara"; *Journal of Ancient History and Archeology*, No. 1.3, 2014.

Goldsworthy, Adrian: *The Complete Roman Army*; Thames & Hudson, 2003.

Graafstal, Erik P.: *Frontiers of the Roman Empire: The Lower German Limes*; Sidestone Press, 2018.

Greta Bridge Roman fort, vicus and section of Roman road; Historic England Blog, 2000.

Harrell, James A., and Storemyr, Per: "Ancient Egyptian Quarries—an illustrated overview"; *Geological Survey of Norway Special*, 12, 2009 (via *www.researchgate.net/publication/281397894*).

Haynes, Ian: *Blood of the Provinces*; OUP, 2013.

Hill, P.R.: *The Construction of Hadrian's Wall*; Thesis, Durham University, 2009 (*etheses.dur.ac.uk/1071/*).

Karavas, John: *The Evolution of Roman Frontier Defence Systems and Fortifications the Lower Danube Provinces in the First and Second Centuries AD*; Thesis, Durham University, 2001 (*etheses.dur.ac.uk/3957/*).

Kennedy, David, and Bewley, Robert: *Ancient Jordan from the Air*; Council for British Research in the Levant, 2004.

Kolbeck, Ben: "A Foot in Both Camps: The Civilian Suppliers of the Army in Roman Britain." *Theoretical Roman Archaeology Journal* 1(1), p.8 (*doi.org/10.16995/traj.355*).

Korać, Miomir et al: *Frontiers of the Roman Empire: Slovakia*; UNESCO, 2014.

Kropff, Antony: "The Guarded river through no man's land"; Westerheem 64, pp. 178–188, 2018.

Ikram, Salima, and Rossi, Corinna: *North Kharga Oasis Survey 2004: Ain el-Tarakwa, Ain el-Dabashiya, and Darb Ain Amur*; MDAIK 62, 2006.

Le Bohec, Yann: *The Imperial Roman Army*; Routledge, 2000.

Lendering, Jona and Bosman, Arjen: *Edge of Empire*; Karwansaray Publishers, 2013.

Livingston, Helen: *Walking Roman Roads in Britain*; Dial House, 1995.

Marchant, David John: "Roman Weaponry in the Province of Britain"; thesis, University of Durham, 1991 (*etheses.dur.ac.uk/1557/*).

Matei-Popescu, Florian: "The Roman Auxiliary Units of Moesia"; Il Mar Nero, 2013.

Matei-Popescu, Florian, and Tentea, Ovidiu: *Auxilia Moesiae Superioris*; Mega Publishing House, 2018.

Mattingly, David et al: *Frontiers of the Roman Empire The African Frontiers*; Edinburgh, 2013.

Mattingly, David, and Hitchner, R. Bruce: *Roman Africa: An Archaeological Review*; The Journal of Roman Studies, Vol. 85, pp. 165–213, 1995.

Milner, N.P. (trans): *Vegetius: Epitome of Military Science*; LUP, 1993.

Parker, Philip: *The Empire Stops Here*; Pimlico, 2009.

PeterD: An Inspection of the Limes of Africa Proconsularis; Forum Ancient Coins, 2014 (*www.forumancientcoins.com/board/index.php?topic=95399.0*).

Pisz, M., Tomas, Agnieszka, Hegyi, Alexandru: "Non-destructive research in the surroundings of the Roman Fort Tibiscum"; *Archaeological Prospection*, Vol. 27, issue 3, 2020.

Pollard, Nigel, and Berry, Joanne: *The Complete Roman Legions*; Thames & Hudson, 2015.

Rankov, Nikolas Boris: *The Beneficiarii Consularis in the Western Provinces of the Roman Empire*; Oxford theses, 1986.

Roxan, Margaret: "The Auxilia of Mauretania Tingitana"; *Latomus*, pp. 838–855, 1973.

Simkins, Michael: *Men at Arms 46 The Roman Army from Caesar to Trajan*; Osprey, 1984.

Simkins, Michael: *Men at Arms The Roman Army from Hadrian to Constantine*; Osprey, 1979.

Southern, Patricia: *The Roman Army*; Amberley, 2014.

Speidel, M.A.: *The Oxford Handbook of Roman Epigraphy*; Oxford 2014.

Tentea, Ovidiu: *Ex Oriente Ad Danubium. The Syrian Units on the Danube Frontier of the Roman Empire*; Mega Publishing House, 2012.

Tomas, Agnieszka: "Canabae Legionis in Lower Moesia"; Sacrum et profanum, 2018 (via *academia.edu*).

Trakadas, Athena L.: *Piscationes in Mauretania Tingitana*; thesis, University of Southampton, 2009 (*eprints.soton.ac.uk/366713/1/Binder1.pdf*).

Various: *Frontiers of the Roman Empire: The Lower German Limes; Nomination File for Inscription on the UNESCO World Heritage List*, Pts 1 and 2; 2019.

Visy, Zsolt: *The Roman Limes in Hungary*; 2003 from www.univie.ac.at/limes.

Vries, Bert de: *Umm El-Jimal "Gem of the Black Desert"*; Al Kutba Publishers, 1990.

Watkins, Thomas H.: "Roman Legionary Fortresses and the Cities of Modern Europe"; *Military Affairs*, Vol. 47, No. 1, pp. 15-25, 1983.

Wilmott, Tony: *Saxon Shore Forts*; Historic England, 2018.

Zaroff, Roman: "The Vandals and Sarmatians in a New Perspective"; Collegium Medievale, 2017 (via *www.researchgate.net/publication/324471860*).

The extremes: from the cold of a Taunus winter in Germany to the heat of the desert on the *limes Tripolitanus,* the Roman frontiers weren't homogenous. However, they did have common duties and threats. The duties were the same everywhere in the empire: maintaining the *pax Romana*, collecting customs dues and taxes, controlling the flow of people into and out of the empire, and watching out for the main external threat—tribesmen from *barbaricum* tempted by the good life over the border.

Photo Credits

Index